3 9094 00998 0747

D1031714

THE VIKING SHIPS

A. W. BRØGGER — HAAKON SHETELIG

THE VIKING SHIPS

THEIR ANCESTRY AND EVOLUTION

TWAYNE PUBLISHERS, INC. — NEW YORK

PUBLISHED IN USA
BY TWAYNE PUBLISHERS INC., NEW YORK.

LAYOUT AND PRODUCTION: DREYERS FORLAG.
PRINTED IN NORWAY BY CENTRALTRYKKERIET,
OSLO 1971.
ISBN 82 09 00030 6 (H.)
ISBN 82 09 00031 4 (IB.)
ENGLISH TRANSLATION BY KATHERINE JOHN.

ON THE JACKET:
LEIF ERIKSON DISCOVERS VINLAND.
FROM A PAINTING BY CHRISTIAN KROHG.

CONTENTS

PREFACE

When the first Norwegian edition of this book was published in 1950, to be succeeded by an English translation the following year, it presented the results of the two most prominent Norwegian archaeologists' lifelong studies of the viking ships, their origin and development. Their technical adviser had been the experienced naval engineer and boatbuilder, Fr. Johannessen, who had taken an active part in the reconstruction of a number of ancient vessels.

Whereas the method of construction has long been established, the question of the origin of these eminently sea-worthy vessels has continued to occupy the minds of modern archaeologists, and finds of later date, as for instance, in Denmark and England, combined with renewed studies of older material, have given some impetus to divergent theories on this essential point. Whether, as Brøgger and Shetelig were inclined to believe, the ancestor of the viking ship is to be found among the primitive skin-boats known to us from Bronze Age rock carvings, or among the dug-out logboats to be found in many parts of the world, is still an open question. The solution lies perhaps in a combination of these two theories.

Since the first publication of this book both authors have passed away, and we have elected to publish this new edition of a book which meanwhile has come to be considered a classic in its field, with the original text unaltered and unabridged.

Thanks to the assistance of the Collection of Antiquities of the University of Oslo it has been possible to provide many new illustrations as well as a few drawings wich indicate more clearly how the ships were constructed.

DREYERS FORLAG

THE BOATS OF VERY EARLY TIMES

Introduction

«Bundin er båtleysir maðurr»
(Bound is boatless man).

West in the sea, beyond Helgeland's skerries,
There swims an isle on the quiet waves
— sang Welhaven, after the old fable.

Myriads of such islands lie to seaward, west of all the skerries in Norway, and they were all reached by men, as far back as there were men in Norway at all. They took the sea for their arena. All the old dwelling-sites of the most remote Norwegian antiquity lie by the sea, from which it follows that all early settlement of our country presupposes the boat, as does its coastwise economic life, thousands of years old. But nowhere does this question of the boat spring more directly out of geographic history than in North Norway, where all the islands in the western sea are inaccessible except to true seagoing boats. The whole record of the ancient settlements from the coast of Bohuslän to Finnmark presumes a boatbuilding and a boat culture which will be the mainspring of the coastal dwellers' history for many thousands of years.

Naturally, therefore, we must first know something of the settlement of our country in old, and very ancient times. The earliest traces go a long, long way back; it must be ten thousand years at least since the hunting tribes of Finnmark, the Helgeland-Fosna coast and Østfold journeyed along the coast and out upon the deep sea, which furnished a great part of their livelihood. And on through whole millennia, it was the same story. We learn it from the dwelling-sites of the Stone Age, which cluster thickly in wide areas along the whole coast. Certainly, the hunting people also penetrated inland, along the waterways and the great lakes, and upward to the mountains and plateaus. But throughout all antiquity, the coast remained the focal point.

Therefore the boat became the mainspring in the life of these tribes: the boat for fishing, and the boat as a means of transport — or one may well say, as a means of settlement. For there was no real qualitative difference between the two; where one is present we shall find the other. Distances were of no account in these old hunting communities. The history of Stone Age settlement is on a grand scale, and this long chapter of our past has wide horizons. Often the expeditions of a hunting tribe involve the covering of great, even immense distances; so does a change of dwelling-place from winter to summer. All this leads us directly to the genesis and history of the boat itself. It is inherent in the very framework of the Norse hunting culture that the boat should rank as high, in technical achievement, as the basic tools of the chase.

It is on this background that the boat appears. Then if we turn to the discoveries of archaeology, the background deepens and the picture is enlarged. On the very ancient site at Viste near Stavanger, we found innumerable bones of deep-water fish: — conger-eel, cod in abundance, haddock, pollack and ling; and there were also bones of the grey seal, the Greenland seal and the porpoise. The grey seal is the king of the deep, and they must have gone far beyond Jæren to secure it. Again, the later Stone Age site at Ruskenes near Bergen had many deepwater fish, including turbot, as well as the fjord seal, the ca'ing whale and the dolphin. Some of the fishhooks in the Ruskenes find are heavy, solid hooks for deep-water fish.

The numerous discoveries in Nordland tell the same tale. An amateur archaeologist in Ballangen, Kaare Petersen, has made a very interesting and valuable study of the fishing-leads which may be found on all Stone Age sites along the Norwegian coast. The Forselv carving in Skjomen depicts a line weighted with oval pebbles, of the same type as we find on the dwelling-sites, and with a halibut hanging on the hook. Another part of the same carving shows a boat with fishing-lines over the gunnel and with a halibut on the hook. The hand-line in use today carries a sinker varying in size according to the depth to be fished. By weighing Stone Age sinkers from sites in Ofoten, Kaare Petersen has shown that they present the same degrees of variation as the modern implements — from 10³/₅ oz.—53 oz. (0.3—1.5 kg.).From this, he concludes with every right that they fished the same depths in the Stone Age, and were acquainted with all variations, from simple shorefishing to fishing at a depth as great as 90 fathoms (about 560'). Such an inquiry tells us a vast deal, both of the fishing voyages and the efficiency of the fishingboat.

Many more observations from archaeological material could be brought forward, to illustrate the leading role played by the boat in the Norwegian economy, as far back as the early Stone Age. The slate spear for hunting seals, and other big game hauled up from great depths, the hunting scenes in the rock-carvings, the hunting culture represented on the sites by tools — all this will help to throw light on the views that follow. The main thing is that we should now raise the question: *What were these boats like?* In this brief introduction we have made, so to say, the heaviest demands on the boat; we have, quite simply, given it all chances. It must have been seaworthy in swell and current, in calm and storm. It was a boat for long voyages, for big objectives, for hunting in deep seas and for deep-water fishing, not merely in fjord and sound, but in areas which even now are a severe test of boat and crew.

It often happens, in debates on the technique and methods of the ancient economy, that the man of practical experience has a juster and clearer eye than the professional scholar. And so it once was here. In 1925, I gave one of my lectures on «The Norwegian People in Antiquity», and said something of their boats. Afterwards I had a visit from an elderly seaman (Th. Ring), who had been present, and had seen the lantern slides of boats in rock-carvings of the Bronze Age. He said that those boats could only have been of one kind — they were skin boats. I asked him to write this down, and now, when I reread his comment more than twenty years later, it seems to me so good as to deserve inclusion. No archaeologist held that view in those days.

«With reference to your lecture,» he writes, «I beg to observe that the Stone Age tribes used vessels made of skin, with ribs of wood. The carvings go to prove that, I should say, because two keels are shown, an upper and an under, with strokes from the upper one, which may be meant either for 'frame-timbers' or crew. The boat's skin casing goes round the upper keel up to the gunnel, while the under keel is put on to protect the hide from stones on landing — as a kind of false keel — and it is carried upwards to protect both ends. These craft were probably flat-bottomed to begin with. The gunnel and the bottom ribwork would be easy to make from suitable tree-trunks, so would the different struts they had to use to keep the hide stretched and give the ribwork enough strength. The craft were driven by small blades of hide fastened to a suitable stick (paddle), and later on by oars when gradually they came to need bigger craft. At the same time it seems most likely that the flat-bottomed boats were found unsatisfactory, and the 'tub-shape' gave way to the boat-shape with two keels. A kind of sail, again hide with a wooden frame, might possibly be used, and then in time they would evolve the yard, mast, and sail with sheets. The hollow treetrunk, the canoe, may have been used, *but for crossing the Skagerak and the Kattegat I think that skin craft would have been more practical.* And then canoes are much more difficult to make than craft of skin, with which the Stone Age tribes must have experimented as to size. The drawing of a ship at Lake Totak seems to me evidence that quite large craft were used even there. I dont believe that outrigger canoes were used at all in our waters.»

These simple and sound views, put forward by an interested layman, were bound to strike the archaeologist as pretty wild in those days — when there was actually no real knowledge of the hunt-carvings, with boats, in North Norway.

Judging by all we have now learnt of the most primitive communities, which we know best through the great series of discoveries in North Norway, it is precisely in these grand-scale northern conditions that we must seek for the beginning, for the origins. Those heaps of large and small implements, which often strike the vulgar eye as a monotonous array of incoherently-shaped pebbles, tell us distinctly what these people lived on, and how their entire way of life was moulded. It was on the chase of creatures good for food — whale, seal and halibut, fish and sea-fowl, besides the elk, the reindeer and the bear. So it became primarily a civilisation based, in great things and small, upon the use of hide. Professor Gutorm Gjessing saw more clearly on this point that anyone before him, when he concluded that the oldest boat up in the north was the *skin boat.* The old, confused idea that the first boat was a hollowed tree-trunk — the log boat, or «eike», or whatever we please to call it — is founded on romantic notions of the life of primitive man. It does not, however, lack all basis in reality, as we shall see later. But only now have we acquired much fuller knowledge of these things, so that we can inquire into the meaning of both types of origin, the skin boat and the log boat. They belong to different cultural milieus, and both are of great antiquity. Then if we add the clinker-built boat of planks — the Norwegian boat *par excellence* — we have the three basic elements in the history of the boat in Norway with which we are to be concerned.

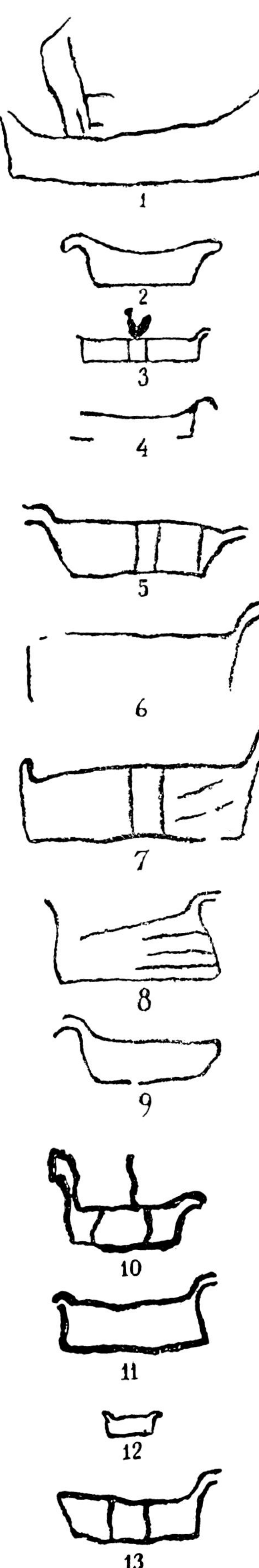

The Skin Boat

It is implicit in the very date of the old North Norway hunting culture that it can have known the boat in only one form, the boat of skin. What it looked like, or how it was constructed, we have no safe means of judging. But we have pictures of fishing-boats in the rock-carvings, and from them we can at any rate get some idea of how it looked. Even though the form does vary to some extent, we may certainly assume that on the whole there was one distinct type of boat in use over the whole area.

It was the skin boat which made possible the settlement of all the western isles, the furthest outpost of Lofoten, Værøy and Røst. This distinctive coastal settlement can now be visualised more and more clearly. While we have still no finds of inland dwelling-sites in North Norway, the outer skerries are growing richer in discoveries year by year. Within the last few years, a number of the furthest North Norwegian islands have produced a whole series of them, which demonstrate the immense importance of sea-fishing. And the impression becomes even stronger as the use of bone is revealed in such great finds as those at Kirkhelleren on Træna, Skjåvika in Hamningsberg near Vardø, and Nyelv in Nesseby — to mention only the most typical. Here we find types of implements almost exclusively for use at sea, hooks, harpoons, fish-spears, forks etc.

In other words, these were boats which could sail or row the dangerous and famous Maelstrom (Moskenstrøm) and the sea of Røst.

Boats that were to be practical out there had first and foremost to be light, so that they could ride the crest of the waves and thus avoid shipping too much water. But they also had to be built strong and pliant, so that they could take the heavy stresses of the sea. Out there, a log boat would very soon break up, even if it were stabilised with outriggers. It would not be easy enough to handle, would cut through the sea and fill. Nor would a bark canoe be easy to use, for it would lack solidity. Whereas the skin boat, rightly constructed, has all advantages.

The pictures of fishing-boats that we have in the rock-carvings really provide quite rich material for study. So far they have been known only from North Norway carvings — Skjomen (in Ofoten), Rødøy (Tjøtta, Helgeland) and Evenhus (Frosta, Trøndelag). In our illustrations on pages 12, 13 and 14 we have reproduced all the known examples, 36 boat pictures in all. The

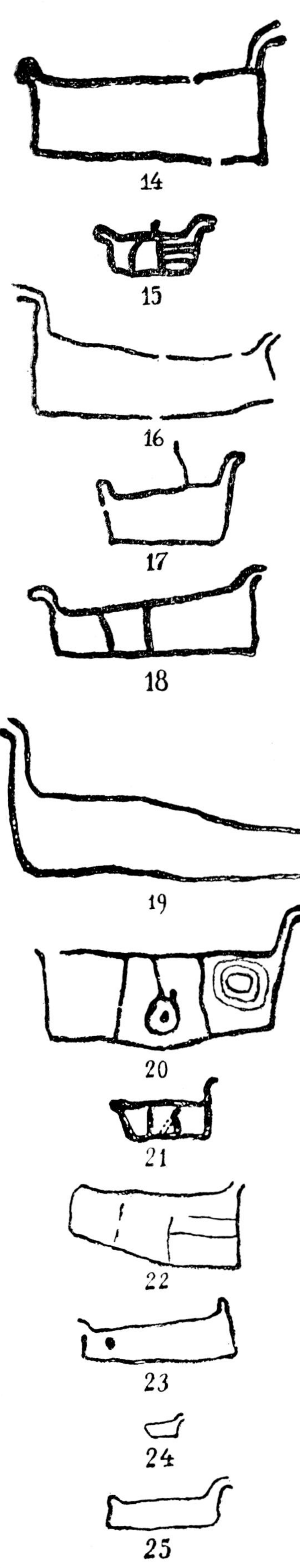

drawings are small, sometimes to the point of miniature (No. 24, Evenhus); the biggest of the boats (No. 19, Evenhus) measures about 4'7" (1.40 m.) on the rock.

The boats in the Skjomen carving (No. 1—2) are both very interesting and enlightening. They are of different sizes; boat No. 1 is almost 4' (1.20 m.) the other only 1'17" (48 cm.). The big boat, No. 1, is very typical of the whole group. The prow is rather higher than the stern; the stern curves outward and seems to end in an animal's head. The smaller boat is of the same shape, but the prow is lower and has a stronger forward sheer.

Of very special interest is the boat from Rødøy, No. 3.

It is distinctly drawn, with gunnel, keel-line, and steep lines fore and aft. The bow has something of an arch, the stern seems not to have. But the most striking feature of this boat is that there are two crosswise strokes which *divide it into three bulkheads.* And in the middle space there sits a hunter, executed in simple outline. This boat is the old Norwegian skin boat which was built in different sizes, for the single hunter and for big expeditions, but keeping the same type for all. Quite certainly we should not be able to pronounce on this, if we had not the rich and excellent material of the Evenhus carvings, No. 5—36. Every one of these drawings offers important, interesting problems; they all tell us something fundamental of the old Norwegian skin boat in the early hunting period.

Evenhus lies in Inner Trøndelag, so here we are not on the sea as at Skjomen and Rødøy. The hunting area was the great, inner Trondheimsfjord, which can be rough and testing enough, and the carving itself depicts seal, the most important object of the chase in sea-hunting. The boat drawings — the richest gallery we have of skin-boat drawings, more than 30 examples — seem at first glance to offer a confusion of forms, but if we look more closely they assemble into one definite archetype with variations. The hull is, practically speaking, the same in all, and the design of the prow, especially, is amazingly uniform, curving upwards in what can be a really high and stylish curve (Nos. 7, 19, 20, 26, etc.). This form is quite beyond any ever reached by the Greenland skin boats. One would not have supposed that a skin boat built on ribs could give such opportunities for elevation of the prow. Here it is quite unmistakable, and is such a constant feature in all the boats that we must assume the Stone Age tribes had found some natural and easy way to solve the problem.

We are assuming throughout that the drawings are valid as examples of how the boats really looked. The nature of the carvings gives us a right to do so. It is not till later that the drawings become formal and conventional. But here, at Skjomen, Rødøy and Evenhus, we may assume that every drawing is a sharp, exact rendering of the hunter's reliable experience and memory of every detail in the boat's lines. We have therefore every reason to dwell somewhat longer on these drawings. This applies particularly to the elevation fore and aft, and the transition from the keel to the prow and stern. Almost without exception, these transitions are strikingly abrupt, almost right-angled. In extreme cases we get such broad, nearly amorphous and completely square hulls as, for example, Nos. 14 and 34. Such a hull would be inconceivable in a plank-built boat, and quite incompatible with the log boat. With the skin boat, on the other hand, it is fairly natural. The best and most spontaneous evidence of this is given by the little skin boat made by Nansen and Sverdrup in 1888, when they had come down from the Greenland ice cap to the head of Ameralikfjord. If we compare the photograph of it with the boats from Evenhus, all doubt is dispelled. It looks exactly like a picture of a boat in the rock-carvings.

The stern, too, has a fairly consistent character, frequently ending in an upward curve; Gjessing suggests that the Skjomen boat No. 1 ended in a kind of animal's head.

Most of the Evenhus boats are drawn with distinct bulkheads, like the one at Rødøy: see especially No. 7 and No. 18. But only one of them depicts a man in the middle bulkhead, like the Rødøy boat. So one inevitably wonders why the hunters, or voyagers, are not shown in the boats except in these two cases. Here we have a difference in kind from the ships of the Bronze Age, which almost regularly feature strokes for the crew. In general, there are some details in these boat-drawings, particularly those from Evenhus, which spring from motives other than a wish to represent the structure. One of these boats in the Evenhus carving (No. 20) has concentric circles near the bow, and these have been interpreted as «the boat's eye». Other boats in this carving (most markedly Nos. 8, 34 and 35) have a number of horizontal strokes in the fore part, which can scarcely refer to structure. It is most natural to assume that both the circle and the horizontal lines had an ornamental and/or magical significance, presumably they stand for painting on the sides of the boat. One might perhaps explain the crosswise strokes in the same way. Reference has been made, in this connection, to the crosswise strokes which appear constantly in animal drawings of the hunting age. A similarly painted decoration, clearly magical in character, is found on Aleutian skin boats; there we have both crosswise strokes, as on the Norwegian boats, and various curved lines, circles and round spots.

In shape these boats carved in the hunting period are often strikingly suggestive of the Eskimo *umiak,* the «women's-boat». The likeness between the boats in the Skjomen carving and the *umiak* is especially great. Of all hunting pictures of boats, the Skjomen carving, on the whole, is the most strongly naturalistic in style, and there, accordingly, we must expect the shape of the boat to have come closest to reality. And a comparative study of Arctic skin boats leads to the conclusion that the open women's-boat is in all likelihood the most aboriginal of the Arctic boat-types which have been preserved.

The kayak, Gjessing says, is far less widely diffused, and considerably more specialised in form. It never had a place in Norwegian life, belongs chiefly to the American Arctic, and only reaches its highest and most functional development with the Greenland Eskimos. Kayaks are also to be found in East Siberia, among the Chukchees and Koryaks, but they are rare, and are completely lacking the slender elegance of the Greenland kayak. Nor are

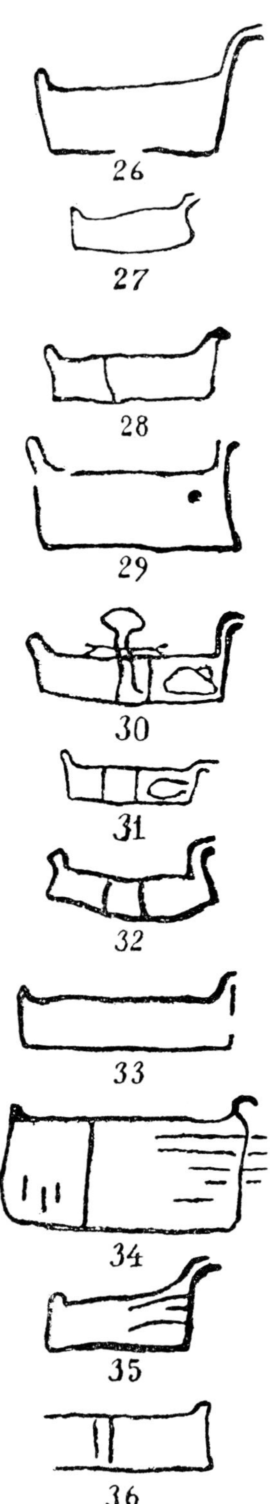

Rock carvings depicting various types of skin boats. Nos. 1–2 are from Skjomen, 3–4 from Rødøy Nos. 5–36 are all from Evenhus, Frosta.

 skin boat from the 19th. centu-y. The Nansen-Sverdrup «half-oat» built by the two Norwegian xplorers after they had crossed he Greenland ice-cap and had rrived at the head of the Amera-ik-fjord on the west coast of reenland (1888). The boat con-ists of a ribbing made of bran-hes, covered by skins which the xplorers had brought with them or various purposes. Oars and eats presented the greatest prob-em. Nevertheless, the two men ianaged to row the boat down the jord to Godthåp in 6 days. The oat shows striking resemblance to he boats seen in the Stone Age ock-carvings.

the kayaks of Alaska and Canada to be compared with those of the Greenland Eskimos.

While the kayak is only to be found in part of the Arctic area, and may be traced there in a steadily improving technical form, the open *umiak*-form exists, so to speak unchanged, over the whole Arctic, from the Samoyed in the far west of Arctic Siberia, to Greenland. If we except the few and clumsy kayaks of the Chukchees and Koryaks, the boats of all Siberian Arctic tribes have almost invariably the appearance of the women's-boat, whether they are quite small, intended only for one man, or large craft holding a crew of up to twenty. The cultural continuity in the diffusion of the women's-boat from West Siberia to Greenland is entirely clear. There is no break in the diffusion, and the form is the same. Even in ancient times, boat-skeletons were being exported across the Bering Strait. In the development of the whole social order of Arctic tribes, both in Siberia and North America – for instance, everywhere among the Asiatic and American Eskimos – the women's-boat has been of fundamental importance.

Here it is tempting to conclude that the resemblance in form between the boats in our rock carvings and the Arctic skin boat of the *umiak* type springs from a real coherence of tradition. Gjessing, who first suggested the idea, has also gone deeper into it. There is no doubt that the *umiak* has a very ancient, primitive stamp. Among the Chukchees and the Siberian and American Eskimos, communities are built up with the *umiak* and its crew as a social unit.

It should be mentioned also that new rock-carving discoveries on the shores of the White Sea have produced drawings of boats of much the same type as the skin boats in North Norway carvings.

Here we depict, after Gjessing, one of the boats in the Skjomen carving side by side with the skeleton of an Eskimo *umiak*. The Skjomen drawing gives no structural detail, but its outline, at least, is very like that of the Eskimo boat. As may be seen, the latter is built over a frame of ribbing and then clad with skin. Here the structural details naturally varied with conditions in the different territories – bone and wood for the ribbing, usually sealskin for the hull.

)utline of a boat from the rock-arvings in North Norway.

'keleton-drawing of an Eskimo umiak» (women's boat). The si-nilarity in form between the ty-es of crafts is apparent, see also he photograph of an umiak on he following page.

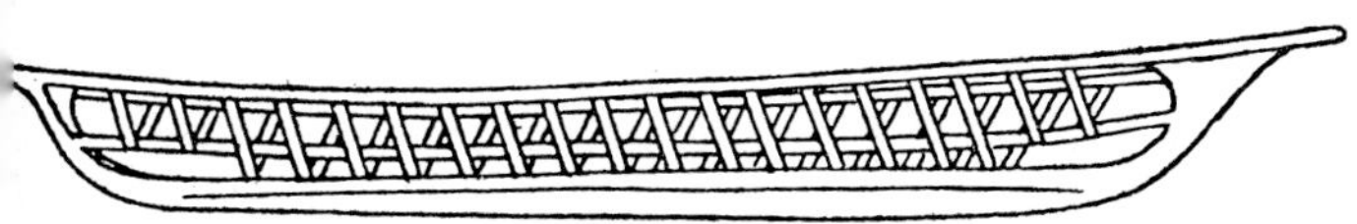

An eskimo «umiak». Photo: Etno-grafisk Museum, Oslo.

In this country we know the *umiak* best from our popular ideas of the Greenland women's-boat. Nansen's classic picture of it has remained unsurpassed to this day.

«Indissolubly bound up with the tent life of the summer was the big travel-boat, in Eskimo called *umiak*. By Europeans it was named the «women's-boat», because, in contrast to the kayak, it was rowed almost exclusively by women.

«This boat is up to ten or twelve metres long, and is is completely open. It has a wooden ribbing, which they make of driftwood, and is covered with sealskin. It is very narrow in proportion, and flatbottomed. It is easy to row, but the form makes it an uncomfortable and a bad sea-boat, and so the Greenlanders make for shore with it as soon as there is much wind. It has quite commonly a little sail to set up in the bow. Sailing, however, is not a thing the Eskimos have mastered, or been very keen on, in the past at any rate.

«These boats are so roomy that one of them could take a whole household with all its belongings — tents, sledges, dogs, children and grown-ups. They were rowed by up to half a score of women, and when there were so many they could make good speed. The usual steersman was the house-father, while the other men of the family followed in their kayaks.

«In the women's-boat the Greenlanders kept moving all summer through, from one hunting-ground to the next. Where there were reindeer, they spent a month or months hunting up along the fjords, and lived in luxury and mirth.

«In those days they could sometimes undertake long voyages, both on the west and the east coast. For instance, on the east coast families might travel from the Angmagssalik area, 65$^1/_2$°N, all the way to the trading-posts west of Cape Farewell, and back again — which meant a distance of 500 miles each way. They did not usually go fast. One of the two women's-boats we met on the east coast near Cape Bille in 1888, was southward bound, and did not reach Paniagug, west of Cap Farewell till two years later; a stretch of only 300 km, which I should think we could have travelled in a week or two in our boats. But as soon as the Eskimos have reached a place where seal abounds, they put ashore, pitch camp, set about hunting and live high. If autumn or winter is at hand, they choose a good place and build a winter house, to resume their travels in the spring or summer when the ice allows them to move on. In this way, the women's-boat I have referred to had spent three years on the journey from its home at Umivik, nor was it likely to spend much less time getting back again. The other boat which also was going southward from Cape Bille got as far as Nanuseq, and wintered there. But then the father died, and they turned round and started on the long journey home to Angmagssalik, after what might be called a fruitless errand since they had failed to reach their destination, the trading-post, which was not more than 110 km away. Journeys along the west coast were of course much easier and quicker, since there was no floating ice to hinder them.»

Nansen adds that while thus wandering about, they avoided too much isolation in their own settlements. They fell in with other people, and all the summer through there was a life and intercourse by which they profited in many ways. They were livened up, their interest in the chase was stimulated and in various respects their skill as hunters improved. «So it was not at all strange that the Greenlander's fairest dreams of happiness should be bound up with the women's-boats and the tent.»

Even though this picture by no means covers what the skin boat meant in the Norwegian Stone Age, it gives a good view of the inner life of a hunting society. In Greenland the *umiak* was the travel-boat, not the hunting-boat. And the geographical conditions never turned the Eskimos into seamen, as they did the Norwegian tribes of the Stone Age. From other places in the Arctic zone we have other pictures of the *umiak*.

We may now regard it as something more than a general assumption that the hunting-boat, throughout the whole Stone Age in North Norway, was the boat of skin. It simply cannot have been anything else. And then we must assume a continuity of tradition from the ancient culture of Finnmark to the skin boats of the later slate age.

But if we have arrived at this point for the purely «Arctic» Stone Age, the question still remains whether the Stone Age boat in South Norway and the west was also the boat of skin. Here we have to grope much more in the dark, because material is wanting. There are no boats in any carvings of this period from East or West Norway. This has a simple explanation in their subject-matter. Practically all of them depict the hunting of deer and elk; we have only a couple of exceptions, the grampuses in the carving from Skogerveien, Drammen, and the whale in the drawings from Åmøy near Stavanger. Nevertheless, there are two things we must bear in mind when trying to think out this question. The cultural milieu of the early and later Stone Age in East and West Norway, different as they may be, shows that many of the tribes lived on sea-catches; therefore they had boats, and doubtless also good boats, for expeditions and journeys. And the earlier phases of this hunting culture depend on the preparation and use of skin, just as the Arctic Stone Age did. We may express it by saying that all the earlier periods of Stone Age society throughout the land, and even a good stretch of the later period, are «skin-age» that is, the use of skin for clothing, houses and boats was fundamentally important. But it does not necessarily follow that the boats were of skin. They might quite possibly be wooden also. To get an understanding of the larger problems, we must embark on a provisional discussion of the three-sided question: the skin boat, the log boat, and the clinker-built boat.

The Log Boat

Here we mean by this the simple, hollowed-out log of wood, the *eike,* as it has also been called in so many parts of the country, chiefly in the east. It is in the nature of things that the log boat should be a product of the forest, as the skin boat is a product of the treeless Arctic landscape. Therefore it must be remembered that, as far as we now know, all the discoveries of settlements in South and West Norway, even the earliest known, belong to a period when the forest had reached these areas. There is an exception in a number of Stone Age finds from Østfold which may be considerably earlier than the forest age. Further, one may draw attention to the larger context here, the wide perspective one acquires by keeping to the broad outlines: that distinct period in the geographical history of northern, and more especially of western Europe when the great forests spread over the whole zone, and set their mark on certain hunting cultures of the age. Its most distinctive settlements, attached to lakes and inland waters, are known from Britain, Denmark, North Germany, Scania, the Baltic countries and Finland (the continental period). A find like that at Viste near Stavanger proved that Jæren, in this early Stone Age, was covered with forest, a habitat of elk and bear.

It is quite natural to suppose that the hunting tribes who were then living in those wide areas, employed the forest timber to make boats — the log boat, even though they doubtless knew the skin boat.

The log boat has been found over great tracts of Europe. Perhaps it is best known in the Swiss lake dwellings of the Stone and Bronze Age — the *monoxylon,* as it is called by archaelogists in western Europe. In the lake-dwelling at Robenhausen there was a big, handsome log boat, about 12'(3,60 m.) long. Others have been found at Möringen. In the lake-dwelling in the Lac de Chalain there was a log boat together with a quantity of stone and bone implements. It is no less than 31' (9,5 m.) long, a very good-sized craft, and into the bargain very elaborate. The prow is beautifully arched and shaped like a spur, while the stern curves backward, ending like a swan's neck.

In England, Wales and Scotland the log boat has been found in many different places. In 1926, Cyril Fox published a number of valuable particulars on these monoxylon finds. His starting-point is the boat from Llangorse, which was found in a lake in 1925. It is now in the Welsh National Museum. «The first impression of the craft which I received,» says Fox, «as it lay in a boathouse after being drawn up from the bottom of the lake,was confirmed on closer study: it is by no means just a hollowed tree-trunk, but a most shapely vessel, built by men who had evolved a high degree of craftsmanship.» The boat is made out of a splendid, solid oak log, and about two-thirds of the diameter of the trunk has been used. It is about 16'5" (5 m.) long, the beam is about 2'2" (65 cm.) the height midtship about 1'4" (4 cm.)0. The prow curves upward, and lies about 1'8" (50 cm.) above a horizontal base-line. The marks left by the tools are so distinct and

og-boat from Numedal. Now in e Norwegian Maritime Museum Oslo.

clear that it is possible to say, with fair certainty, how the boat was made. In Fox's view, they employed iron axes and chisels. In the stern a very well-shaped seat had been contrived. There can be little doubt that the Llangorse boat derives from the early Iron Age and from a Celtic tribe.

But that does not imply that it is independent of much older traditions of a pre-Celtic age. Among the many other monoxylon finds, some have been placed with certainty in the Stone Age. There is, for instance, a boat found in the Clyde in 1708; in it lay a handsome, ground stone axe of the late Stone Age. In a log boat from Kent there was a ground stone axe, as well as a flint axe and a flint scraper. In a boat found in Cambridgeshire, there was a barber's knife of the later Bronze Age type. The well-known boat find from Glastonbury can be placed about 100 B. C. Certain other finds can also be placed in the Celtic Iron Age, yet others in the Roman Iron Age. Fox also mentions a discovery which can be placed in the fourth century A.D. A log boat from Loch Arthur in Scotland has a prow ending in an animal's head.

The Scottish archaeologist Munro held that in Scotland, at least, they went on making log boats down to our own time. Reliable information proves that they were used in certain places till the 1870'ies.

For more than four thousand years — and probably far more — the log boat has been in use in certain districts of England, Wales and Scotland. It was created in the Stone Age, and it goes on through all the different types of population in those thousands of years — pre-Celts, Celts, Anglo-Saxons, Picts and Scots. But the most vital feature of these log boats is that they belonged distinctively to *lakes and rivers;* it is not likely they were ever used as sea-going boats. Fox's account of their geographical distribution makes this quite plain. Nevertheless, it was not merely a question of small, simple boats. The discoveries in the Fens include long, massive boats more than 49' 3" (15 m.) long, boats which might hold a crew of ten. Perhaps they are just as likely to have been warships as trading ships.

It is curious that no log boat has been found in any of the ancient Danish settlements of the forest age. In the big find from Holmegaard in Sealand there are a few small, short paddle oars, but they may just as well have been used in skin boats.

Otherwise, discoveries of log boats are very common in Danish bogs and lakes. Professor Johannes Brøndsted kindly informs us that nowadays the Danish National Museum in Copenhagen usually receives from five to ten reports of such discoveries every year. Dating is in most cases difficult or impossible. So far the most important are some recent finds, as yet unpublished, from Aamosen in Sealand, which Troels-Smith, by an analysis of pollen, has been able to date to the barrow period of the later Stone Age. But the finds undoubtedly belong to different periods. The National Museum has, for instance, a report of a find from Tissø, Sealand, in which the boat showed plainly the repairing of a crack, which had been mended with iron staples. And in the Odder Museum in Jutland there is a boat carved with runes, seemingly from the early Middle Age. Brøndsted says there is evidence from different sources that the log boat was in use right up to the mid-nineteenth century, both in Jutland and on the islands. It was used only on lakes and other quiet waters. The types described in these reports appear to correspond exactly with the *eiker* which have been dug up, even with those from Aamosen which can be placed at the beginning of the later Stone Age.

In *Sweden* also the discovery of log boats in marshes and lakes is very common. Excellent information has been supplied within the last decades, by Ph. Humbla (1935) and Albert Nilsson (1943). Humbla's conclusions differ widely from the reflections which have just been urged. But on a thorough sifting of the now abundant Swedish material, it is not impossible that we may reach agreement on the main points. Few investigators have gone so deeply into the genesis and history of the Nordic boats, therefore his point of view deserves ample space.

He begins by mentioning a notable discovery – a *bark boat* – in Vestergötland. It is made of bark in one piece, of beech or elm. Some paltry ribs of wood supplied the frame and the support, and between the frame-timbers and the bark there is a strip of leather; the whole suggests a kind of sewing or lashing. Humbla, however, takes the view that it is the history of the log boat, in broad outline, rather than that of the skin boat, which will elucidate the evolution of the boat from its most primitive types down to the in many cases perfect constructions of the Iron Age.

There can be no doubt that on lakes and calm waters, the log boat answered its purpose as a means of fishing and transport. The question is only whether the devices used to stabilise this primitive craft – outriggers or a higher gunnel – can have any relevance to the evolution of a sea-going boat. Humbla here mentions local types of the log boat, which had the form of double logs. These may be said to represent the final result of generations' work on the log boat. In this way it became broad and capacious, reached a sufficient height above the water, and was relatively easy to handle. It answered adequately the requirements of a craft for calm, untroubled waters, and on lakes, creeks and fjords it has survived to this day.

In Norway there has been a find of a triple log boat, which was sunk in Lake Lønning, in Lønningsdal, near Bergen. It was crude and primitive, and had no doubt been used to ferry cattle on their way from one pasture to another.

But the log boat obviously had great drawbacks. It was not so much the mass of timber it required for building. But it was crank, and rode the water badly; and it was heavy to row, paddle or pole.

Now the question arises, how far they could break with their ingrained repugnance to making a hull of many sections joined together; or such, at least, is Humbla's theoretical reflection, according to the theory of evolution worked out by him. And it is highly plausible, as he develops it. But we are always coming up against the main theme, which in my judgment cannot be ignored: the deep and irremediable cleavage between inland and coast, between the lake tribes and the sea tribes. What they did on quiet streams, and on the creeks and sounds of enclosed waters, has absolutely no bearing on the great and difficult problem of building a sea-going boat. If it were all these inland tribes who had picked up a little boating on rivers and lakes, and finally put out to sea — if it were as simple as that, the problem would be solved. But that is against all historical reason. I will go so far as to say that if all the inland tribes, right down from the Stone Age, had worked at the improvement of the log boat — and it was bad enough — they could not have provided the coastal and sea tribes with a single idea of any consequence towards the development of the true boat and the ship. The boat for use on the coast and ocean was not created by the landlubbers of the forest age in any part of North Europe, not if there were thousands of ancient log boats to be found over the whole area. Indeed I actually believe that the reverse is true: that all the little boats in the Norwegian rivers and lakes of our own day are copies of the coastal boats. *It was the coast and ocean which conquered the interior, and not the other way round.*

Humbla can point out quite truly that in Swedish rivers there are *eiker* built of several strakes, which might suggest the log boat as their origin. He thus draws up a fine old-fashioned typology of evolution, on the recipe: from the log boat to the flat-bottomed *eike,* made out of planking and with sheers fore and aft — the intervening links being the double log boat and the simple and composite *eike.* But it all comes to nothing, when we recall the difference between sea, river and lake. There was not much that they could teach each other. Think of a fishing community on the west coast of Norway where the log boat never can have been of the slightest use, and we come back unawares to Sigvat Skald's[1] profound scorn and downright terror of that absurd craft, which he judged so harshly because it could not live on the sea. He knew what the sea was.

These considerations do not prevent a number of the views we owe to Humbla from being highly valuable, since no one else has paid such heed to all the structural problems arising from the evolution of the boat. Although it is impossible to go along with him in his interpretation of the facts, as he sees them, nevertheless there is the greatest interest in observing his attempts at clarification.

In the Hjortspring boat, Humbla finds a connecting link between the log boat and the craft of planks, with keel, prow and stern. He maintains that the «spread out» log boat the «soft dugout» — with stretchers, ribs and lashing-cleats — is the type of boat which led up to the Hjortspring and later

[1] Icelandic skald from the Viking Era.

also to the Nydam boat. Even the viking ships, with their peculiar system, must be supposed to have developed similarly from the log boat with a strake on it. I need hardly say that I regard this theory as mere deskwork.

Most recently, in 1943, Albert Nilsson has produced an admirable study of a number of log boats in Småland. Here, for instance, there is a name for one distinct type; it is known as *klovaskepp,* a boat whose floor consists of two *klover,* two cleft sections of log. The objects of Nilsson's study are boats from the three great lakes, of Åsnen, Bolmen and Sommen, and he advances a more general consideration which is of great interest. The boats from these three lakes cannot be regarded as different phases in the evolution of more modern forms. Åsnen's comparatively «perfect» log boats, which were in use right up to the present century, could not be given any further development in their own kind. The boats from Bolmen and Sommen, on the other hand, present a stage in evolution from the log *eike* to the plank-built *eike.* Here the Sommen boat is the more primitive, in that not merely the keel lacks but the prow is «dug out», while that from Bolmen has a prow of the more advanced type.

It must not be concluded, by the way, that the evolution of more modern forms, on the three lakes, took place through any mutual contact. The technical emancipation from more primitive forms (log boat to plank-*eike)* occurred in the three lake districts independently, as it did in other parts of the country.

In comparison with the coastal boats, those of the interior are considerably less affected by the larger context and the various historic impulses. But here too there are zones of culture and methods of diffusion, which, however, in the main have still to be worked out.

In the Baltic areas the log boat is very well known, but in specific forms which may suggest many reflections as to age, spheres of origin and evolution. We find that it is known in practically all the Baltic regions, and on into the north of Russia, and further on throughout Siberia, and then in kindred forms over large tracts of North America — everywhere as a boat distinctively of lakes and rivers, nowhere as a sea-going boat. Even though there are many gaps in our knowledge, all goes to show that we are here confronting something very ancient.

It seems we may now take it as established that the log boat, even in its most developed form, was used only on rivers and lakes. As a river boat it belongs to those territories where *rivers played a leading part in communication,* and only there did it reach any technical development. This could never happen in Norway, where communication by river is very limited. And after what has now been stated, it seems less and less credible that the log boat should in any place have been the ancestor of the sea-going boat. We are left with an impression that the log boat was not capable of much development, that even with the wonderfully fine technique arrived at in Estonia, Siberia etc., it remained the same old log boat, confined in all respects to its own possibilities.

The log boat in its ordinary simple and crude form is well known in certain parts of Finland, Sweden, Denmark and Norway. A few words on the Norwegian log boats will be of interest. Their real sphere is the lake and forest country near the Swedish border. Not a few are known in Glomdal. I cannot say whether they are to be found in Gudbrandsdal, Valdres or Hallingdal; I know of no one who has seen them, though it would be surprising if they did not exist. Numedal has one, from Dagali, and Telemark, among others, one from Tuddal.

But from the whole of South Norway and Rogaland, with all their river-valleys, lakes and coast, not one discovery of log boats has been reported. One possibility is named by Færøyvik – a «double boat» of hollowed tree trunks from Bykle in Setesdal, used up to our own time. In the west we know of only one find, the triple boat already mentioned (p. 20), from Lønningsdal, Os, near Bergen.

Then they crop up again north of the Dovre. The Trondhjem museums have four specimens, one of them from Meldal. This one is said to have been built in 1820, and was used on the river as late as 1912. It was made out of a single massive pine log. All are from big-river country, where they fit in naturally.

These Norwegian log boats have never come in for much scrutiny from the technical-historical point of view. A little has been written on occasion about the Glomdal boats. They are mostly or predominantly lake boats for fishing, but of course were also used for ferrying and transport at a pinch. It is quite clear that in a good many of these cases we are confronted with old Finn Boats. Some of them had outriggers, as the Finlanders' old boats also had, and the oars they used were bound with osiers. They looked like milk-troughs, says Lønborg. But the form must be older, in Glomdal also. The normal length seems to have been round about 13' (4 m.).

These Norwegian log boats are perhaps the simplest, least varied and least elaborate in all Europe. And indeed the main reason for this seems fairly evident. The rivers of East, South and North Norway were beyond doubt admirably suited for communication, but owing to our climatic conditions it was most practical that this communication should take place in winter, when the ice made roads and bridges, so to say gratis. Therefore with us the log boat was in the main a fairly primitive craft, in no great social esteem; the simple little boat for lake fishing, with the rudest technical equipment imaginable.

What we can say as regards certain of the Nordic countries, and Norway in particular, is that the log boat never occurs in those districts where they had most need to create a *sea-going boat.* The position is not quite the same for countries verging on a shallow North Sea – Holland, the Frisian regions and West Jutland, where the sea has quite a different physical and technical character from that of the ocean round the coast of Norway. To make a boat which will bear and last up here is very different from making one for the southern part of the North Sea, although of course it may be truly said that a boat is a boat everywhere. But in the case of Norway we can say at least that the idea developed by Behn, that the log boat is the «primary» form of the ship, or at any rate the form which played the biggest and most vital part in the evolution of shipbuilding, is a complete mistake. It does not get us anywhere.

One of the reasons why the log boat failed to develop much in Norway lies in the circumstance that here the rivers were not used for *long voyages*. Therefore it remained essentially a fishing and odd-job boat of the simplest kind, on lakes and short stretches of river. To men on any part of our long coast, the boat, big or small, is a necessity of life. An old Faroese proverb expresses this dependence of the coastal dwellers: *Bound is the boatless man.* To inland dwellers it is still of use, but comes far down the list of indispensable necessities.

So we would seem to have reached this point at any rate: in Norway the log boat never gave any positive foundation for the development of the plank boat, although it may have one or two derivatives. The foundation must be sought elsewhere.

In our approach to this problem, we have the same good indications.

First and foremost, it is to be remembered that the skin boat has ribs, one of the structural factors in the Norwegian boat of later days. There are no ribs in the log boat.

Next we must bear in mind one of the supremely vital features of the Norwegian plank boat: the thin planking which is the basis of its elasticity at sea. Hitherto we had not thought that Norwegian carpentry with the stone axes of the Stone and Bronze Age could have achieved those amazingly thin planks which are the indispensable condition for the Norwegian sea-going boat. According to Bøe's judgment of the Valderhaug boat (see below), that view must be changed.

Finally, the basis of the sea-going boat is the *keel;* an invention which takes generations, and indeed centuries, to reach its ultimate solution.

These three factors may be called essential. We shall turn more light on them in time. But first we have to glance at that remarkable interlude which is called

The Bronze Age Boats

Apparently we know a great deal about them, in actual fact our concrete knowledge is extremely slight. But we have masses of material, which has given and always will give rise to any number of debates, and great divergencies of view.

First of all, of course, we have the rock-carvings with all their drawings of ships, both in Norway and Sweden; we have ships carved on Danish bronze knives; we have the large image of the universal Bronze Age culture, which presumes not merely occasional craft, but downright seafaring; and we have the find, thus far unique, of the remains of a Bronze Age boat from Valderøy, Sunnmøre.

This find is old, but not till 1942 was it set in place, by Professor *Johs. Bøe.* On the most easterly point of Valderøy there still exist the mighty ruins

ʾart of a pine strake found at Val-ʾerhaug, Giske, Sunnmøre. Holes ‹or the seams can be seen along ‹he upper, left edge. Bergens Uni-ʾersitet.*

of a giant cairn, which, despite centuries of constant havoc, gives an impression of enormous strength even now. It is called Valderhaug. It was «excavated» in 1824—27, and Bishop Neumann, by whom the digging was initiated and supervised, in 1827 wrote down the observations of the workmen, which he checked on his account. Bøe has given a full resumé, from which the following may be extracted. The mighty mound contained a central grave, in the middle of the floor. Here lay a big flat stone, and on it the remains of a boat or ship. It may be assumed that this arrangement in the centre, with the boat-fragments, formed the original purpose of the mound. And the dating seems to be pretty clear. It must be from the early Bronze Age.

Except for a newly-discovered Bronze Age boat-grave in Scania, these are the only boat-remains of such antiquity to have been found in the North, so the discovery may well be called rather sensational. And we look somewhat closer at these ancient bits of board. They consist of several fragments of *pine* planking, two of them obviously pieces of a ship's side, with planks so laid that the lower edge slightly overlaps the one before, but not riveted. They are *sewn* together (with bast or something of the kind—pigs' bristles, Neumann says in 1827), the seam was finished off with treenails, and there was some kind of material between the planks as caulking. One of the fragments has a lashing-cleat: cf. the Nydam ship.

Here we have full technical agreement with the boat from Hjortspring on Als in Denmark, which is of the much later Bronze Age or early Iron Age, and with the old Iron Age boat from Halsnøy in Sunnhordland. Both will be discussed later. In the 1920's our great boat specialist Bernhard Færøyvik annexed these remnants of the Valderhaug boat, and established that the planks were sewn together with twisted *gut,* that there was *wool* in the caulking, and that seam and caulking were impregnated with some matter which might be birchbark oil, tar or resin. In every strake there had been holes bored for the seam. Færøyvik says he has met no instance in the North of any similar finds—boats made of planking sewn together with sinew or gut. The Valderhaug boat is the only one, and it must be considerably older than the boats from Hjortspring and Halsnøy.

Everything, says Bøe, goes to show that we have here the genuine remains of a boat or rather *a ship of the Bronze Age,* and probably from an early Bronze Age burial. It is the first, and of its kind so far the only one in the North. Whether the boat was whole or nearly whole when it was placed in the grave remains uncertain. Quite possibly they buried only some pieces of it, to represent the entire craft. Although the fragments which were found,

›rwegian historian of the 18th century

and which are now in the historical museum of Bergen University, do not give us a complete picture of the Bronze Age ship, its appearance and dimensions etc., yet they provide most striking clues for an appraisal of the history of the boat in Norway. The most important point is that we have here a *plank-built boat* as far back as the early Bronze Age. The planking is quite thin, in its present condition barely $^3/_5$", but since it has never been treated, of course we cannot say how thick it was originally. None the less, we are here faced with one of the most vital chapters in the history of our early boat-building. Even though this boat, in the eyes of a shipwright of the Viking Period, would be very «primitive», it leads in direct line to the boat-building we know of in our early Iron Age.

The great new question thus arising is: Where and when did they begin to raise the hull in this way, with strakes hewn thin and laid with the edges overlapping? Though there is no trace of ribs, it is fairly self-evident that they were used here. And it is no new feature. The old skin boats had ribs.

For the time being, the question must remain unanswered. For though we have pictorial matter of unique richness, in all the likenesses of ships in the rock-carvings, they do not give us reliable information on the structure of these boats.

These rock-carvings have been under discussion for a number of years in Norway and Sweden. The most important question has been this: Are they the likenesses of real ships and boats, or are they mere symbolic drawings, bound up with the cult, magic and ritual of religion in the Bronze Age, and without basis in reality? From all this discussion it seems plain that they were certainly connected with religious practices. But it is equally certain that they reflect a milieu where ships and boats did play a leading part in real life. Pictures («photographs») in our sense they are not. Yet to this very day, one may see things as the rock-carver saw them. A day of sunshine on the sea. In the far distance rows a boat; it stands out on the horizon, peopled from stem to stern. The picture is exactly like one of the simpler boats in the rock-carvings. The curve from prow to stern, and—like black silhouettes with no more form than simple strokes—the men on board. This impression, which I have received many times, is just like that expressed by the rock-carver in the simplest drawings.

It is different with the more complex pictures, where details and development involve so many nuances. But they confirm the view that these are pictures of real shipbuilding in the Bronze Age and the early Iron Age. A number of important detail-studies of the various types of boat and ship have been made by both Norwegian and Swedish archaeologists — Arthur Nordén, Gutorm Gjessing, Per Fett etc.

Starting from the big rock-carving group at Bardal in Beitstad, Trøndelag, where at least 350 ships are represented, Gjessing has laid a foundation for the dating of the big main groups of ships. It is of great importance there that he has pointed out ship-drawings which correspond to well-known decorative themes on bronze objects. This applies especially to the big, heavy ship-figures, often of massive proportions — ships which vary from 9'10"

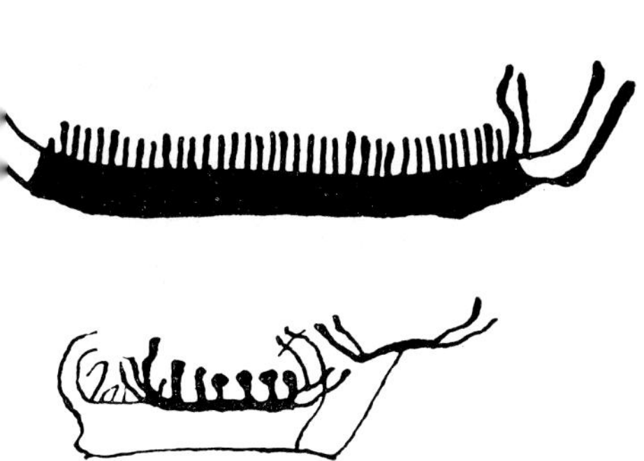

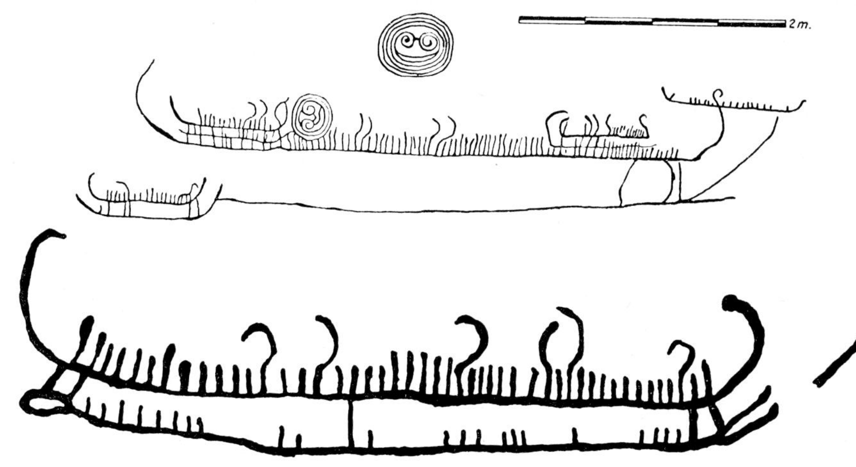

Ships from Bronze Age rock-carvings at Bardal, Trøndelag. The examples shown here illustrate the various stages in the development of shipbuilding in the earliest times.

(3 m.) to nearly 15' (4½ m.) on the carved surface. The biggest ship has no less than 81 «crewstrokes». They are also impressive in technique, with broad, powerful lines, and are, pictorially speaking, complicated ships, with curving prow and stern, gunnel and keel-line etc. The dating proves that these ships must belong to the later Bronze Age, or perhaps even to the late Bronze Age and early Iron Age. We have splendid ships of this class in the rock-carvings of Østfold and Östergötland, Uppland etc. In other words, Gjessing believes it to be clear that we can trace, throughout the whole Bronze Age, a constant evolution of the ship from its earliest and simple forms to the great «chieftain-ships» of the late Bronze Age. On this route there are many phases of extremely varied character. The famous ships from Bakkehaug in Skjeberg has a prow and stern ending in horses' heads, and that from Bjørnstad in Skjeberg also has an animal's head at either end. With the curved line taken by the «keel» in the fore part of the ship—see for example the ship from Bakkehaug—these latest shipdrawings are brought into clear contact with the Danish ship from Hjortspring, whose structure and date we know.

A couple of the most outstanding finds in this latest group may be discussed separately.

On this basis one can look backwards through the large material of rock-carving ships, and classify the figures. Among Nordic investigators, there seems to be agreement that the earliest type, the so-called «*Herrestrup boat*», goes right back to the Stone Age. It is a very simple drawing, made up of one curved line and a few crew-strokes. And here too one can distinguish between an earlier and a later group. This class belongs, in general, to the early Bronze Age, and can be found over the whole extensive rock-carving areas of Norway and Sweden.

Later than this class are the ships with *keel-boards*. And here again one can distinguish an older group, with well-marked gunnel and keel-line. The latter is decidedly prolonged and bent upwards. Both prow and stern have a strong upward curve. The later group gives smaller ships with strongly upward-curving prow and stern and rounded keel-line. Both these go on into the later Bronze Age (age group 8—9).

Finally we have the latest group, which has already been examined, and which takes us straight to the Hjortspring ship.

Both Gjessing and others have now shown that the «rock-carving» delineation of boats is continued into the earlier and later Iron Age on rocks and standing stones. We shall glance at this material in connection with the later Norwegian boat-building.

Many investigators, both Norwegian and Swedish, have, by the same means as Gjessing, brought chronological order into the pictorial renderings of ships in the rock-carvings.

In their work on the Rogaland carvings, Eva and Per Fett have distinguished two main series of boats. The earlier is the *skin* boat, which is a legacy from the boats of the early Stone Age and maintains itself well into the Bronze Age. The later is the «wooden ship», which seems to have arisen in the late Stone Age, develops gradually throughout the Bronze Age, and continues as the plank boat of the Iron Age.

Thus the hiatus is, as it were, the «jump» from skin to wood. The structure otherwise is common to both. This jump was made as far back as the Stone Age. It shows the technical civilisation of the Stone Age in a new perspective. We have found it hard to believe that Stone Age axes could be used for splitting logs up into planks, such as we see them in the fragment of the Valderhaug boat. But then in actual fact we may observe that even in bronze there are no axe-tools very well adapted, in our eyes, to the making of planks. In this the Bronze Age made no technical advance on the Stone Age. Our understanding of these basic technical problems is very slight; we have been blunted by modern technique.

The question has been discussed with a modern shipwright, and with our specialist on viking ships, Mr. Fr. Johannessen, and on the basis of these discussions we can give a number of important facts.

The transition from wood to skin will not be easy to explain well. At first one might suppose it must be easier to stretch skins on a timber skeleton than to carve planks of wood, then fit them in and sew them to the framework. But this is more than one can take for granted. The use of skin for boats requires a long and complicated process. The milieu out of which it grows is a typical and one-sided hunting culture connected with the sea (seal). The plank grows out of a forest age milieu, which, to be sure, preserv-

Rock-carvings from Hornes in Skjeberg, Østfold.

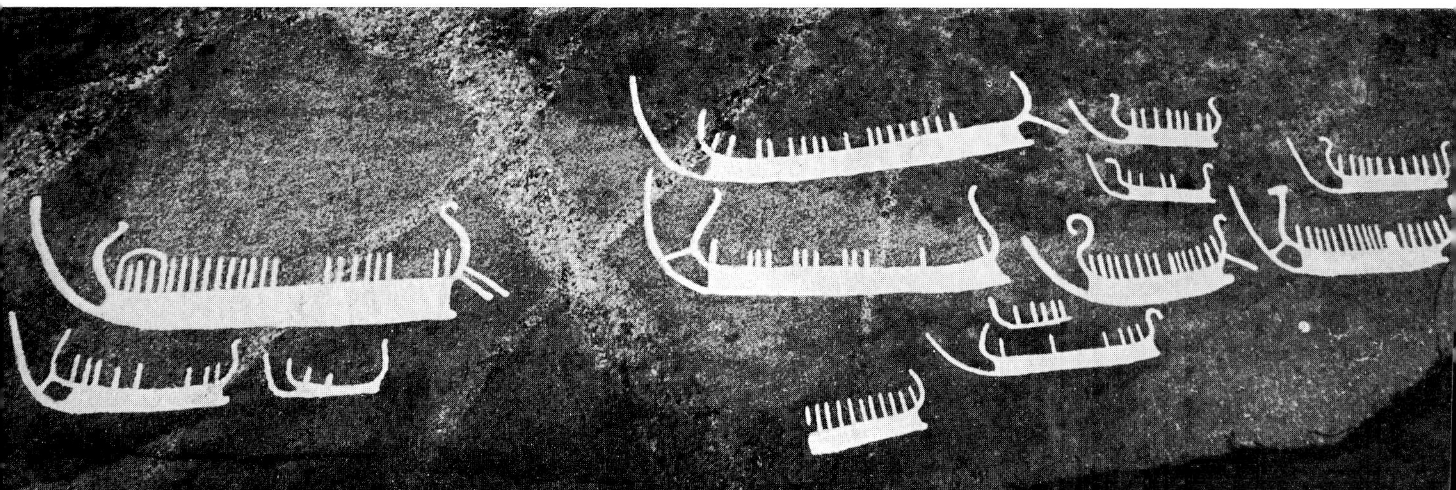

'he Bronze Age ship in the rock-arving at Bjørnstad, Skjeberg, Østfold. This is one of the most amous rock-carvings in Scandina-ia. Photo: Sverre Marstrander.

ed the hunting accent in its own way. In these general conditions it may be possible to find an explanation, based on purely archaeological circumstances and material.

It is certain that the change-over constitutes a real *invention,* experiment leading to a discovery. The milieu must have been a wooded sea-coast. The discovery may have been made in several places. That it should have anything to do with the log boat is definitely improbable as regards Norway.

If we follow the evolution of the rock-carving ships, the plank boat does not start up from nothing. In the older drawings we find the keel and gunnel as two straight, parallel lines, both of which end fore and aft in upward curves. In the more developed pictures, the cross-strokes between gunnel and keel are to be interpreted as ribs. The crew on board is indicated by a monotonous series of upstrokes above the gunnel.

And so far everything seems plain. Only with the next questions do we have obscurity and disagreement. Our best judge, *Shetelig,* holds that the ships were rowing vessels, since we have no proved instances of ships depicted with mast and sail. And this could have been a very conspicuous feature in a profile drawing, were the crew shows up so plainly above the side. The oars are not usually included in the drawing. But we have a few fine ships' pictures in which it can be clearly seen that they rowed with loose paddle-oars, short and broad-bladed, with no attachment to the gunnel. This applies to the picture in a rock-drawing at Skien, and also to the famous Brandskog ship from Uppland in Sweden.

According to Gjessing and Fett, it is plain that several rock-carving ships depict a *rudder* (North Trøndelag, Rogaland); it is interpreted as a side-rudder, and if so, pretty clearly on the starboard side. They belong to the later group, and indeed it is very possible and probable that the rudder first appears with the big ships of the later Bronze Age and early Iron Age.

Shetelig's opinion is that the boats and ships of the rock-carvings were lightly built, low, open rowing-boats. There was plainly no obstacle to building them very long, with lofty prow and stern, which often end in stylish decorations, animals' heads, spirals etc. A number of ships' figures have designs which might suggest some decorative painting on the sides. This, as is natural enough, applies chiefly to the latest of the big ships. Obviously, when we talk of crew-strokes it is not implied that we can reckon up the crew statistically by the number of strokes. There are drawings in Østfold with more than 70 strokes, and big ships in Rogaland with over 80. All we can say is that they were able to build really large craft. In certain pictures the crew are drawn as human figures, and in a few of them we see great shapes depicted, chiefs, who, with raised weapons, tower above the throng of ordinary seamen. These are the age's mighty gods, formed in the likeness of the chief. Pictures like this tell clearly of the first bloom of early Old Norse ship-building on the coast of Norway.

Rock-carvings from Borgen in Skjeberg, Østfold.

Thanks to the harmony already mentioned between the big ships of the later rock-drawings and the Danish find, the Hjortspring boat, we now know definitely how at least the later Bronze Age ships were built. The main features in the building were a broad *bottom plank without an outer keel,* finishing at either end in a free «beak», and two *gunnel-planks* with thickened edges, meeting in the lofty prow and stern. Between the keel-plank and the gunnel, two similar cross-pieces are thrust in, which «close» the hull fore and aft. The planking of the sides is next adapted to this skeleton, and propped internally by frame-timbers, ribs. Alongside the normal type, pictures occur with many variations, indicating that the method of building varied somewhat with the time and place. A mere scrutiny of the pictorial matter from Østfold, Bohuslän, Rogaland, Trøndelag, and the rich areas of Uppland and Östergötland reveals many local types, and also forms which differ with the period. Shetelig says that in the rock-drawing of West Norway many ships occur in which the stem goes vertically upward from the «keel-plank», while the latter shoots straight out in a little free beak. Here it is taken that the stem was mortised into the keel-plank, and then the gunnel and planking of the sides were fixed to it. Shetelig adds that on a closer study of the pictures from this point of view, we should undoubtedly reach a clearer insight into the evolution of Norwegian shipbuilding in the Bronze Age, and should identify more local types. Such an inquiry would be best conducted with the help of a boat-builder.

Johs. Bøe states that the pictures on the slabs of rock from Mjeltehaug on Giske (Sunnmøre) indicate purely local boat-types, which were peculiar to Sunnmøre as far back as the early Bronze Age.

Shetelig's interpretation of the drawings of ships, that they had no mast or sail, is borne out directly by the boat from Hjortspring, in which there is not a trace of any fitting for mast or sail. So they were built for rowing, and the rowing was clearly done with paddle-oars. Here, then, the question arises whether these ships were ocean-going. At first sight it appears a fairly hopeless enterprise to row a good sized craft over such waters as the Skagerak and the North Sea. But it would be a mistake to draw the conclusion that these ships did not cross the sea. In the introduction it has been shown from indirect evidence, that even in the early Stone Age dangerous waters were being crossed in boats of skin. We have also indirect evidence that they must have crossed even the *great* waters, where they had to be several days at sea. (Montelius on direct contact between England and Sweden in the Stone Age.) And yet we cannot get away from the fact that they *were not* acquainted with sail and mast. In this point, therefore, the structure of the boats differs decisively from later shipbuilding in the Iron Age.

Nevertheless, to judge from a large source-material, it seems clear that the Bronze Age was an age of seafaring, the first we know of. In a lecture to the International Archaeological Congress in Oslo in 1936, I tried to show the probability that some tribes of Western Europe and the Mediterranean created in the Bronze Age the first great seafaring period, in which they not merely sailed along the main coasts, but put out to sea and sailed the ocean. It is probable that this applies especially to the later Bronze Age.

The ship in the rock-carvings at Brandskog, Uppland, Sweden. Notice the characteristic «beak», or prolongation of the keel fore and aft, and the animal heads on the prow and stern. The crew is standing up and paddling the ship. Probably from the early Iron Age. After Arthur Nordén.

It is implicit in the very idea of a bronze industry that it should have done much more to develop seafaring and communications than did the production of raw material in the Stone Age. The manufacture of bronze requires supplies of copper and tin, metals which have to be obtained from widely different regions. Therefore it builds up quite new organs in the working life of the European communities. The whole process naturally develops knowledge and skill which can only be employed by trading and shipbuilding firms with an understanding of both production and markets. The prevalence of the raw materials to some extent marks out the new connections and routes. All this continues to flourish for some centuries, during which the forms and dimensions of transocean shipping are constantly enlarged. Then in the transition period, when iron really begins to make its way in Europe, the old bronze commerce and seafaring enter on hard times. There is a notable falling-off in the demand for tin and copper. The old shipping and commercial firms are reduced, and the great age of seafaring is over. And soon all the geographical knowledge which had been gained through the centuries becomes a legend. The Bronze Age maritime period is followed by the continental world-picture of the first Iron Age, which set its mark upon geography for twelve or thirteen hundred years, until the new epoch of discoveries and seafaring arrived, and had to build up again almost everything that had been assembled by the great maritime civilisation of the Bronze Age.

In this wide European milieu the Nordic Bronze Age ships have their place. Even though our picture of them lacks reliable detail, we can at least feel sure that the skin boat is gradually replaced by boats built of wood, cut in whole planks, with the structural details of the skin boat as a basis. We can see this most plainly in the big ships of the later Bronze Age and early Iron Age. And there the way lies open for the appearance of the Nordic Iron Age boat. Towards a picture of its evolution we have gradually acquired a good store of matter, chiefly from finds within the last generation.

The Plank Boat in the Iron Age

The line of this evolution has been traced by Shetelig. Its point of departure is the Danish *Hjortspring boat,* already mentioned, from Als in South Jutland. This is still of the Bronze Age type, but can be dated as belonging to the first Iron Age, some centuries before the start of our chronology. Here we make acquaintance with the technical details in the structure of the rock-carving ships. The Hjortspring boat was deposited in a bog, together with a quantity of weapons, as a victory offering after a battle. Therefore it must have been a war craft. It is an open rowing-boat with twenty paddle-oars in all, but without oar holes or rowlocks – that is, a fairly primitive ship. And as has already been said, it has no fitting for a mast. Indeed the whole structure makes it obvious enough that such a fragile craft would not have stood such a thing. For it is built in this way: The bottom of one broad plank and over them two planks on either side. The uppermost of these is the gunnel, with a thicker edge contrived out of the same piece. The keel-plank and the gunnel both continue as a free beak shooting out at either end of the hull. This gives the boat the same characteristic profile that we know so well from the rock-carvings.

The boards are very broad and quite thin, hewn out of lime wood. They are *sewn* together with cord, and the stitches and seams are caulked with resin glue. The inner skeleton of the boat is a quite complicated ribbing of slender hazel branches, fixed to the planking by lashing them to cleats contrived in the boards. These ribs, a kind of imperfect frame-timber, are reinforced by crosstruts, and there are props inserted under each thwart. By way of rudder there were two steering-oars, one at each end of the boat.

Compared with such perfect boats as the Gokstad ship and the Tune ship, this craft is undeniably very primitive, frail in build, too open and vulnerable on open sea. Another curiously primitive feature is that the planks have noe joints, but are prepared in one piece. And yet we are by no means dealing with a clumsy noviciate. The separate structural features are well calculated, and the execution shows a finished craftsman-ship at all points. The aim which they had set themselves – a light, manoeuvrable ship capable of taking a large crew – is achieved completely. All the woodwork is as light and thin as possible, yet at the same time with the greatest possible resistance, even in all the joinings of seam and cord. It can be said with certainty that we have here an old tradition, inherited from the boat-building of the Bronze Age. On this foundation they continued working in the Iron Age. The basic features persist right down to the Viking Era.

odel of the Hjortspring boat, und at Als, South Jutland. oto: The Norwegian Maritime useum, Oslo.

The new development taking place in Roman times and in the period of the migrations can be followed both in late rock-carving pictures and in boat-finds from Norway and Denmark. It was again Shetelig who worked out the points at issue. The first hard problem to crop up was especially the structure of the stem. The old form with the keel-plank shooting out in a beak, of which the object is not quite clear, and which goes with the insertion of a cross-piece, intended possibly to cleave the sea in the bows, was an over-complex yet an insecure device for such a vital part of the craft. The need for stronger and more seaworthy boats must soon have made itself felt.

In the ships of the Kårstad carving, Nordfjord, the interpretation seems to be that the stems are attached to the keel at that point where he hull is «closed», and that the planking on each side is fastened to the stem itself, not to an inserted cross-piece. The beak of the keel-plank thus becomes a superfluous rudiment, and indeed a weak point, dangerous to the whole craft. So it is done away with. The ship appears in this simplified form in the carving from Roskar, Sunnmøre. The beak has vanished from the keel, while the stems are still cleft at the end into two horns, as a reminder of continuity with earlier stages.

We see this advance completed in the *Halsnøy boat,* Hordaland, the oldest craft we know in Norway, which has been minutely analysed by Shetelig. In the whole method of building, the Halsnøy boat has close kinship with the boat from Hjortspring. It is built of pine and has light, thin planks sewn with thin root-fibres, and also sewn to the stems, with coarse tarred thread. All the joints are caulked with strips of red woven material, dipped in tar. The planks have cleats contrived in them, with holes for lashing the frametimbers. The top strake has a solid thickened gunnel, cut in the board itself. A completely new feature and a great advance is that the top strake has *rowlocks* for the oars. The boat is no longer paddled, but is rowed in the proper sense.

The very ancient Danish ship from *Nydam* in Slesvig is constructed like the Halsnøy boat, with planks laid so that the lower edge of each one slightly

Rock-carving with ship and ru at Kårstad, Nordfjord, probab from the early Iron Age. Pho Bergens Museum.

Cast of a rock-carving at Roskar, Sunnmøre. Bergens Universitet.

overlaps the one below, but this time *riveted with iron nails.* The clinker-built plank boat is from this time forth — the early migration period — the Nordic boat, which will be steadily improved until it finds its climax in the Gokstad ship. Even though the Nydam ship represents a great advance in many ways, it still has certain glaring weaknesses. For instance, it has no true keel, only a broad keel-plank, on the most massive scale indeed, but still not adequate to resist pressure on the bottom out at sea. It is a legacy from the building methods of the Bronze Age, says Shetelig. There is an attempt to counteract it, by giving the hull an absurdly narrow and abrupt profile in section. Oars are still the only means of propulsion, and they are noticeably short, so that the strokes must have been something between rowing and paddling — what in the Mediterranean was called Turkish rowing.

The splendid burial-find from *Sutton Hoo* in Suffolk, which came to light in 1939, also contained a ship. The date of the grave is fairly certain — the

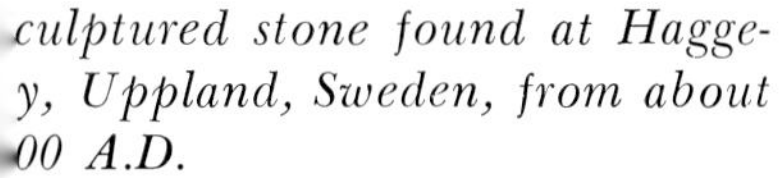

culptured stone found at Hagge-y, Uppland, Sweden, from about 00 A.D.

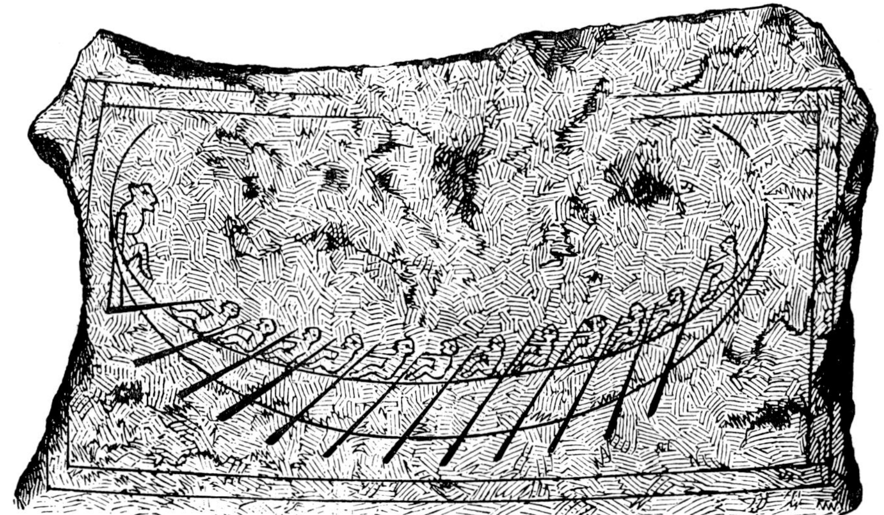

first half of the seventh century. In the centre of the huge grave-mound stood the ship, about 80 feet long – that is, a little bigger than the Gokstad ship. Even though many details have been lost, the general picture of the ship is clear. A slenderly built craft, with strongly projecting stems, and no sign of a mast – unquestionably near akin to the Nydam ship. This find, so far unique in England, proves that Nordic and Anglo-Saxon boat-building followed much the same structural lines, and passed through more or less the same stages. And despite the fact that Halsnøy, Nydam and Sutton Hoo are all rowing vessels without mast and sail, after the English find we need have no doubt that they were sea-going ships, capable of covering long stretches of ocean by rowing alone.

The next stage in the solution of these complex nautical problems is to be found in the big boat from *Kvalsund* in Herøy, Sunnmøre, excavated in 1920 by Shetelig. It is a large craft for ten pairs of oars, built in the main on the same principles as the Nydam ship. The connection between stem and keel, frame-timbers, gunnel and rowlocks is executed in the same way in both. But with the Kvalsund ship there appears something quite new, showing a decided technical advance. It is a question of the keel and rudder. The ship has still, indeed, quite a broad keel-plank, not a fully-developed keel as later in the viking ships. But this keel-plank has an external keel on the under side, the whole in one piece. We may express it by saying that the keel is still only a modest effort, a kind of thick runner along the middle of the bottom, but enough to strengthen the boat against the pressure of the sea, so that the bottom could fill out and give a good deal more stability. In other words, the hull could be built broader, with greater carrying power and more room on board. And instead of the broad, whole strakes of Hjortspring and Nydam, we now have narrower and more strakes, scarfed from several pieces. Presumably experience had taught them that it was a superstition to believe that broad, whole strakes without joints were so strong. It is soon to be recognised among boat-builders that the ship will have much more elasticity at sea with a hull made out of many boards joined together.

The invention of the keel, which we meet here for the first time in the Kvalsund boat, was the first great step forward to the form of the Viking Era.

It is of equal importance that here we first meet with the classic (Nordic) treatment of the rudder. They had indeed used rudders even earlier, in the form of loose steering-oars, but their connection with the ship was too loose and inadequate, at least for a sailing vessel. In the Kvalsund boat the rudder

The ship found at Nydam in Slesvig from the 4th Century A. D., now in the Museum Schloss Gottorp.

Runic stone at Tullstorp, Malmøhus län, Sweden, from about 1000 A.D.

is attached very efficiently to the ship's side, aft the starboard gunnel, with a tiller thrusting crosswise into the ship.

All these constructive details made it possible for the boat to carry *mast* and *sail*. And thus the foundation had been laid for that North Sea voyaging which increases through the migration period and alters the whole geography of ancient civilisation.

The large boat from Kvalsun Herøya, Sunnmøre. Here, for t first time, we see the solution the problem of the keel and t classic arrangement of the rudd. This boat could have both m and sail. From a model in Berge Museum.

In this section of the book we shall not enter on the history of the *sail* outside Nordic boat-building. The presentation here makes it quite plain *when* sail-carrying boats and ships appeared in Norway. The Kvalsund ship is the first stage. Nor shall we discuss why it was that such good seamen as the Scandinavians did not arrive at the sail earlier. Probably there were more reasons than one. There is no doubt that races outside Scandinavia had reached some use of sail. Here it will be enough to mention that Caesar found sailing-vessels in use on the Atlantic coast of Gaul – or what is now the north-west of France. He refers to the craft of the Veneti, powerful and high-built, with a strong sheer in prow and stern. They carried sails made of hide, and though designed for rowing as well, they were definitely sailing-vessels. Against them Caesar's rowing-craft made a poor show; they were of the old Mediterranean type, not very seaworthy, and without a trace of sail. But these vessels of the Veneti had no influence on the evolution of Nordic boat-building.

The Kvalsund boat is not more distinguished by its improvements in technique than by its marked aesthetic quality – the fine lines of the hull, the proudly rising curve of the stem, which has no practical object, but is designed exclusively to make the vessel handsome and stately. Embellishment, again, brought in two ornamental pieces, which we call *brander,* finishing off the top strake where the planking joins the stem, and lightly decorated on the outer surface. The full length of this ship, which to all appearances could sail the sea, is about 59' (18 m.), and the beam is rather more than 9' 10" (3 m.) thus it is still a narrow boat in proportion, and not very deep-drawing, only about 2' 7" (80 cm.).

With the Kvalsund boat, shipbuilding in Norway reached the first phase of sea-going sailing-ships. Though it is still a long way from the more accomplished viking ships, in the judgment of Shetelig and Fr. Johannessen we can say that it belongs rather to the new period than to the old. And now we are really beginning to have fairly reliable data on the history of boat-building. We know its evolution from the skin boat of the Stone Age to the later Bronze Age boats made of whole planks, ending with the Hjortspring boat, which we can place about 300 B.C.

The next clear link is the Halsnøy boat, which may be placed about 200 A.D. With this simple litte boat of all work, in which the paddle oars give way to rowlocks, begins the introduction to a new phase in the history of Norwegian boat-building. It has practically the same profile as modern boats of the west coast. The many scattered finds made in the west before and after the Kvalsund boat show that the same building methods were diffused along the coast from Møre, Trøndelag to Nordland.

The Nydam boat reveals the next step, and Shetelig dates it at 300—500 A.D.

Then comes the decisive new era, with the Kvalsund boat, which can probably be placed about 600 A.D. — the great age of the migrations and the prologue to the new great age of Norwegian seafaring. This is the time of the heroic legends in the west, with all their memories of feats at sea, their battles between «kings» in Rogaland and Hordaland, indeed as far up as North Norway. It was in ships like this that the first voyages were made across the ocean to the western isles — voyages beginning in the seventh and eighth centuries, and leading later to discovery and colonisation.

What now remains to be accomplished in boat-building is the achievements of full strength and solidity in the keel part, so that they could raise a proper mast and employ sail at sea in all weathers. This takes place in the centuries between the Kvalsund ship and the Gokstad ship, the years from 600 to 900, as Shetelig describes later in this book. Instead of the old keel-plank there appears a true keel, with a strong vertical cross-section, gi-

'he imprint of the ship in the urial mound at Sutton Hoo, Suf- olk, from the first half of the 7th 'entury A.D. By courtesy of the 'rustees of the British Museum.

ving the bottom of the ship an ample and sturdy shape. The parts most vital to the shoring of the hull, which were formerly the gunnel and thwarts, now move down to the water-line, and take the form of an especially solid strake, and internal cross-beams from top to top of each rib. The underwater part of the ship, on which all really depends, is thus protected by a structure at once strong and elastic, while the planking above the water is built more simply, nailed to knees attached to the cross-beams. It was through these innovations of keel and cross-pieces, which may look simple enough, that it became possible to give the ship an efficient spread of sail.

The old type, from Nydam on to Halsnøy and in part to Kvalsund, was too crank and frail. Now the keel could give support to a solid substructure, and the beams hold up the mast. Above the keel, and resting on the frame-timbers amidships, they placed a massive block of oak with a mast socket and partner. The rigging was as simple as possible, one large square-sail, and the mast without any appreciable support from shrouds or stays. In this connection Shetelig recalls an old experience of our seamen. They used to say that the boats sailed better when the masts had give in them, without shrouds. And now the structure lends itself to canvas. The Gokstad ship, about the same length as the Nydam ship, is twice as broad, with a proportionate increase in carrying power, an ample form, and correspondingly high-built. This led to yet another innovation. In ships with such a lofty gunnel, they can no longer very well use rowlocks. *Oar-holes* are introduced in one of the upper strakes, as we see in the Oseberg ship and the Gokstad ship.

Now, at any rate the Gokstad ship and Tune ship were seagoing vessels. Formerly we knew less about fjord boats and odd-job boats. But in this field too, the excavations and studies of recent years have changed the situation.

Here we have most light on the fully developed small craft from the Gokstad find. On the ship were discovered fragments of no less than three boats. The old «seaport boy», Nicolaysen of Bergen, saw at once that here was something really remarkable. Fundamentally, he says, they can be considered even more remarkable than the Gokstad ship itself, since they must be the only ancient craft of this kind which are now known. Nicolaysen and his successors had not experience enough to manage the reconstruction of these three unique boats. That was reserved for our time, when we were working on the big ships of antiquity, to get them properly restored and moved to the new hall of viking ships at Bygdøy (1926—1948). Our specialist on the structure of viking ships, Fr. Johannessen, has now restored two of the three boats, and given a description of the largest, which we shall quote in brief. It is 31'11 1/2" (9.75 m.) long, and the beam is 6'1 1/5" (1.86 m.). It is built entirely of oak, with five strakes on each side. They are almost incredibly thin, and the whole boat is extraordinarily light and slender in build; nor do the ribs (six in number) err on the solid side. The whole transverse connection is very like that still employed in the west and north. The thwarts were loose, and rested on the ribs. The floor-boards were of thin pine. This boat was rowed with three pairs of oars in rowlocks, attached to the inner side of the top strake. It was steered with a rudder, attached aft to starboard,

he large ship's boat of the Gok-ad ship. Altogether there were agments of three boats found in he Gokstad mound. Two of them ave been completely reconstruct-d by Fr. Johannessen. They have n almost incredibly thin plank-ng, and the whole structure is xtraordinarily light and slender. he boats were rowed in rowlocks ith grommets. In these craft we oubtless see the foundations of he present day fjord and fishing oats used along the Norwegian oast. The Viking Ship Museum, slo.

just as in the big ships. There is no mast; in that respect the boat is on a level with the earlier stages. And yet it is difficult to imagine a boat with finer, purer lines than this Gokstad boat. There can scarcely be a rowing-boat on the coast in our time to equal it. In this boat we can doubtless see the type of the ordinary fjord or fishing boat for domestic needs.

The many connecting links in the line of evolution we have here attempted to trace, the numerous transitions, and above all the multitude of local variations in boat-building on the coasts of Norway, are coming gradually to light with all the new discoveries made every year of individual ships parts, and sometimes of whole boats. When Shetelig published his account of the Kvalsund boats, he also drew attention to the reports of similar finds in West and North Norway. We may assume, he says, that many of these boats found in our marshes are victory sacrifices, offerings of war booty after a fight. It is the nature of things that a large number of these finds should not be very easy to date. Besides, the majority of them include only separate parts of boats: chiefly such things as billets for, or half-finished, boat-stems, pieces of keel, frame-timbers, strakes, rowlocks, and occasionally oar-blades, balers etc.

By no means all these finds can be regarded as sacrificial finds. A number of them consists, as has been said, only of more or less completed *ship-stems.* We have them from Rogaland, Hordaland, and other parts of the coast. Some have also been found on the Norwegian Atlantic islands. On a typical find of this description, Shetelig, in 1923, made a report which is very illuminating. It is from Haukanes on Hufteren, Austvoll, in Hordaland. In the course of a big ditching job in a marsh, they found, along with pieces of a boat-keel, *three stem-posts* for boats. One of them is only rough-hewn; the other two are rather more fashioned, but even they are not quite finished.

The keel is also rather rough. All the pieces are of oak. None of them have been used; there is not the least sign of their having been fitted to each other or to the planking. «I have speculated a great deal on this,» Shetelig writes later, «and then I heard that boat-builders of the west country still preserve bits of material sunk in water, preferably in the sea — especially material for stem and stern-posts, keels, frame-timbers.»

There is a similar find in Stavanger Museum: three unfinished boat-stems of oak, discovered in marshy ground on the farm Gard in Skåre. And in Sunnanå, Ryfylke, the stern-post for quite a big boat was discovered in a marsh.

Of these numerous marsh finds, our expert Bernhard Færøyvik says that they belong to various types of boats; some to heavy cargoboats (barges), others to more lightly built and faster-sailing craft. It is curious that several are of types as yet unknown in Norway, but found in other contries. Such, for example, are the Galtabäck boat in the west of Sweden, and the Danzig-Ohra boat in East Prussia (probably a nest of vikings).

In addition to these many individual finds of pieces in marsh land, recent years have brought forth more discoveries, of boats for the most part entire, which have greatly enlarged our knowledge. Therefore they deserve a few words. We mention them here in no precise order of time or place.

To a stage before the Viking Era belong the two boats which were dug up in 1940—41 in a marsh in Fjørtoft, Haram, Sunnmøre — that is, just north of Kvalsund, Herøy, Færøyvik reckons that we have here a twelve-oar boat and its after-boat, as it was called in old Norse — a four-oar dinghy. The reconstruction of the big boat shows a craft much the same size as the Gokstad boat just mentioned, about 16'4" (10 m.) long, but slightly broader and deeper than the Gokstad boat, fairly sharp-bottomed, and with a high sheer. The keel is of oak, with no apparent fitting for a mast: a biggish boat, therefore, without sail. The frame-timbers and all the «inner wood» are pine, while the planking is again oak. As usual in the small boats it is quite smooth, without lashing-cleats for the frame-timbers. It is riveted with iron nails. The caulking is done with wool and cattle-hair. The boat had rowlocks, with long oars, and a side rudder of pine. The thwarts and floor-boards were also pine.

The small boat from Fjørtoft was, as has been said, a four-oar dinghy, built of pine. It is a highly curious feature that, as Færøyvik points out, it is built like a barge in the middle and like a boat at both ends, — something hitherto unknown in the old Norwegian shipwright's craft. Instead of a proper keel it has a so-called «sliding-keel.» The planking is unusually thin, there seem to have been only two strakes on either side, and it is fastened to the frame-timbers (three in number) with treenails. The boat was about 18'8" (5.7 m.) long, much broader than the smallest Kvalsund boat, and flat, so that the rowers sat rather low.

Per Fett, who dug up both these boats, believes that we have here a fairly obvious example of a sacrifice. The boats were drawn up on land, the big boat foremost, with the dinghy behind. Neither of the boats was destroyed,

Rowlock with grommet-hole in one of the boats in the Gokstad find.

as at Kvalsund and elsewhere, and these were not graves. For one thing, not a single antique object was found.

Færøyvik goes thoroughly into the dating of these two boats, by comparison with the Kvalsund boats, etc., and finally reaches the conclusion that they can probably be placed in the same era as the Kvalsund boat, the 5th—8th centuries A.D.

Yet another bog find came to light in the Bergen Museum's excavation of 1945, from the farmstead of *Rong* in Herdla, west of Hjeltefjord north of Bergen. Bernhard Færøyvik, who was in charge of the excavation, has reported on the find. He points out that it is the third sacrificial find to have been dug up in West Norway in recent years. The Kvalsund find was the first (1920). Here two boats had been smashed to pieces and thrown down into a boghole, and afterwards covered with many layers of turf. The Fjørtoft boats were the second find. Here, as has been said, the boats were whole and sunk in the marsh. The Rong ship had been broken up, and the separate parts buried in the bog.

Only very imperfect fragments of the ship were left. The most conspicuous piece is a strong and heavy mast-partner of oak, just like the one we have in the Tune ship. There are also bits from different parts of the boat, all pine, including part of a strake, the strongest section of the ship, which we call *meginhufr,* the headboard. Defective as it is, the type and dimensions of the Rong ship can be approximately fixed. It was about 44'3" (13.5 m.) long, with a beam of about 9'2" (2. 8m.). It had eight spaces (eight pairs of oars), and probably rowlocks, not oar-holes. It was what we call a little karve: see Shetelig's description. And in Færøyvik's opinion we may assume that the Rong ship is more or less contemporary with the Tune ship: that is, from the period about 900. It is also closely akin to the one Shetelig dug up in Grønhaug on Karmøy.

The special feature of the Rong ship is the heavy mast-partner. Færøyvik points out the interesting detail that no such partners are found either in the *jekter* (sailing coasters) or fishing-boats of West Norway in more recent times. In this connection he gives certain observations on the *sailing* problem, which may be quoted here in part. In such close-sailing craft they needed, he believes, not only solid sockets and partners, but also both shrouds and stays. They raised the mast obliquely from the after end, and slipped the lower mast-end down into the socket in the step. Then they raised the mast vertically, and locked it firm with one or two square blocks of wood. After that they went on to shroud and stay it. Probably the mast was lowered while they rode in a head wind or calm. Or they rowed a short or longer distance up into the wind before raising the mast and setting sail, as they do in the square-sail boats of our time. Fishermen commonly row up into the wind, either along shore or out on a fjord, and thus they can cover long stretches at a time under sail. For instance, if one has to sail a few miles across a fjord, and wind is «scarce», the thing is to row up a little distance into the wind, and then one can make the whole stretch under sail. Tacking takes longer in a narrow sound than rowing. On stretches of open sea, on the other hand, fishermen would rather sail than row. For one thing, because the boats get less spray under sail. Fishermen know what a struggle it is to raise the mast in an eight or ten-oar boat in a rough sea. That was why it mattered so much, if they were to raise the mast for sailing on the open sea, that it should be firmly socketed and keep steady, even if the boat was rolling as they made fast the stays and shrouds. It might be equally necessary to have the power of lowering the mast in a trice, in narrow sounds where tacking was impossible. From all this one can see how vital it was, in these old boats, that they should be able both to raise and lower the mast as quickly and easily as possible.

One other marsh find of a boat in recent years may be mentioned. This is the boat from *Bårset* on Nord-Kvaløy, north of Tromsø, dug up by Soot-Ryen in 1931, which was the object of a profound and basic monograph by G. Gjessing in 1941.

Here again we have a boat which was smashed up before being buried in the bog as a sacrifice. What came to light on excavation were imperfect remnants of a big boat; there was enough, however, for a reconstruction to be made with confidence. We have here an open rowing-boat, about 42'7" (13 m.) long, beam 8'8" (6.24 m.), sharp-pointed fore and aft, built all of pine. It carried eight or nine pairs of oars, and probably had rowlocks and rudder of the same type as in the Kvalsund boat. It has six strakes; the lower ones are riveted, while the upper are partly sewn, and partly nailed with treenails. The ribs are lashed to cleats contrived in the planks. The frame structure, with whole ribs from gunnel to gunnel, is exactly the same as in the Kvalsund boat. Altogether, there are a great many features in this Nordland boat from Bårset which recall the «Kvalsund stage», earlier than the Gokstad-Oseberg stage. Gjessing holds, therefore, that the Bårset boat can be placed in the 8th century.

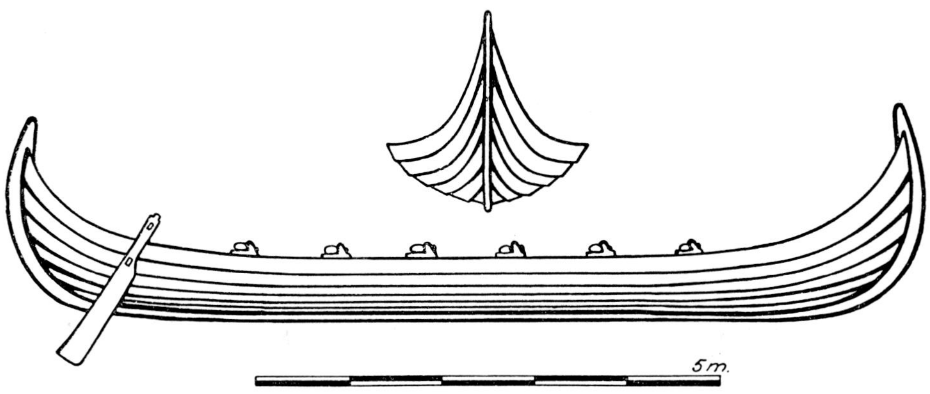

A drawing of the boat found in a bog at Fjørtoft, Haram, Sunnmøre, from the Viking Era or earlier. No mast, rowlocks for six pairs of oars. Bergens Universitet.

In this comparative study, Gjessing has put forward a number of views on boat-building in North Norway, and also in the west and east. For instance, he has posed a question of great historical significance: Where was this boat built? The islands off this coast never had pine forests. We must go up the fjords to look for it, and here the nearest are Lyngen, Ullsfjord and Balsfjord. But, judging by all we know from archaeological sources, there was no permanent Norwegian settlement up these fjords. So we inevitably ask ourselves whether the boat can be a product of the «Sea-Finn's» boat-building. We know from many sources that these people were good carpenters and shipwrights, from the Middle Ages down to the 18th century. In many fjord-side villages, they actually lived by boat-building. For several centuries, Salten, Tysfjord and many others supplied the whole of Lofoten, Vesterålen, Værøy and Røst with boats. We hear that in the 16th century they were building *jekter* for northward voyages, and that every year they paid a boat over to the sheriff as a tithe on their industry. Snorre relates that in the winter of 1138—39 Sigurd Slembe was living on Hinnøya, and that he then had two boats made for him by the «Finns» up in the fjords. They were sewn with sinews and had never a nail in them, the knees were of willow, and there were twelve oars on each side. This is obviously what the North Norwegian skald Eyvind Finnson calls the *håløygske fura* (North Norway pine-boat), which was bound with sinews, and an excellent sailer.

All the same, there can be little doubt that the Bårset boat is Norwegian-built, and not Sea-Finnish. Gjessing conjectures that it was built up in one of the fjords, most likely Lyngen, Ullsfjord or Balsfjord. He points out that a strikingly large number of these inner, thickly-wooded fjords were named in the early Iron Age. This applies primarily to the many names in *angr,* the old Norse word for fjord. There we have Ballangen, Herjangen, Gratangen, Lavangen, Salangen, Malangen, Kvænangen, Porsanger and Varanger. They show that the Norwegians of the islands and the coast did travel up the inner fjords, both on hunting and trading errands (Varanger), and to run the shipbuilding concern they had up there.

Gjessing imagines the position to have been that the Norwegians were already building their own boats in the early Iron Age, and that Lappish

(Sea-Finnish) boat-building on a large scale developed later, by degrees, during the Merovingian and Viking Periods. It naturally took some time for contact between the two races, the North-Norwegians and the Lapps, to get under way. Constant and prolonged spells of boat-building up in the fjords may well have greatly interfered with the Norwegians' pursuit of the chase. And so they gradually left most, or at any rate a good deal of their boat-building to the Sea-Finns, so as to rationalise their own economic life.

Throughout this sketch of the history of the boat in Norway during ten thousand years, we have tried to keep strictly to the archaeological sources. We have had to ignore the data of philology and legend, though often there is important information to be gleaned from such material as well. The account we have been able to give is, in the nature of the case, somewhat defective, yet it is much more ample and has far more continuity of line than would have been possible a bare generation ago. We can now see the line from the skin boat to the clinker-built plank boat, and onward to the sea-going boat with mast and sail. The intermediate stage is the boat of entire planks without joints. And the great problems were the treatment of prow and keel.

At present we can hardly get much further. But when we think how much more has been learnt through antiquarian discoveries in less than 30 years, there seems every reason to believe that the next generation will increase our knowledge considerably.

In one sphere especially, we have not yet gone very far: in regard to the share of different provinces and districts in the solution of the various problems of the sea-going boat, and the development of different boat-types by adapting them to the prevailing wind and weather, to the skerries and the fjord, the voyage to the great sea-banks in the 16th and 17th centuries, and much more.

This account barely touches on the fact that we possess in Norway, and the Norwegian-tinctured countries of the west, a considerable material of boat-finds from what we call *boat-graves,* of the Migration Age and probably still earlier, but chiefly of the Viking Era; they have been found in hundreds. They occur also in another Nordic region, with features highly characteristic of the history of boat-building: that is, in Swedish Uppland, which has the finest boat-graves, next to those of the Norwegian viking ships. Here we have the celebrated finds from Vendel, Tuna, both on Fyris and Mälaren, and both completely overshadowed by the kingly boat-graves from Valsgärde, which have been brought to light by excavation since 1928. So far eight boat-graves have been found in all, most royally fitted up with burial furnishings which are unique in their age. They belong chiefly to the 7th and 8th centuries, and their closest parallel is the grave at Sutton Hoo in Suffolk already mentioned. The most fantastically furnished Valsgärde grave is (No. 6) the one dug up in 1931. Of the boat itself practically nothing remained, but the rivets lying in the ground gave a complete idea of it. It was clinker-built, and oddly enough the planking was of pine. The boat must have been about 32' 10" (10 m.) long, with four or five pairs of oars.

'he prow-ornament for a boat, und in a bog at Midtvåge, Onar-eim, Tysnes. Probably from a ipwright's stock of halffinished aterials, kept in marshes and ɔgs in order to stay fresh and pple. Bergens Universitet.

Boats-graves belong essentially to Norway and Sweden; in Denmark there are practically none. All we can infer from this is a difference in actual *burial custom,* not in boat-building. For they could undoubtedly build just as good boats and ships in Denmark as in Norway and Sweden.

One single, but in compensation splendid ship-grave has been found in Denmark, at *Ladby,* Kertemindefjord, on Funen; it was excavated in 1935—36, and is now on view within the mound itself. Here they found a viking ship of the Norwegian size, built in the same way, and with a burial outfit very like what has been found in the Norwegian graves: for instance, a magnificent bronge dog-leash, a number of dogs and horses, and so on. The whole thing — ship, mound, etc. — tallies so little with Danish burial custom in the 10th century as to have raised the fancy that it may be the grave of a Norwegian chieftain of a royal house in which these burial customs were observed. There have even been conjectures who he might be. But the significance one can attach to such a random thought must be exclusively historical, as a reminder of the constant feuds between the royal families of Norway and Denmark, starting when the two kingdoms were «united», and continuing throughout the whole Middle Ages. A discussion of this point, however, lies beyond our scope. There is no doubt that from the point of view of structure and development the Ladby ship could just as well be Danish as Norwegian; indeed it is much narrower in proportion than the Norwegian ships.

For the development and detail of the boat-types and ships themselves, we have material of great importance in the rich and interesting *Gotland sculptured stones,* dating from the 6th to the 11th century: material which, properly used, should also throw light on the history of Norwegian boat-building in the same period. But, here not least, one has to bear in mind that sailing the Baltic and sailing the North Sea are very different things. The pictures, which in the later periods are very detailed, represent both cargo-boats and more distinctive sailing-vessels. This material cannot all be brought in here. One of the points most vital to our theme, however, is that on these sculptured stones as far back as the 8th century, we find mast and sail, and the sail is a *square-sail,* with reefing-lines and all appurtenances. We knew so much already from our viking ships. But here we can see far more detail. The mast is stayed, and in addition there are many shrouds to keep it firm under sail.

These leading points in our old ships, a mast which is invariably placed amidships and a square-sail with lines to swing it round in all directions, even to secure it high up against the wind, are central points in the whole

Sculptured stone found at Hejnum, Gotland, representing a fully equipped ship. Probably from the 8th Century A.D. After Lindquist.

history of seafaring in North and West Europe, Hull, mast and sail, and starboard rudder, finally have merged into one, into a well-tuned little orchestra where every voice is part of the united harmony. The hull, built of the thinnest planks over a skeleton of frame-timbers, makes of the ship a perfectly elastic instrument at sea.

So far, the most accomplished specimen we have is the Gokstad ship, and even that, presumably, is a mere stage in the perfecting process.

It was a Swedo-Finnish expert, (Hornborg) not one of ourselves, who wrote as follows: «Around the year 800, the Northmen are the foremost shipbuilders and seafarers in the world.» He adds some details on the Gokstad ship, which may be quoted here.

It has usually been reckoned that the mast of the Gokstad ship was about 42' 7" (13 m.) high. It was stayed right forward and «sideways» aft, with stay and backstays. The yard, again, has usually been reckoned at 32'—35' (10—11 m.) long. This makes the area of sail about 70 square metres; so that its dimensions are rather small for that size of craft. Yard and sail were managed by cordage running from the yard-arms (braces) and from the lower corners of the sail, as we see in the Gotland reliefs.

In Hornborg's view, the Gokstad ship can scarcely represent the Northmen's true sea-going ships. It is, one might say, only the beginning. Not till the Viking Era do they become increasingly evolved. It is believed that the

tail from one of the Gotland ·lptural stones representing a ly equipped ship, found at ·angride. 8th Century A.D. After ıdquist.

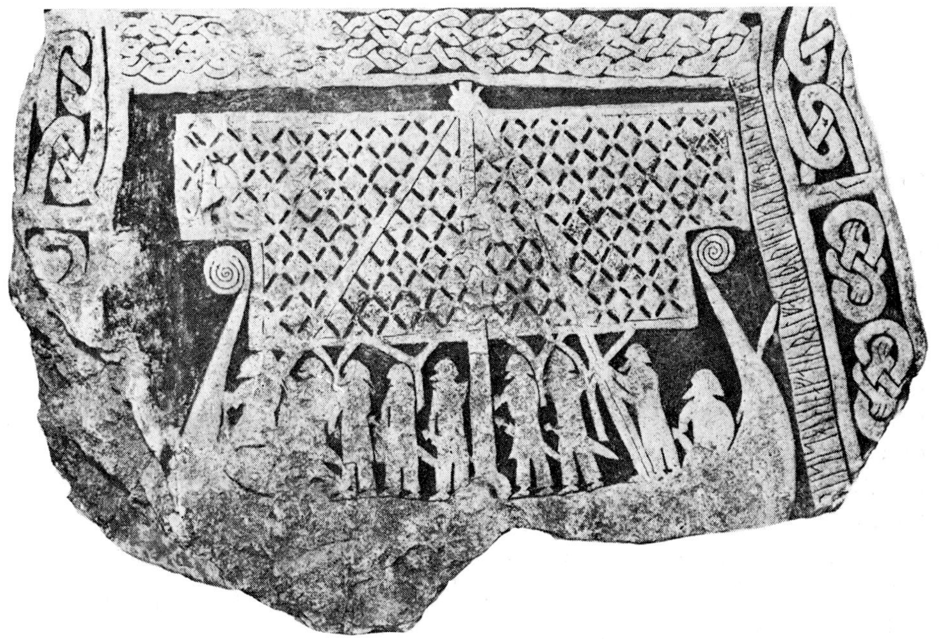

Long Serpent, built about 1000 A.D., had a keel of about 145' (45 m.), which means 160' (50 m.) from stem to stern, and 34 pairs of oars, while the Gokstad ship had 16 pairs. The average North Sea ship would probably have about 20—25 pairs of oars, and a length from stem to stern of 80'—95' (25—30 m.) at most. Such a ship must have carried about 80—120 men.

We shall conclude by touching on one further point about the Norwegian boat-graves. According to the list drawn up by Shetelig we possess well over five hundred at least, so that the conclusions reached by Bernhard Færøyvik rest on extensive evidence. He maintains, undoubtedly with perfect justice, that the type for smaller boats was stabilized long before the Viking Age. And in the west especially, it remained fairly constant for many centuries.

The information Færøyvik gives here, on boat-building in the western provinces, is of such interest as to deserve a short account in this place, though strictly speaking it refers to practice in our own day. But there is every reason to believe that we have here a fixed tradition dating back to fourteen hundred years ago, when boat-building in these districts made head, and was adopted as a trade by numbers of the western peasantry.

In Gloppen, where Gustafson examined an old boat-grave, there was a whole parish occupied in building boats as a domestic industry, and selling them to fishermen, often as far south as Bergen. This Nordfjord boat was sea-going. Sometimes a Gloppen boat-builder would tie five boats together, and row and sail right down the long fjord, then south to Gulen in Ytre Sogn, where he would sell his boats.

In Sogn and Sunnfjord there were often boat-builders who went round the district, and built boats on commision for this man or that. If the boat-builder himself owned the forest, the buyer had to order his boat a year ahead. Then the boat-builder could fell the material in winter, take it home by sledge, and saw and cut it up, so that it could season well before he started the construction. The buyer had to collect the boat himself.

The men of Nordfjord, on the other hand, sent their boats. A farmer who went in for boat-building required great experience and knowledge to select the material. The timber was best felled a year in advance. The strakes were cut out or sawed and laid out to dry. The timbers for cross-beams, knees, stem and stern had to be sought for among crooked trees. If the boat was to be absolutely sound, the whole strake, from prow to stern was best made from the same tree. The boards of equal thickness have about the same elasticity. A few big trees could thus provide work for a household through the winter, and not a little extra gain. Father and son worked together. Thus an art is passed on. If a boat-builder had a reputation for being especially accomplished, young men would serve an apprenticeship with him. On every farm, the building averaged five or six boats a year. If the son took over the farm early, his father would keep on the boat-building, and then the figure might go up to 10—12 boats a year. For the whole of Gloppen it might be about 250 boats a year. When they were building *jekter* and big boats, several builders usually combined. When the last Nordfjord *jekt* was building (in 1881) four «masters», each with his assistant and a smith, worked all together — nine workmen to a *jekt.*

In the 9th-century boat-grave at Holmedal, *Sunnfjord,* of which Shetelig has given so detailed an account, including a technical description of the boat itself, there was a ten-oar boat. Structure and workmanship were in the main just like those of the boats they went on building in Sunnfjord right down to our own day. Boats were built everywhere in Sunnfjord; many, indeed, were wanted for the herring fishery in these parts. The old boat-building families kept up the craft. Between the heavy seasons on the land, they built both boats and *jekter.* For going after the basking shark ten or twelve-oar boats were employed. In these they used white sails to attract the shark; the boats were painted white for the same reason. Right down to our own time, they also used the old *skutill,* the harpoon for this fish, the same shape as that of the Viking Era and earlier. The Sunnfjord boats were strong and safe, good sea-boats, rather flat-bottomed, and with especially strong bottom boards. There are boats here which had seen up to 100—150 years of service! The Sunnfjord boat was more for skerries, while the Nordfjord boat, with sharper lines fore and aft, was better for deep-sea fishing.

Færøyvik has also given a full and very illuminating account of the *Sogn boat,* starting from the 9th-century boat-grave at Brekke (excavated in 1931). It was a four-oar boat of about 17' 2" (5.25 m.). — The Sogn boat, right up to our own day, was perhaps the one most resembling the viking ship. It had a handsome «sheer», with high prow and stern. It is best fitted to the peculiar wind conditions in Sogn, squalls, topping waves, currents and short seas. As late as the 1930s, there were 10—12 boat-builders in Sogn who turned out four and six-oar boats of the same type as we find in boat-graves of the Viking Era.

Incidentally, it was a special feature of these Sogn boats that they were fjord boats pure and simple, answering capitally in the often dangerous Sognefjord. They were not found, for instance, at the mouth of the fjord, in Solund and other districts. Here is an amusing fragment of social history, which must be very old indeed. Every autumn the fishermen of Solund sailed their boats, *jekter* and small freigthers up the fjord with fish, often the whole seventy-odd miles to Lærdal. The men of Hallingdal and Valdres came across the fells to meet them and buy the fish. They called those of the outer fjord the *sea-men.* These latter would exchange their fish for butter, cheese, timber, bark, potatoes etc. But not one boat from Sogn did they take back to Solund!

On the *construction* of all these west-country craft, Færøyvik has much interesting and valuable information. Here it would take us rather too far from the subject to go deeply into it. The notable thing is that the building method, principal measurement, etc., rig and sail have remained virtually unchanged for much more than a thousand years. Indeed, even the names and phrases for the different parts of the boat have been the same from age to age. The bigger boats had square-sails, just like the viking boats. The mast length equalled the «girth» of the boat at the mainsail thwart. The girth is a line round the middle of the hull. The mast they reckoned only to the bolt for the sail-pulley; the masthead was not counted in. For the reefing-lines of the sail, strips of walrus-hide were used right up to our own day.

An account of boat-building in North Norway, from Åfjord to Salten and further yet, would yield the same infinite wealth of details, with their source in ancient boat-building right back to the Migration and Viking Periods. And this conservative line is really not so strange. With sail and oars as their motive power, after a few centuries of experiment, the coastal dwellers had already, fourteen hundred years ago, achieved buoyant boats so finely planned, in all the hundred requirements and details, that they could be improved no further. Only with new demands, a bigger spread of canvas and the invention of a foresail to balance the mainsail, and above all with the appearance of the engine, do we get the first radical change in the thousand-year-old boat-type. Its adaptation to the sea had lain in its unrivalled elasticity. It worked, so to speak, *with* the sea. The modern demand for speed, for quick arrival, means giving up that point. The strength which is required today lies in the power both to cut through the seas and fight *against* them.

The most interesting feature in this building of smaller boats, which thus maintained itself for hundreds and hundreds of years, untouched by wars, changes of kings and dynasties, higher political developments of every kind, is this deep substratum of folk-culture. The big ships vanished with the wars and the Norwegian royal line. The little boats remained indissolubly bound up with the life of the peasantry. Just as the dialects of popular speech preserved the ancient language of Norway, so the peasant boat-builders conserved the full harvest of that vast social effort which is linked with the Norwegian boat.

Decorative element from the bo
of the Oseberg ship.

THE SHIP-GRAVES

The Other Ship Finds

As we have seen from the preceeding account, Oseberg, Gokstad and Tune are not the only burial-mounds to contain good-sized ships. We have also a very few others which are worth mentioning.

The first Norwegian ship-grave of which we have any information was found on Rolvsøy, Østfold, in 1751, not far from the place where the Tune ship later came to light. The Rolvsøy ship is described as a big, open vessel with a clinker-built, oak planking.

In Vestfold we have the Borre ship, now unfortunately nonexistent. According to relatively reliable accounts of this find, it seems to have been very closely related to the finds at Oseberg and Gokstad, further south. The Borre ship was found in 1852, during a clumsy excavation of one of the big royal burial mounds in that area. The vessel had been placed in the mound with the bow pointing south-west west. It was clinker built, about 55' 3" (17 m.) long, and contained a similar wealth of furnishings to that found later in the Gokstad and Oseberg ships. Most of these unfortunately vanished during the digging. There was a quantity of riding and driving gear, some of it beautifully decorated, a cart, a sledge with carved shaft, some harnesses, a saddle, etc., besides at least three horses and one dog. A few objects were preserved, and are now in the Archaeological Museum of Oslo University.

They give a strong impression that the grave was furnished with exceptional magnificence.

At present, five splendid royal mounds remain at Borre, and it is highly probable that at least two or three of them contain large ship-graves similar to those of Oseberg and Gokstad. Their excavation must be left to coming generations.

Beside those of Østfold and Vestfold, there are ship-graves on Karmøy; one of them at Storhaug in Avaldsnes, excavated in 1885 by Anders Lorange, the other at Grønhaug in Bloheien, excavated in 1902 by Shetelig. The ship at Storhaug had a keel 65' (20 m.) long, against the 56' (17.6 m.) of the Gokstad keel. The splendid furnishings of the grave show that it was fully equal to those of Oseberg and Gokstad, but as conditions in the mound were not favourable to preservation, there was very little left.

The ship at Grønhaug was smaller, approximately 48' 9" (15 m.), about the same size as the Borre ship. This grave had also been furnished with great richness, but had suffered heavily from plundering. The whole character of the Karmøy ships places them in the same group as the Vestfold ships and graves. Shetelig connected them up with Harald's royal manor at Avaldsnes. They certainly belong to that family native to Vestfold – the royal line which so to speak fostered the custom of burying one's dead in ships.

That other royal families in Norway also adopted this distinguished burial custom is shown by two other ship finds. One is the grave at Myklebostad, Nordfjord. But here the ship and all the burial furnishings were burnt at the funeral, and there is very little to be gleaned from the ashes, except that it was a splendid funeral and a fair-sized ship, judging by the fact that 44 shields were burnt with the ship. According to the custom, the shields were hung along the sides of the vessel and hence give us some indication of its size. By way of comparison we may mention that the Gokstad ship had 64 shields, 32 on each side.

The other is the big ship-grave at Skei in Namdalen, excavated twice in the 18th century. The accounts are somewhat confused, but with our present knowledge we are able to reconstruct the grave in broad outline. It contained a big ship with a burial chamber and two human skeletons, cf. the Oseberg ship. The presence of a sword indicates that it was the grave of a man.

At the time of Gerhard Schøning there was generally believed to be a tradition that this mound had been raised over two Namdal kings, Herlaug and Rollaug, of whom there are such vivid accounts in the Saga of Harald Fair-Hair. Unfortunately it is no longer possible to establish whether this really was a tradition, or whether it had originated with the reading of Snorre in the 18th century.

It is, by the way, an undeniably striking fact that neither at Tune, Borre, Oseberg, Gokstad nor Karmøy was there a single local tradition of historical character concerning the graves. What was related as such during and after

agment of a tapestry found at augen, Østfold. From about 900 .D.

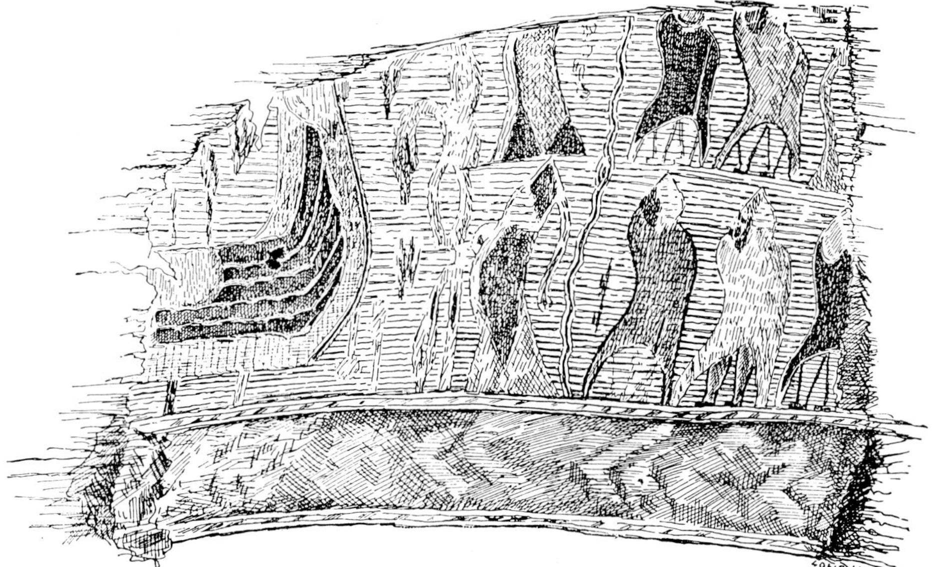

the excavations, sprang up, as it were, of its own accord, simultaneously with the diggings, at the prompting of local historians. The question *when* the traditions disappeared is of great interest, and one that well deserves a separate inquiry. Most likely it happened some time in the 16th century, a period of great decline in national traditions.

How the Viking Ships Were Found

The discoveries took place over a period of 40 years. The Tune ship was excavated in 1867, the Gokstad ship in 1880, and finally the Oseberg ship in 1904.

The Tune ship was found about 16 miles north of Fredrikstad, on the east side of Rolvsøy. On the farm of *Haugen* there was a huge grave-mound which has been called the Boat Mound for a long time, although it is doubtful whether the name actually originated in antiquity. There had been some digging in the mound before, but in the middle of the 1860's the people on the farm began to cart earth from it. In the summer of 1867 they hit upon a ship, and before this was reported to the archaeologists of Oslo University, a large part of the vessel had been uncovered. Then the digging was stopped until professor Oluf Rygh and his assistant, engineer B. Chr. Arntsen, could undertake a proper excavation, in September and October.

The mound, which was roughly 260' (80 m.) in diameter (the second biggest grave-mound in Norway) lay at the top of a slope going down to the river Glomma, so that it could be seen far and wide from both sides of the river. Within this mound the Tune ship was placed at natural ground level, pointing north and south. The inside of the ship was lined with moss and juniper bushes. A square burial chamber had been erected over the stern, of oak planks driven vertically into the ground close to the gunnel. The roof was flat. Very little remains of the grave furnishings, but it is clear enough that it was the grave of a man. We are told that rust stains from the hilt of a sword, a spearhead and the boss of a shield could be discerned in the bow. Inside the burial chamber were found some charred human bones together with those of a horse which had evidently been buried standing up. There were also two glass beads, some matted cloth and some small pieces of wood with carved ornaments in high relief, depicting *inter alia* human figures. The middle section of a ski is said to have been found near these other things. Of the objects found before the arrival of Professor Rygh, only the carved pieces of wood, a wooden spade and a handspike have been preserved.

As with two of the other ship-graves, the mound of the Tune ship had been broken into and the grave plundered. The carved wooden figures show that the furnishings originally must have been very fine.

Dating a find of this nature is very difficult when so little has remained. Most likely the interment took place towards the end of the 9th century, or somewhere around the year 900. This is indicated by the carved ornaments.

The Gokstad ship during the excavation.

Apparently Rolvsøy was at that time the seat of a family of powerful chieftains, for there are a number of these huge grave-mounds in the area. Beside the Tune mound there are graves at Rostad, Valle and Haugen. The latter contained a large timbered burial chamber. These finds are probably relics of a line of Østfold kings, just as the Oseberg and Gokstad finds are the vestiges of a Vestfold line. But whereas we have considerable historical knowledge of the Kings in Vestfold, we know nothing of the Østfold chieftains, and there are no traditions concerning them.

Right across the Oslo Fjord lies Vestfold, the ancient realm of the *Yngling* kings, and here the Oseberg and Gokstad ships belong.

The Gokstad farms lie in the parish of Sandar, near Sandefjord, less than a mile from Lahelle Bay, where there must have been a loading berth in ancient times. On a flat, treeless plain belonging to Lower Gokstad there is a large grave-mound which throughout the past century at least, had been called the King's Mound. According to legend, a king with all his treasures had been buried there, and in 1880 people began to dig. The digging was stopped so that the mound could be examined properly, and the same spring the excavation began under the supervision of Mr. N. Nicolaysen. This discovery was to stand out as our most remarkable archaeological find for more than a generation, and in many ways it still is. The mound was about 162½' (about 50 m.) wide, and 16¼' (about 5 m.) high. The prow of the ship was uncovered already the second day, and after 2½ months the excavation was completed.

The Tune ship had been partly preserved by the presence of *blue clay,* and the Gokstad ship had benefitted even more from this. The ship had first been carefully dug down into the clay, with the prow pointing towards the sea, and then the burial chamber built of timber and the mast cut off level with the chamber roof. Inside the burial chamber a chieftain was buried, laid out on his bed in his finest apparel, with his arms beside him; in all probability a king. The remains of the skeleton were examined by Professor K. E. Schreiner, and was found to belong to a man about 50 years, 5' 10" high, and of powerful build.

A number of things where found in the ship. Foremost among them were the remains of three smaller boats, found in the bow. Two of them are now in the Viking Ship Museum in Oslo, fully restored. They closely resemble the ship itself, and are of much the same type as boats used up to the present time, especially on the north-west coast of Norway. These boats had been equipped with oars and a tiller, and were rowed by means of rowlocks with grommets. In the bow there were also the remains of one state bed and at least six plain beds, all made so that they could easily be taken apart. Only two of them could be fitted together again. Mention has already been made of another bed, the one in the burial-chamber.

Before the mast a quantity of kitchen utensils were found. Among these, particular mention must be made of a huge bronze cauldron which may have served to cook the food for the crew, a large pot-hook, several cutting-boards, plates, a number of buckets, some small wooden cups and trays and two candlesticks.

Among the other wooden objects preserved was a piece of board which could be used for two kinds of game. One side was marked out for a game that is still in use today (mill). Several wooden spades were also found, clearly those used in building the mound, and finally, a carved sleigh.

In the grave-chamber were also some smaller objects that deserve mention, *viz.* some pieces of silk worked with gold thread, pieces of dark wool cloth, the remains of a leather purse, some gilded bronze and lead ornaments for leather straps, an iron celt and an iron belt buckle.

After the gravegoods had been placed in the chamber, it was closed. At least 12 horses and 6 dogs were killed and placed just outside the ship. An interesting and characteristic feature was that a peacock, naturally a very rare and costly creature, was inside the ship, while all the other animals were outside. Finally the whole ship, except the burial-chamber was filled with blue clay, over that was placed a layer of moss and twigs, and then the mound was built up over all.

The King's Mound at Gokstad had also been forced in ancient times. The spoilers had broken into the grave chamber from the port side, and here they had made a large hole both in the chamber and in the side of the ship. One must assume, therefore that the grave originally contained a good deal more. The grave can be dated by the ornamental bronze mountings and various other things, to about 900 A. D.

The Oseberg find was made in 1903 and excavation took place next summer, 1904, under the direction of Professor Gabriel Gustafson.

The find occurred at Oseberg-Ødegården in the parish of Slagen, about half-way between Tønsberg and Åsgårdstrand. The grave-mound lay on a plain just north of Slagen church, close by a small river running down to a bay east of Tønsberg. The site is now about 2½ miles from the sea and

'he Oseberg ship in the grave-ɩound.

about 49' (15 m) above sea level, but in viking times the distance to the sea was appreciably less. The flat Slagen valley is otherwise without historic monuments of that period, and one may well assume that in earlier times the soil was marshy and unworkable. When the Oseberg mound was placed here, it was perhaps to save the trouble of dragging the ship too far inland. Originally the mound was an impressive sepulchral monument, about 130' (40 m.) wide and 18' (6¹/₂ m.) high, but it had sunk considerably, and did not look very monumental when the excavation began.

Within this mound, covered by a heap of stones, lay the Oseberg ship. The mound itself was built of peat which formed an absolutely hermetic layer over the grave. The bottom of the grave was of blue clay, as in the Tune and Oseberg mounds. The combination of a peat cover and a blue clay bottom caused the woodwork to be excellently preserved both in the ship itself and in all the antique objects found with it.

The ship lay with its prow pointing south, towards the sea, as did the Tune and Gokstad ships. It was made fast inside the mound by a hawser tied to a big rock near the bow. Behind the mast was the burial-chamber, and here two women were buried. Owing to the subsidence of the mound the ship had been severely damaged. In the bow, where the pressure of the stones and peat had been greatest, the bottom of the ship had been badly broken, and in the burial-chamber it was the same. The ship could not therefore be lifted in one piece, but had to be taken up in fragments and restored later. The objects placed inside it had been similarly crushed and spoilt, often completely smashed.

A queen and her bondwoman were buried in the Oseberg ship. Professor Schreiners examination of the skeletons revealed two persons, aged respectively 25—30 and 60—70. From various circumstances he thinks it may be concluded that the young woman was the queen. The older woman was almost completely disabled by arthritis, palsy and spondylitis. Both had been laid in the big burial-chamber. Here they had been given beds, quilts, pillows, blankets and clothing, as well as tapestries, with which the chamber was hung inside. In addition, the queen had with her in the grave several chests, one of which was whole and could be opened, and the contents taken out. It held lamps, scissors, a cotton-box, a batlet, etc. There was a wooden bucket containing wild apples, several of which had been picked when ripe and had preserved their flesh and peel. Various other pails were also found. Two looms had been placed in the grave-chamber and there were also four exquisitely carved animal-head posts, complete with «rattles». These posts are among the finest objects found in the grave.

The Oseberg grave, as well as those of Gokstad and Tune, had been broken into in ancient times. The spoilers had entered from the south side of the mound, making a passage about 10' wide towards the bow of the ship. From there they had gained access to the gravechamber, cutting a hole in the roof.

In the stern was a fair amount of kitchen utensils, — two iron cauldrons, one with a stand consisting of tree iron claws, two small axes with intact

The Oseberg ship during the ex-cavation. The stern seen from the starboard side.

wooden handles, a kitchen stool, sundry wooden dishes, ladles and knives. An ox was laid out on two oak planks, and a hand-mill was found under one of the floor-boards.

The bow was particularly rich in gravegoods. Here lay a four-wheeled cart, three beds, a loom for tablet weave, a small chair, two tents, the framework for a kind of house and various items of ship's equipment, such as oars, an anchor-stick, a baler, tubs, gangplanks, nails etc., besides a wide range of smaller objects, mostly contained in two buckets. A round pole carved with runes was also found here. 13 horses, 3 dogs and 1 ox were found in the mound inside and outside the ship, many of them killed by severing the head from the body. Thus the head of the ox was found in the plain sled, which in turn had been placed on the largest of the beds. The body was outside, near the port bow. There were tethers with poles for several of the horses, and chains for the dogs.

The remains of a number of plants were found in different parts of the ship, — in a chest and a pail in the burial-chamber, and in various containers in the bow. Thus there were about 50 wild apples of two main sorts, wheat, cress seeds, a plant dye (woad) which was used for blue before the advent of indigo, walnuts, hazel nuts, etc. The earliest find of woad in the North was on a dwelling site at Ginderup, Jutland, of the Pre-Roman Iron Age.

By a comparative analysis of the plant remains in the Oseberg ship and of the peat in the mound, Professor J. Holmboe established that the burial must have taken place in the late summer, in August or, more probably, September.

The age of the grave can be determined by a number of details in the ornamentation. We may now venture to say that the Oseberg Queen was buried in the latter half of the 9th century.

The ship itself is considerably older. The decoration of the prow and stern dates it to about the year 800 A. D. In other words, it was an old ship when it was used as a grave-ship for the young queen. On archaeological grounds we may state with reasonable certainty that the Oseberg ship is about a generation older than the ships from Gokstad and Tune.

All the objects found in the Oseberg ship were examined and treated by Professor Gustafson when the restoration of the ship itself had been completed. It was no easy task to conserve these thousands of wooden fragments, and piece them together so that the finished articles could be exhibited and preserved for all time. After extensive experiments a method was found which proved superior to all the others for the treatment of this find. All soft woods (beech, pine, ash, etc.) were boiled in a solution of alum, then dried and impregnated with linseed oil. By this means the fragments maintained their form and volume, so that they could be pieced together afterwards. The Oseberg find consists mainly of fragments; one of the sledges was in 1068 pieces, and each piece had to be boiled in alum, dried and impregnated with linseed oil. The entire restoration of the gravegoods was carried out in this way, with the greatest of precision by Professor Gustafson and his assistant, Paul Johannessen.

e animal-head posts as they re found in the Oseberg grave-ound.

Some of the most fragile objects could not be subjected to such hard treatment as boiling in alum, and have been preserved under water. As an additional precaution, exact copies have been made of the most valuable and fragile objects.

The biggest and most remarkable object found in the grave was the four-wheeled cart. The wheel-base is quite simply constructed. Each of the large beech-wood wheels is fastened to an axle, and the front and rear axles

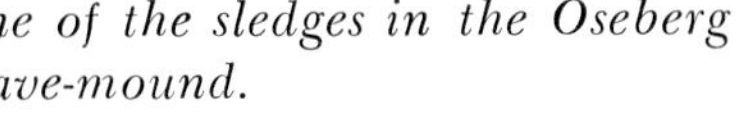

ne of the sledges in the Oseberg ave-mound.

are connected by a long centre bar which forks at the back. The ends of the fork are bolted to the rear axle. Mounted on the front axle are two ash shafts with finely carved ends. The pieces connecting the axle and the shafts are also beautifully carved with animal designs. On each axle there is a base for a trestle. The ends of the trestles are carved to represent a man's head. The front trestle is of beech, the rear one of oak. The semi-cylindrical body of the cart is mounted on the trestles. The body consists of 9 boards fitted onto two end pieces. The outside of the body is decorated all over with carvings in most interesting and curious designs. It is not very likely that this cart was ever intended for practical use, probably it was a sacred vehicle for religious ceremonies. This would explain many cryptic aspects of the decoration.

Of the three state sleighs found in the ship, two had runners curving upwards at both ends, while the third, like the simple sled, had an ordinary toboggan form. On all three the body is placed loosely on the underpart without being fastened to it, and from the way it looks today, one is inclined to believe that the bodies do not belong to the underparts found with them. Bodies and runners are decorated with carvings which vary somewhat from sleigh to sleigh. A particularly curious feature is that these small sleighs were intended to be drawn by two horses. The shafts are also lavishly carved, and this augments the impression of splendour encountered throughout the find.

Next to the cart and the sledges, the most outstanding objects in the find are the wooden posts carved with animal-head designs, the so-called animal-head posts. They are carved in various styles and constitute an extremely interesting and important part of the Oseberg find, because they show the wide divergence in artistic conception from one artist to another. On one of the animal-head posts the head is especially well poised. The neck is smooth, and the lower part of the post has a broad section decorated in a purely geometric pattern. The head itself has an animated pattern in relief. It is surprising to encounter an artist with such a sense of contrasts who at the same time maintains a clear and controlled compositional balance. Others are more uncertain in this respect, with a stronger, almost agitated plastic treatment of the subject matter. As for the purpose of the animal-head posts, we can only hazard a guess. They were used in driving, in connection with the iron «rattles» found with them, but the details of their function have not been established. Like the cart, they probably had something to do with religious ceremonies.

The beds found in the ship were in such bad condition that it was impossible to reconstruct them from the original parts.

Fortunately it has been possible to make exact copies of them. The big bed, some 6½' (2 m.) square, is particularly interesting. The head has two broad posts, ornamented with carved animal heads with open mouths and tongues stuck out. The work is somtimes carried right through the posts, so that these are pierced. The animal heads were probably placed there to protect the sleeper. The two other beds are plain and more commonplace. The bottoms were made of fresh twigs and provided some elasticity. The only chair found in the ship is also of interest; it is made of beech with a

Verge-board heads with painted symbols, from the Oseberg ship.

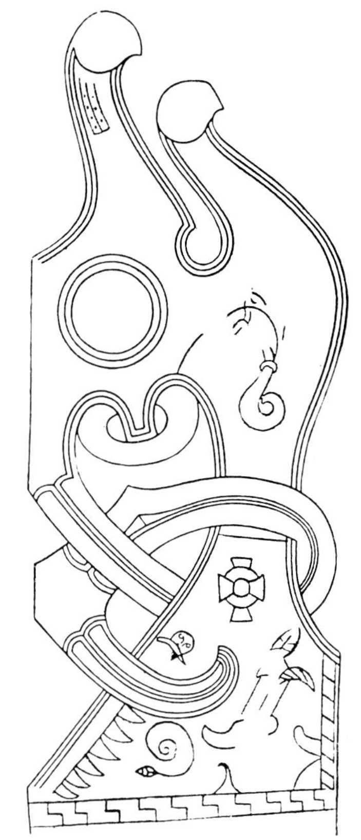

'he Academic Head. 'nimal-head post from 'he Oseberg find.

box-formed underpart and back. The seat was missing, but must have been made of bast or rope. A copy has been made of this chair which to our knowledge is the oldest to be found in Norway.

Of the three chests in the find, one is of oak, bound with iron and further adorned with tin-plated nails. Another small oak chest contained, among other things, grains of wheat. In the profusion of tubs, pails, vats, buckets, ladles, dippers and porringers, there are a couple of objects that deserve special attention, — the richly ornamented pail and the so-called Buddha-bucket. This name refers to two enamel ornaments at the ends of the handles which have an unmistakeable resemblance to Buddha figures. The bucket is of English or Irish origin, and the resemblance to Buddha is of course quite accidental.

The great importance of the Oseberg find is largely due to the exceptional wealth of wood-carving which gives us unexpectedly detailed information on the art of the period. It is particularly interesting because the wood-carvings illustrate one of the most radical stylistic changes that took place in the ornamental art of the Viking Era. But the importance of the find rests also on the profusion of household implements that have been preserved, and which gives us a better impression of the pulsating life in the royal household than any other find.

In connection with the many textile remnants found in the ship it may be of interest to examine the various tools pertaining to women's hand work. Primarily we should mention a small upright loom found in the chamber. It is made of beech, and had been used for weaving in the primitive, ancient way, with warp-threads only and no weft. This method of weaving is still in use in some rural Norwegian communities for making trimmings for table-cloths, towels, carpets, etc. There was also another kind of loom, for making ribbons, belts, etc. This loom consisted of several square tablets of pine and beech, with a hole in each corner. Here we may also mention a reel for yarn, some small balls of yarn, a cotton-box, a beautiful little pail with bronze ornaments and a pair of flax beaters. The numerous flax combs found in other grave-mounds of the Viking Era indicate that flax was widely cultivated at the time.

The Mound-Breakings.

In 1880, when Nicolaysen was excavating the Gokstad ship, it really seems as though he hardly noticed that there must have been people rummaging the mound long before him. Finally it was, so to speak, forced upon him, as he gradually discovered that large parts of the port side had been «torn open». Ten or twelve rafters had been cut out of the roof of the grave-chamber, many of the floorboards were missing, the heavy mast partner had been cut up, and on the starboard side numerous ribs and pieces of the strakes had been chopped off. At last it grew clear and plain that there had once been trespassers in the mound.

Head posts from the Oseberg finc Left the Baroque Head, right th Carolingian Head.

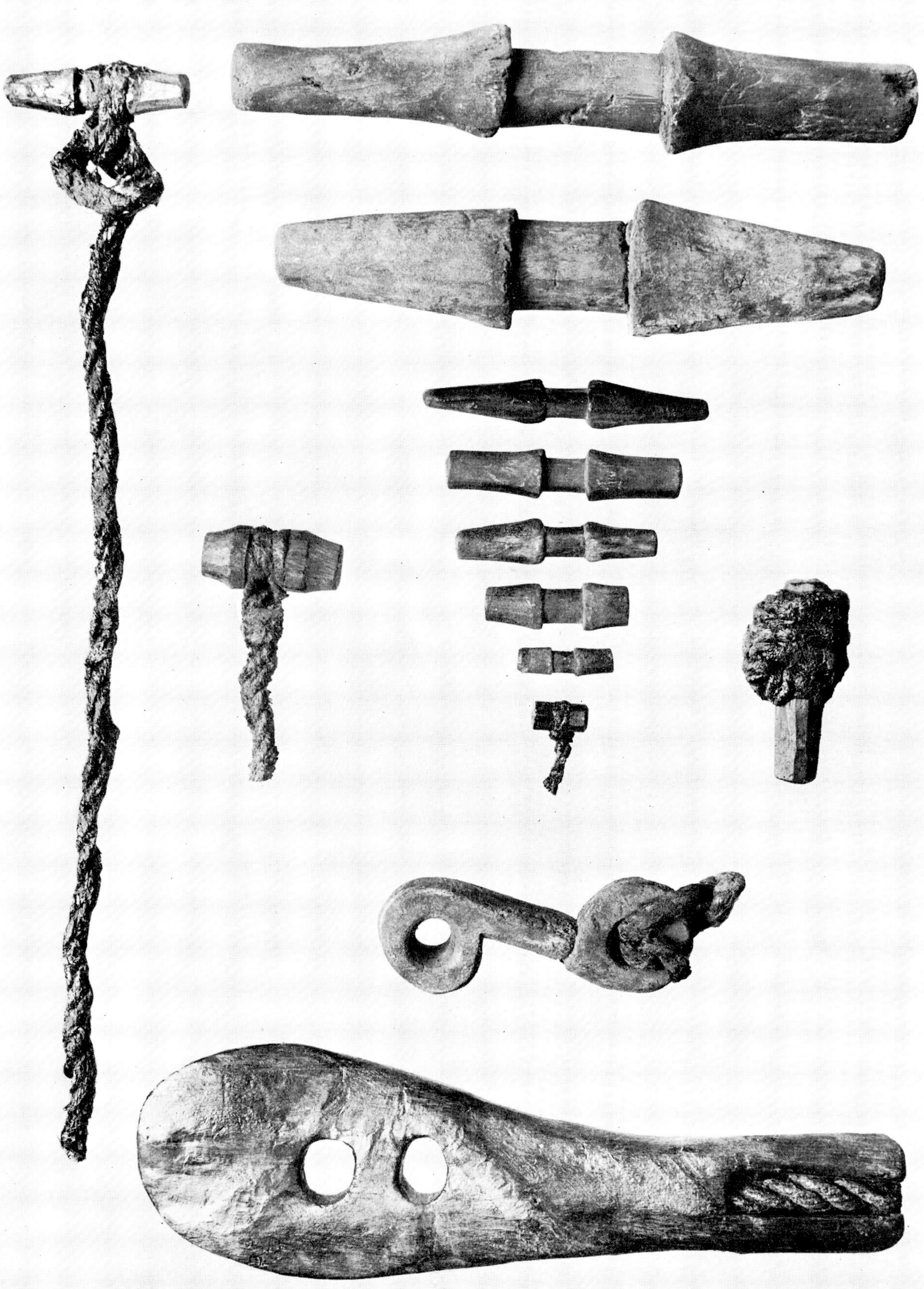

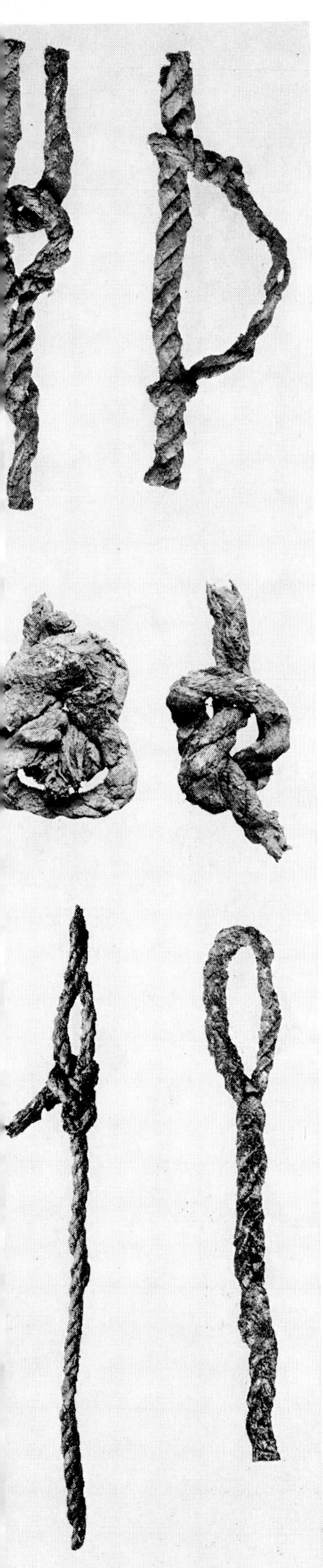

When the Oseberg ship was excavated in 1904, Gustafson, who had a different archaeological background, realized at a very early stage that the mound had been entered before. In its upper layers he found divers fragments of the serpent-spiral on the prow, and of the carved gunnel, but chiefly things which, as it turned out later, must have been inside the burial-chamber. A great sensation was caused by the human bones which were scattered about in this layer, and most of all by the fact that they were the remains of two women who had been buried in the grave-chamber. Almost all the skeleton remains were found in this upper layer.

We have always taken it for granted that in both cases, Oseberg and Gokstad, the tokens were of grave-robbery, of plundering for gold and silver or other valuables. We have supposed ourselves to be facing an impiety which must derive from an age when the people had lost all respect for pagan monuments.

But if we reexamine the facts brought out by the investigation, it gradually appears that this common view cannot be sound. The best basis for a judgment of the whole matter is supplied by the careful, elaborate excavation-plans drawn up by Shetelig of precisely this part of the dig. These exact plans give us important information whose bearing has not been properly estimated until now. One of the first things to strike us is that very little remained of the skeleton of the Oseberg Queen, while that of her bondwoman was almost complete. The explanation is very simple. We must bear in mind that both women lay in the burial chamber in the middle of the ship. Those who broke in obviously meant to remove the Queen in particular from the grave. During the process they were noe very fussy and bones were spilled here and there. We can see that they lifted the skeletons out of the beds and wrapped them in quilts and blankets, and everything got into some confusion. The explanation may be simplified by putting it this way: *They intended to steal the Queen from the grave.*

There are a number of other details which throw a new light on it all. The beds from the burial-chamber had been chopped to pieces. If they were really after gold and silver or other treasures, what would have been the point of chopping up the Queen's state bed – of killing it, as one might say? Besides, we can conclude on analogical evidence that the Queen had neither gold nor silver with her in the grave. Several other observations made in excavating the top layers of the mounds at Oseberg and Gokstad point the same way. The object was to «annihilate» the deceased and render *the grave uninhabitable.* This mode of thought, which is so strange to us, had full validity for the people of that age.

With this, the mound-breakings appear in a completely new light. Luckily there is enough source-material for us to penetrate deeper into their real meaning. We find it in the relation of both dead and living to the grave-mounds.

In Norway the grave-mound became as it were a common property of folk thought, something natural and spontaneous which was particularly well adapted to the Norwegian temperament. The dead man *lives* in the

Wooden beckets, shackles. knots and hitches found in the Oseberg ship.

mound, he is a *mound-dweller* and a *mound-farmer* and so indeed he remains in the teeth of all Christianity, up to the present day. His home is in the mound, the grave, and there he lives the life of the dead. This belief was ineradicable. Christianity and the Church tried to do away as far as possible with the customs, the cult of ancestors, and feasts and toasts for the mound folk. It did so cautiously and hesitatingly. Perhaps in no other field has paganism retained such vitality among us, right up to the present day. Folklore, folk-poetry and legend give profuse expressions to this whole theme of fellowship with the dead.

The grave was protected in all possible ways, and this to protect not merely the dead man, but also the living family, for there were no stronger ties than those between the living and the dead. The grave was not the end of life, but its continuation. The living had a sacred duty to make a secure home for those who entered it. And the dead had power to bring the living good or ill luck. Therefore relations with the dead were not an unmixed joy, but also full of unremitting fear and anxiety. And that is why the feasting for the dead is so indissolubly linked with dread and insecurity. Against the weapons of the dead the living are exposed and helpless. Only the few, the chosen who have «supernatural» powers can challenge the dead if need arises.

From Danish and Swedish runic inscriptions we know some of the formulas of grave-protection and commination. They are mostly directed against «evil powers» which were as dangerous to the dead as certain evil powers could be to the living. This is not to say that the formulas are directly pertinent to the mound-breakings, but they do help to throw light on these acts as such.

The formulas give a valuable insight into the duality of the relationship. On one hand, an immense rallying of the strongest magical forces to ensure the dead man's peace and well-being in the grave: on the other, an equally immense rallying of magical forces to keep him in the grave and prevent «walking». The curse falls on anyone who disturbs the peace of the grave, not merely because he ruins «life» for the dead, but quite as much because he ruins it for the living.

If we could imagine a total break with these ideas on the advent of Christianity, it would be easier to understand the mound-breakings. But it was not like that. The relation between living and dead still remained the same, equally strong and intense, with changes which emerge only by degrees. The explanation must be sought elsewhere. We find it in the traditions of the saga and legend, and see how they chime with archaeological reality. There we discover that the actual mound-breaking theme derives its force from the same world of which we caught a glimpse in the protective formulas. The dead man's grave-goods play a certain part; he himself defends them in the grave, both for worldly and religious reasons. But the true cause of the mound-breakings is different and far more vital.

The motive for the great mound-breakings of saga and tradition is as clear as day. They are directed not against the humble and obscure, but the depar-

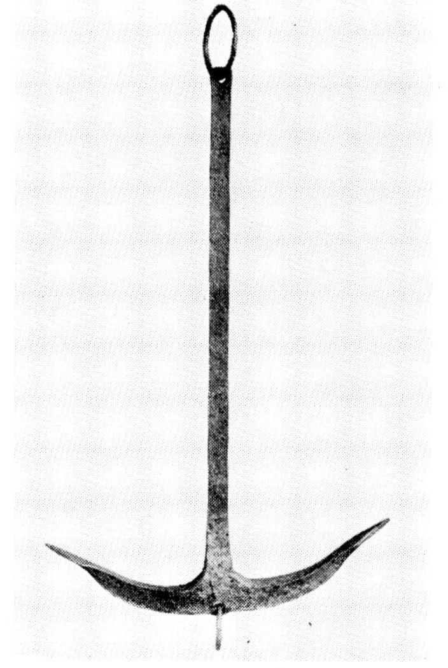

The Oseberg ship's anchor. I made from first-class iron, bu is too slight to hold even a s vessel like the Oseberg ship. ship was also made fast ashor

he reconstructed Oseberg ship
en from the bow.

ted mighty who have a magic power to bring disaster on the living; or against revenants at odds with life in the grave and with the family on the farm, or the entire district — dead men proscribed among the dead.

Ample material on the inner history of the mound breakings occurs in the sagas, and in more or less incidental statutes of the later Middle Ages. Even if the sagas are legendary, it seems clear enough that they place the mound-breakings in a new and juster light. There can be no doubt that the treasures and the magic animal-head posts in the graves were an important object in these mound-breakings. But the decisive factor was the relationship between the living and the dead, the good or harm that they could do each other. Thus, for example, the stronger the occult powers of the deceased, the more toil and trouble the survivors had to spend on his grave, so as not to be exposed to that most fearful enemy, the «walker» who in the end might drive them out of house and home.

The fear of being haunted by the dead first manifested itself in mound-breakings during the period of disintegration under Earl Haakon and the Olavs. It seems that the legends also began to take form in this period. How important the Christian influence was in this respect is hard to say, but it undoubtedly had some effect. And here we should bear in mind that animals, and even men were sacrificed to some of these mighty dead in the 9th century, which may naturally have contributed to the mound-breakings.

According to the few, but sometimes detailed sources we possess, the motives for the mound-breaking were of two kinds. On the one hand, it was necessary to do away with ghosts who made life unbearable to the survivors. On the other hand it was important to acquire some of the most magical of

Human figures, two men and a woman, from the carvings on the Oseberg carriage. One man has his sword raised, but is being prevented by the woman from striking his mounted opponent.

The reconstructed Gokstad ship seen from the bow.

the family treasures, which were lying in a great man's grave, in order to use them at crucial moments in the family life.

Thus the question of mere plundering falls into the background. It must of course have happened, but as a general explanation it has ceased to hold water.

It is along the lines indicated here that we must seek to understand the mound-breakings at Oseberg and Gokstad.

THE VIKING SHIPS

How the Ship was Built

Our first impression of the Gokstad Ship is that of a complete harmony of line and form. It is a real work of art, with the full curve of the sides that naturally and organically flows fore and aft into the high, pointed stem and stern. Between them the straight line of the keel runs like the nerve of the structure, coming up fore and aft in a bold thrust to cleave the water and fling it aside. The ship inspires the same delight as a shapely living creature, a paragon of its kind, a system of many parts welded into a perfect unity. Every sailor knows from experience that a ship is fundamentally different from anything built on solid ground. A ship is built to swim the sea, to run through the water and shed it again; it should be strong to withstand the wind and the waves, and there should be room on board for people and goods. We all know how a ship labours in a storm, wrestling with the sea, rising and heeling over till all its timbers creak and groan. Then we see that a ship is alive, that it has a personal will of its own to take on a fight with the elements and see it through, then a league of mutual confidence is formed between the sailor and the ship. He knows what he can demand of a ship he trusts. He knows what she can take and he knows her moods. The smell of tar reminds him of many a hard struggle they have fought together, but also of cruises in fine weather. Quite naturally each ship has her own name, often a vivid image. «The Long Serpent» or «The Crane» for a slender ship with a high prow, or «The Reindeer» for the fleetest of all ships. All this comes to mind in looking at the Gokstad ship. It is not the image of a viking ship, it is the ship itself, the ship which sailed the fjords so often in the days of Halfdan the Black (Svarte).

This latter point should be especially emphasized as the misunderstanding still exists that the ships from the burial mounds were not real ships, but ships built especially for burying, as an inferior substitute for a useful and valuable vessel. This is as highly improbable in itself, as otherwise nothing was spared in furnishing the graves; besides which the ships themselves are evidence to the contrary. All the materials are carefully selected, every detail of the construction is painstakingly executed, as is all the craftsmanship; everything is done to fulfil the demands made of a ship in use. Furthermore there is evidence that the ships really have been sailed. A careful examination of the Oseberg ship (by Fr. Johannessen) revealed traces of considerable wear on the hull, especially around the rivets. Partly these traces may have been caused by handling the ship on land, but some marks can only have been caused by the sea. As is natural in a pliantly constructed ship, the holes for the nails have been especially worn, and the plates on the upper part of the keel have dug into the timber. The oar-holes likewise show signs of wear, not very much, but enough to indicate clearly that the ship has been rowed.

;arved head from the trestle upporting the body of the)seberg carriage.

The mast partner had been reinforced with iron bands because it had given way under the pressure of the sails, showing that the boat had also been sailed. On the upper surface of the cross-beams are various cuts and dents, and on the floor-boards there are scratches and drawings, both obviously made by the crew. Wear and tear has also been found on the Gokstad ship, especially on the oars and oar-holes.

The Gokstad ship was constructed for regular use, and we can therefore

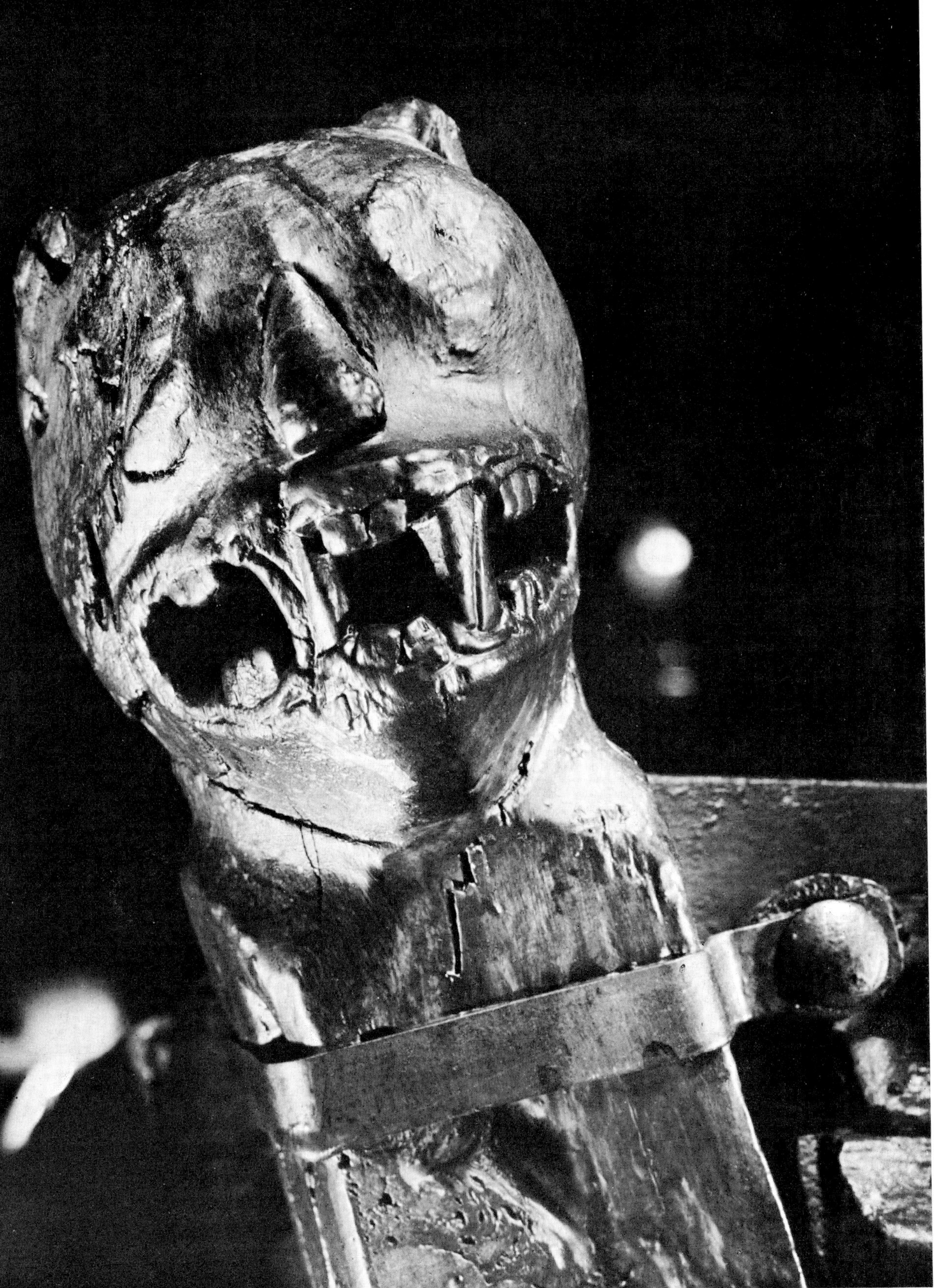

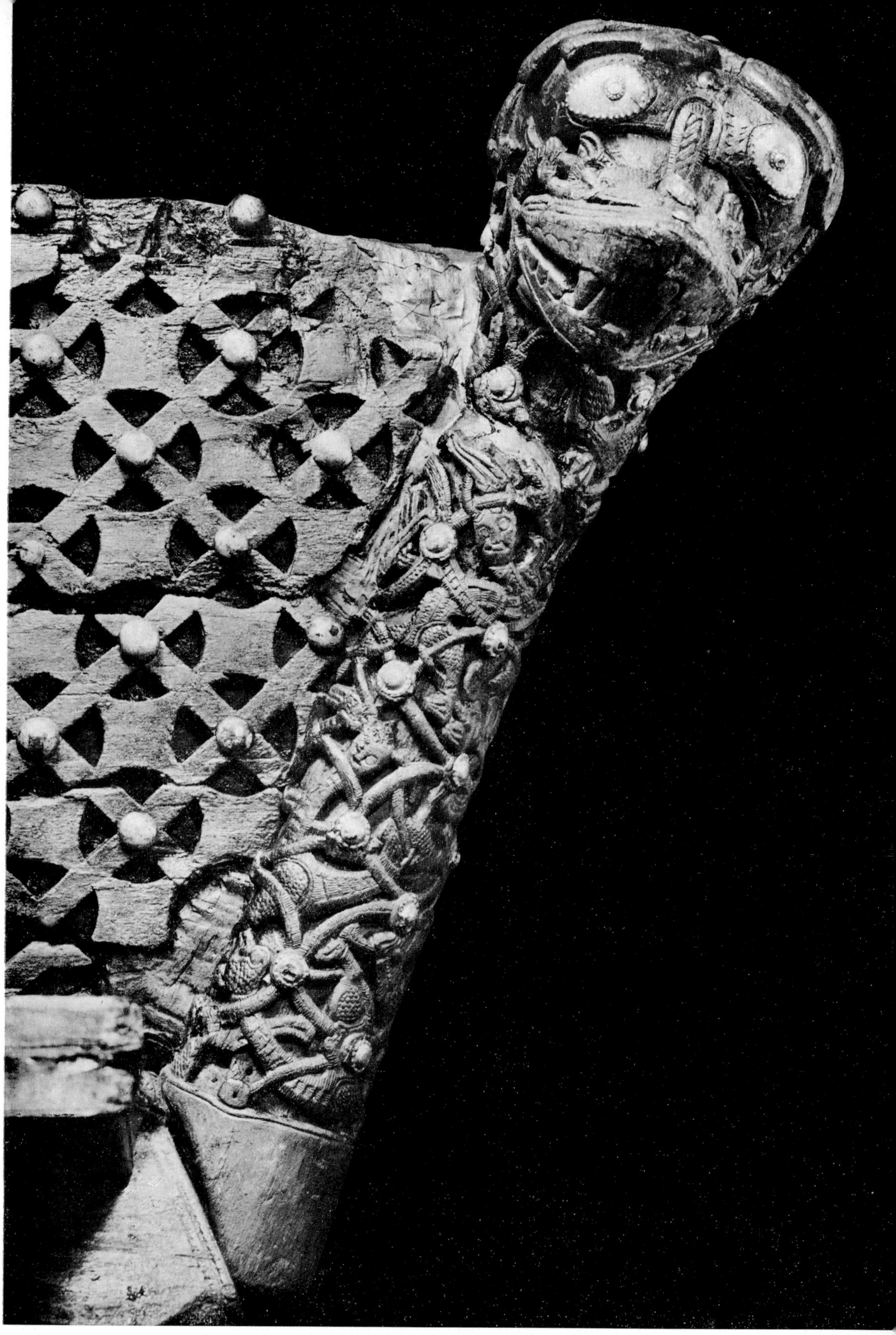

Animal heads on sledges found in the Oseberg ship.

form an idea of what the people of those days demanded of a vessel, and how the shipbuilders of the time solved their task; things that were never really mentioned in the sagas. The ships themselves were frequently referred to, and we also hear of ships being built, but naturally there is no mention of technical details, as these were not pertinent and were familiar to everybody at the time. In the old laws there are certain references to the division of labour in the ship-yards; the master was called the «shipwright», and there were also special, skilled workers who made the keel, stem and stern, further the «filunger» who made the planking and had smaller wages. In describing the building of The Long Serpent (Ormen Lange) for Olav Trygvason, the saga wants to give the impression of an unusually splendid undertaking, and all the various groups of workers with their special jobs are mentioned, as well as the master-wright who was in charge of it all. The most common expression for building a ship was to «erect a ship», as for instance: «This spring King Haakon had a big ship erected in Tunsberg; it was to be called *Suden*» *(i. e.* «The Ship»). The slip where the ship was erected was called the *stocks*. Snorre relates that the stocks where the «Long Serpent» was built could be seen in his days, two hundred years later. Of the tools needed for shipbuilding «The King's Mirror» only mentions the axe, the gouge and the auger. That is all we can glean from literature as to how the ships were built, but the ships themselves can tell us, step by step, how the work progressed.

There were many things to think of before one could begin to build a ship. The design had to be agreed upon in detail, so that everything would be satisfactory, and the shipwright made his preparations accordingly. A good ship was built of oak throughout, and the first step was to select the timber needed for each part of the hull; a long straight log for the keel, particularly strong pieces for the stem and stern, the mast partner and rudder. For each rib a piece of timber was needed corresponding by natural growth to the transverse section of the ship. A large stock of materials for knees and planking was also needed. The materials were as a rule prepared well in advance of the actual building of the ship, and the future owner would long have been on the lookout for suitable trees. The shipwright would also have on hand a supply of the various timber materials, well submerged in water to stay fresh and supple. Such half-shaped materials are not infrequently found in marshes and swamps, where they were stored by the shipbuilders of the past. Thus in Stavanger Museum there are two very nice pieces of oak for the prows of a large ship, found in Sunnanå, Ryfylke. The shipbuilders had some materials to draw on when they received an order, but their stores no doubt had to be supplemented. In any case, the selection of materials would have to be complete, and each piece cut to its proper shape before the construction could begin.

It cannot for an instant be supposed that the shipwright worked from a drawn plan. The boat-builders of West Norway still work in the unbroken traditions of the Viking Era, and build boats flawlessly with a few standard proportions and otherwise by nothing but the measure of the eye. Although the boats built here in recent years have had no more than 5 pairs of oars, we

gures traced on the under side a loose floor board in the Ose-rg ship.

may assume that in former times larger vessels were built in the same way. This was indeed a real art. The joiner formed the keel, bow, stern, ribs and beams, each piece to fit exactly into its intended place in the structure, while the «filunger» prepared the planks, each one calculated to fit into the ship's lines. The responsibility for a successful result rested mostly with the joiner, as he had twice the pay of the others. One should suppose that the prow, stern and keel were a comparatively simple task, even though they constitute the supporting structure of the entire ship. The shaping of the ribs, on the other hand must have required a most skilful hand, as they together (in the Gokstad ship 19 ribs) form the fine lines of the hull. Small irregularities were not always to be avoided, as each rib had been cut out from a piece of timber that was naturally curved by growth, and the planking had to be individually fitted to each rib before all the parts could be joined together. Owing to the peculiar construction of the ship's bottom, as will be explained later, the cutting of the timber was a very complicated process. We are hard put to it to understand how it all happened in detail, but it was the job of the shipwrigh to see that everything fitted in.

The workers must have felt that the worst was done when all parts were assembled and the real construction of the ship could begin. The keel was laid on the stocks, the stem and stern riveted with heavy nails to each end and propped up in the correct position. Next, the planking was built up, always clinker-built in the old ships, the first strake riveted to the keel, and then strake by strake was riveted on, each with the lower edge slightly over-

Ribs and cross-beams in the Go-stad ship.

lapping, and the end of each strake nailed into a rabbet in the end of the ship. The planking was no doubt built up before the ribs were put in, as in many instances the planking is riveted together directly under a rib, and the same applies to joints in the strakes themselves. At the same time it is hard to conceive that the planking could be built up freely without a support to ensure the form of the hull. Here they must have used moulds to keep the transverse section in a correct, symmetrical balance on each side of the keel. When the strakes had been built up to the water line the ribs were put into place, and then it could be seen whether everything had been correctly shaped. There is no way of knowing whether a piece ever had to be discarded and a new one made; in any case we may assume that the under side of the ribs was given a final adjustment when they were being joined to the hull. On each strake, and cut in one piece with it, were cleats, and it was by making grooves of varying depths in the latter that each strake was made to fit exactly into its place. As we know the completed ships today, everything seems to fit perfectly, although slight inaccuracies may be found on a close examination.

The most difficult part of the construction had been completed when the ribs were in place and fastened to the planking. After that, a transverse beam was placed over each rib, from top to top. To each end of this beam a knee was fastened and the upright end of the knee, flush with the side of the ship, served as a hold for the planking above the water-line. Finally came the narrow strakes which continue the planking in a rising curve to the stem and stern. To the bow the decorative pieces were fastened, the posts, and the so-called «spån» and «tingel». Inboard, the keelson and mast partner were placed and secured. A strong block of oak was nailed to the ship's side externally, as a support for the rudder. Then the ship, now completed, was tarred. «A ship is to be tarred as soon as it is built,» says an old law.

When a ship stood complete it was given a name as a token that its life had begun. The saga tells of Olav Trygvason, when he had his first large longship built by the river Nid that: "... it was a sailing vessel, many shipwrights had worked to fashion it. When it was finished it had thirty thwarts, was high of stem and stern, and did not seem large in proportion. The King called the ship «The Crane»". Later, of Haakon Haakonson, that he launched the ship, but first he spoke «and gave the ship a name and called it Krossuden». More will be said of the ships' names in the Saga Era in a later chapter by Brøgger.

The Gokstad Ship, Its Construction and Furnishings.

At the first glance it is evident that the Gokstad ship is a handsome vessel, well built and adapted to its purpose, a work of long experience and fine craftsmanship. But in order really to judge and appreciate it, it is necessary to study the details of its structure, because it is the details that show how thoroughly everything has been tested and thought out. Shipbuilding in the Viking Era was the final stage of a long development, the result of seamanship and technical skill which had gradually achieved that classic standard of which the Gokstad ship is an example. Only a close examination can show us how each part of the ship has its definite function, and how well every detail has been designed to serve its purpose.

The following account is a result of a new examination of the ship (1943—44). The old description by State Antiquarian N. Nicolaysen (1882) was bound to be unsatisfactory as the ship at that time had not been restored to its original form. Now, on the other hand, the dimensions may be corrected from the restored ship. Particularly regarding the stem and stern of the ship, it has been established that they differ from the old measurements in that they rise higher and more sharply. This is naturally a great improvement in the profile of the ship as a whole.

Mr. Fr. Johannessen, a distinguished nautical engineer who has devoted his life to the study of viking navigation, has kindly taken a personal share in the investigations, and has checked our statements of measures and dimensions. We have also had the invaluable advantage of discussing with him the various technical and nautical problems that the ship presents. It is to be hoped that Mr. Johannessen himself soon will publish a thorough, technical account of the Gokstad ship. Meanwhile the present work is the first to give an accurate and complete report on how the Gokstad ship was built.

The Gokstad ship is 76' 6" (23.33 m.) long, between the extreme points fore and aft. Greatest width is 17' 6" (6.25 m.). The height from the bottom of the keel to the gunnel amidships is 6' 4 4/5" (1.95 m). The ship's side above the waterline amidships is 3' 7 1/5" (1.10 m.), and it draws 33 1/2" (0.85 m.). The weight of the hull fully equipped is estimated at 20.2 metric tons. An exact copy of the ship had a tonnage of 31.78 register tons. The ship is built of oak throughout, and consists of keel, stem and stern, ribs with crossbeams and knees, and planking. In addition to this come the special supports for the mast and all other equipment, rudder, mast and yard with sails and cordage, floor-boards, oars, anchor, gangway, baler etc.

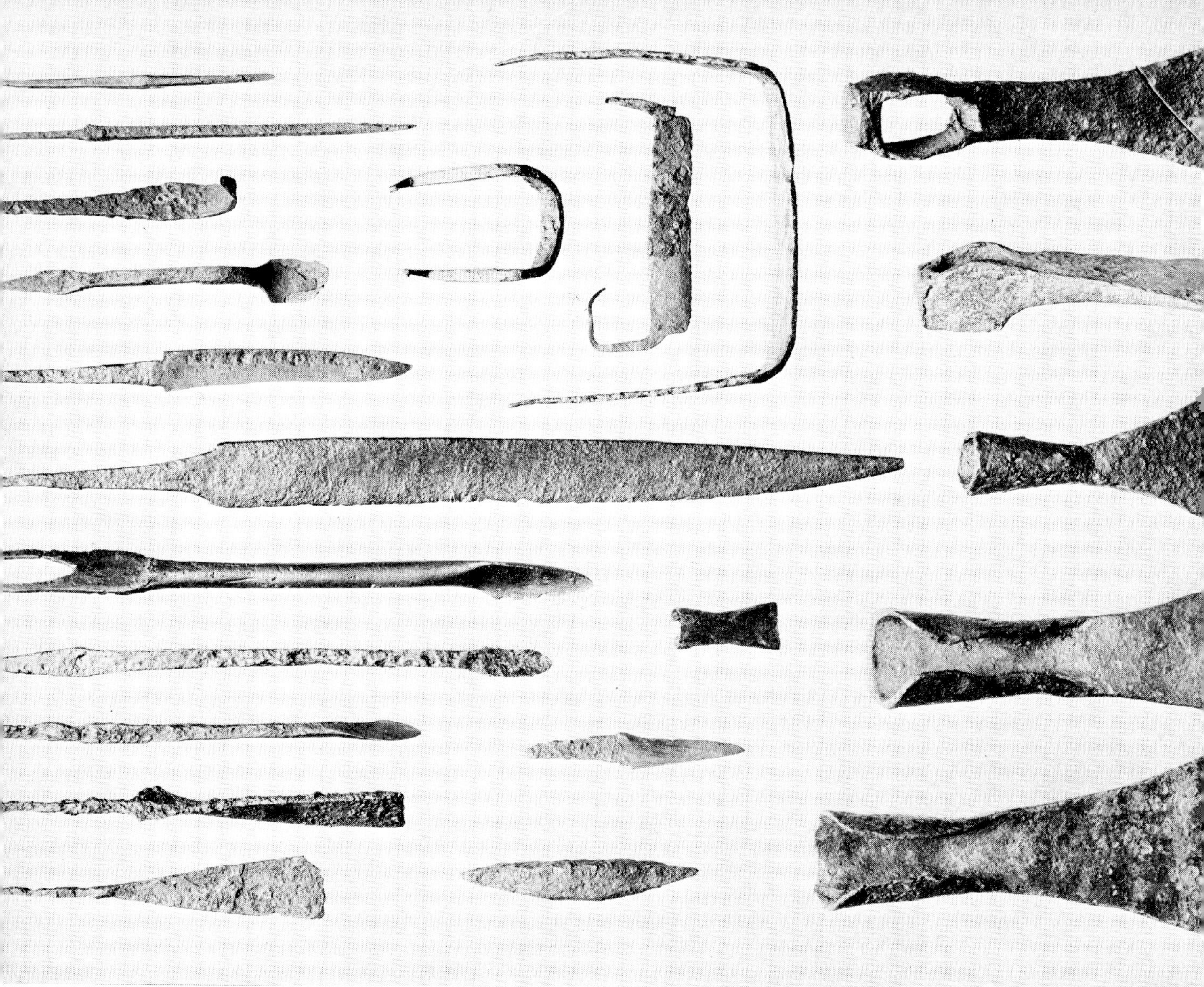

Iron tools found in Norwegian ▮*king graves. Many of them ha*▮ *been used in ship-building.*

The keel is in one piece, cut out from a selected, straight grown oak, and has a T-shaped section. It is 14½" (37 cm.) high amidships, increasing to 16½" (42cm.) aft, and 15¾' (40 cm.) under the bow. The underside amidships is 5" (13 cm.) wide, and the side facing the bottom of the ship 3³/₄" (10 cm.). Each side of the upper surface has a projecting ridge on to which the first strake is fastened. The width on the upper surface is thus increased to 7³/₄" (20 cm.). Simple as it may be, the keel's profile is nicely balanced for the greatest possible strength and the least possible weight. The keel forms a very flat and even arch from fore to aft, so that the ship draws 11¾" (30 cm.) more amidships than at the ends. This is also a masterly feature, as it makes it easier to turn the ship about, causes it to lie high on the water and increases its capacity, as the greatest draught is where the hull is broadest.

We see from this that a shipbuilder in the Viking Era knew how to shape the keel so that it would serve its double purpose perfectly. It reinforces the entire hull lengthwise from stem to stern, and at the same time it gives the ship strength to resist the pressure from below in heavy seas. From the account given elsewhere of older types of ships we have seen that this part of the structure was long an unsolved problem which made it particulary difficult to build ships of larger dimensions. Before the invention of the keel, a broad bottom-plank had to suffice, as in the Nydam Ship. This was a weakness that had unfortunate consequences for the shape of the hull. On the Kvalsund boat, a couple of centuries before the Viking Era, we still have the bottom-plank, but now furnished with a projecting ridge along the middle, giving some strength although it never could be quite effective. In a boat found at Holmedal in Sunnfjord the development has advanced one step further. Here there is a real keel made in one piece with a broad bottom-plank, but with the weakness that the angle beetween the plank and the keel is apt to give way and break under pressure. Finally, in the viking ships, the bottom-plank has been discarded altogether, so that the keel alone can be given the shape most suitable for its purpose. This solution may seem simple as Columbus' egg, but nevertheless it cost centuries of trial and error. Now, for the first time it was possible to sail into the wind.

To each end of the keel is joined a special piece which forms the transition to the stem and stern, both by a slightly ascending curve and by a higher, sharper transverse section. At the ends of the keel the projecting ridge gives place to a rabbet to which the end of each strake is fastened. The keel, transitional pieces, stem and stern are connected by scarf joints. That is to say that the two pieces to be joined are cut at an angle where they overlap, and then they are riveted with sturdy nails, two rows to each joint and four treenails in the upper scarf. In this detail the shipwright also shows great progress from the techniques known from the ships of earlier days. In both the Nydam ship and the Kvalsund boat the connection between the keel and the stem and stern is made by a flat joint (ends of planks not cut obliquely) and overlapping horizontally fastened with treenails, no doubt a less durable method for such an exposed point of the structure. It was this point that would bear the brunt if the ship were to be stranded; even in the times of the sagas it is mentioned several times that the transitional piece might be torn off if the ship struck a shoal.

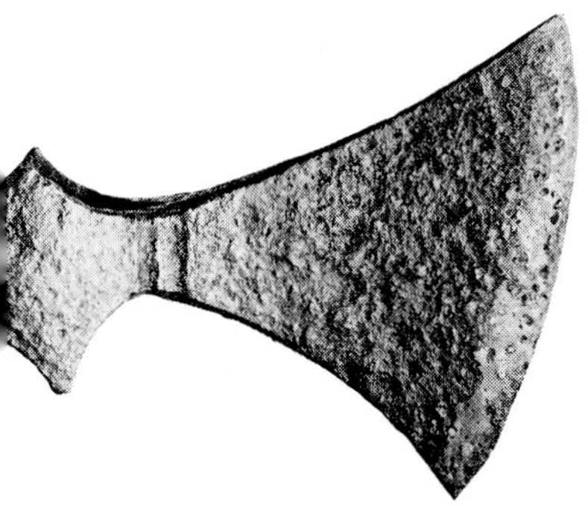

Battle axe found at Kosgården, Åsnes in Hedmark.

The stem and stern are each in one piece, and of the finest materials in the entire ship. Both are unfortunately incomplete now, as the tops have rotted away. The piece that remains of the stern measures 9' 9" (3 m.) cord length, that of the stem slightly less. Greatest width is 17¾" (45 cm.) with a sharp profile, narrower at the stem, the inner side having a rabbet into which the ends of the planking are nailed. What remains of the Gokstad ship is enough to show how the stem and stern rise in an elegant curve from the keel, but it is unfortunately insufficient to tell us anything about their height or how the tops were made. Only one little thing is discernible, just at the edge of the remaining piece of the stern. Here there is a moulding that follows

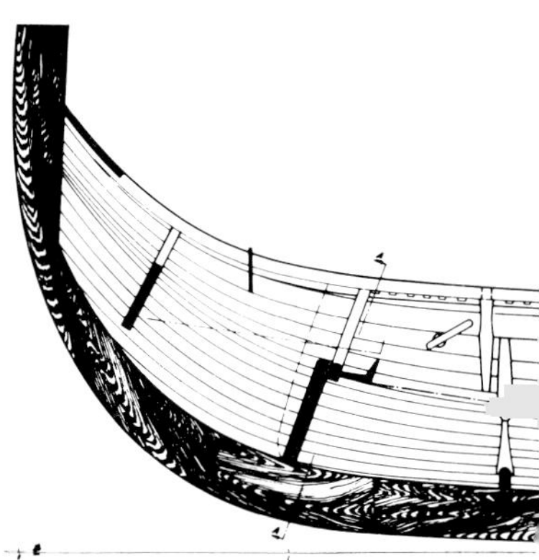

the inner side of the stern in a uniform curve. The curve is interrupted, but begins again after a short intervening space, now ascending vertically. The lines here show with certainty that the stern has broadened appreciably toward the top, but give no indication as to how the top was finished. It is, however, permissible to point to a closely analogous case, *viz.* the stern of a rather large vessel found in the marshes near Sunnanå, Ryfylke. The size of this stern is about two thirds of that of the Gokstad ship, and thus it gives a fair idea of the vessel to which the stern belonged. Here too, just as in the Gokstad ship, there is a characteristic break in the transition from a uniform, projecting curve to a vertical line. Here the top is intact, cut into a high point which rises flush with the edge of the sheer strake. There is a stern of a similar shape on a drawing of a boat made on a floor-board of the Oseberg ship. Evidently this was quite a common way of terminating the stern in the Viking Era, but that is naturally no proof that the Gokstad ship had just this same form. On the other hand it is evident that the Gokstad ship did not have a dragon head of the type found on the Oseberg ship, although it may have had a similar ornament in another form. The dragon-head was usually detachable, as we know from the saga: «Now Olav Trygvason is afraid, he dare not sail with the head on his ship.»

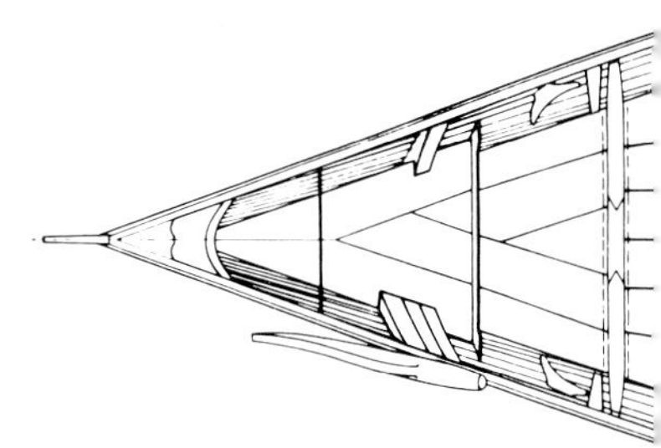

Bard is the old name for the ship's prow, and that accounts for the name of Eirik Jarl's ship «Jernbarden» (jern = iron) which had iron pieces fastened to the stem. The word *barde* is also used poetically for ships in general.

Joined to the keel, stem and stern is the «*planking*», the «*skin*», which forms the bottom and sides of the ship. The planking of the Gokstad ship consists of 16 strakes, each overlapping the one below, and fastened to it with round-headed rivets driven through both planks from the outside. On the inside the nails are riveted over a little, square iron plate called a clinch-plate (*ro*). Only on a small part of the ship, close to the stem and stern, are the clinch plates on the outside, as there was no room for using the hammer on the inside. With this exception, riveting on the outside was considered slovenly and unsightly. The nails used in the Gokstad ship are about ⅖" (1 cm.) in diameter, and have intervals of about 7¼" (18.5 cm.). All joints in the planking are made as scarf joints with three nails across, of which the two on each side are driven through the adjoining strake. An old rule in those days was that two joints should not be placed directly one above the other. Should this happen it was considered a defect, the ship was *pieced*. This has been carefully avoided in the Gokstad ship. Another fine point was that the outer end of the scarf-joint always pointed aft, so as to shed water and ice when the ship was in motion. A competent man would naturally see to it that all such rules were observed in the construction of his ship. While the planking was being built up, all grooves and joints were caulked with animal hair. Loose, woolly threads, approximately as thick as a finger, were spun loosely together into a thick cord, presumably with a thin, hook-shaped twig like those still used with the boatbuilders in North Norway. The caulk was dipped in tar and placed in a groove near the lower edge of every strake, so that it was pressed tightly together when the plank-

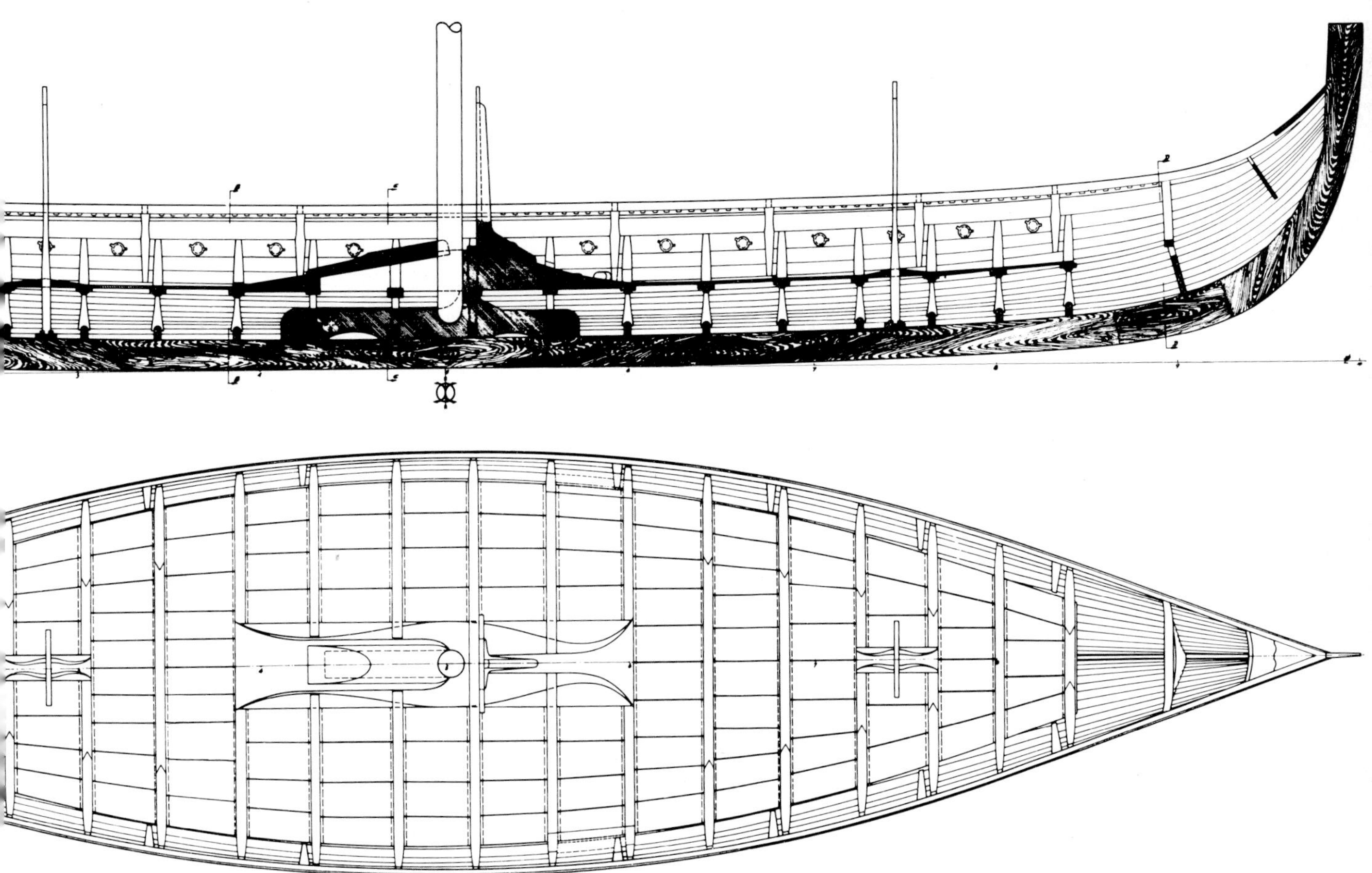

keleton drawing of the Gokstad ip.

ing was riveted. Every seam and joint was carefully caulked, as were the joints between the planking, keel, stem and stern.

The caulking was mainly done while the ship was under construction, but in a few places it was done later, probably after the ship had been put into use. The tarring of the completed ship also contributed to the tightness of the vessel.

Every part of the planking is carefully formed according to its function. The first 9 strakes from the keel, forming the bottom below the waterline, are of elastic planks 1" (2.6 cm.) thick, mostly lashed to the ribs with withy, and not nailed. It is a very curious construction, a legacy from the early, primitive stages of ship-building, still used in the Viking Era although at that time a more simple technique could surely have been found. On the inside of the planking, in the middle of each strake and in one piece with it, are rows of protruding cleats. This is a very nice piece of carpentry, as the cleats are cut out during the process of reducing the boards to the desired thickness. The cleats are so placed that each one is directly under its corresponding rib, and through each cleat two holes are made, one on each side of the rib. Then two holes are made through the rib, on both sides of the cleat. Next, lashings are put through the holes of both ribs and cleats, tying them

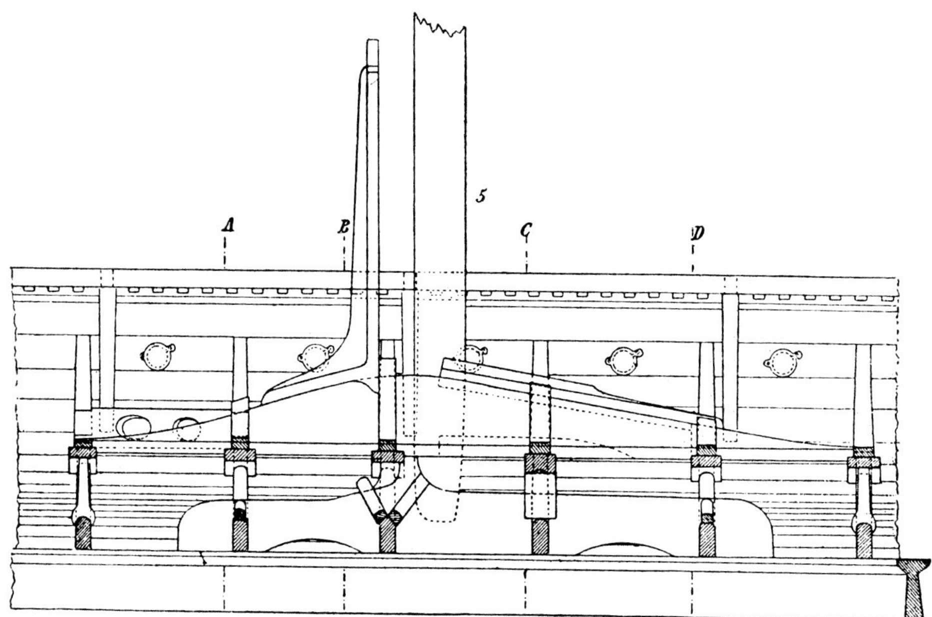

The powerful supporting stru ture for the mast in the Gokst ship.

together. The cleats are so cut that the upper edge of the plank is against the rib, while the lower edge is outside and overlapping the plank below. In the Gokstad ship, lashings of fine spruce roots were used.

This construction is used for the second strake and those above, up to, and including the eighth. The first, garboard, strake is riveted on to the ridge on the side of the keel and to the second strake, with no other fastening. The 9th strake, the last of the strakes below the waterline, has no lashing cleats, but is fastened to the ribs with a treenail. At the point of contact between the rib and the planking there is a broad cleat that begins as a ridge approximately in the middle of the strake, so that the lower edge can be placed outside the strake below. Thus we see that the various strakes differ according to their place and function in the hull. All this had to be carefully planned, measured and cut before the planking was riveted together. By a close examination of the ship one almost feels as if one could follow the movement of the sure and well-trained hands that worked here.

One cannot help asking why this cumbersome method of building ships was still in use in the Viking Era. There was no need to be frugal with iron for nails and bolts; iron was used widely for all kinds of purposes at the time. There can be no doubt that Norwegian shipbuilders could have made a more secure junction of ribs and planking in the ships, as we know it was done in the smaller boats. This peculiar construction of ships must have had advantages which caused its continued use, and was probably closely connected with an essential feature of the viking ships, *viz.* the thin planking, keeping them light and supple in spite of their size. Light, supple ships were easy to row and sail, and also to lay up when they were not in use, as was the custom. If the planking were to be riveted to the ribs, a much heavier structure would be needed to withstand the pressure of the rough sea, otherwise the nails would give way.

The vikings therefore kept up the old-fashioned method of construction which had originally been a necessity, in order to retain all the advantages of a light and supple ship. Ribs and planking connected in the manner described can give without breaking, and it also increases the elasticity of the ship to the advantage of its sailing performance. In the days of the sailing ships it was well known among the more experienced sailors that an old ship which had loosened a bit in the joints sailed better than new ships, and the same observation was made with the copy of the Gokstad ship which sailed the Atlantic, as mentioned elsewhere. The structure was strong enough for vessels no larger than the ships used in the Viking Era. A riveted planking forms a kind of fused shell which is very resistant, the ribs in the viking ships were not intended to keep the planking together, solely to reinforce the hull, and preserve its shape.

The first 9 strakes, forming the bottom of the ship, are all equally thin; after these comes the heavy 10th strake which is 1¾" thick midship. This is a particularly heavy plank forming the junction between the bottom and side of the ship, and at the same time serving to reinforce the hull lengthwise. This plank is also the support for the tops of the ribs and the transverse beams which are the lateral reinforcements of the structure. The 10th strake is also riveted to the tops of the ribs in order to make an absolutely secure fastening.

When the tenth strake was finished *the ribs* were put in and lashed as mentioned above. The Gokstad ship had 19 ribs, strong pieces of oak, each formed from one piece naturally grown in a U-shape corresponding exactly to the shape of the hull. The distance between the ribs is constant, a little more than 3', leaving the space known by experience to be required for an oar-stroke, with one oar for each rib. The ribs are rounded smoothly on the upper side; on the side facing the planking they are cut flat, with a ridge running down the middle. Through the ridge are drilled two holes for each strake. The rib is not fastened to the keel nor to the first strake. One detail here deserves special mention: in the Nydam ship which has no keel, the ribs are lashed to the bottom-plank in the same manner as to the planking. At a later stage, the Kvalsund boat has a bottom-board with a weak, outside keel, and cleats inside made in one piece with it. These cleats support the ribs, but are not lashed to them. In the Viking Era there is no connection between the keel and the ribs whatsoever. With a fully shaped keel the vikings must have found it more practical to let keel and ribs function independently, here too probably with an eye to making the ship more supple under sail.

On the other strakes the ribs and lashing-cleats were fitted together and lashed with fine spruce roots. These were threaded through the corresponding holes in the ridge on the under side of the ribs and in the lashing cleats on the strakes.

The extreme ribs fore and aft are made as high bulkheads, with the sides cut in a series of little steps, fitting closely to the strakes in the planking and nailed to them. There is a small opening in the bottom of the bulkhead over the keel, to allow the bilge water to run through. The bulkhead aft is also formed as a support for the rudder, as will be described later. Far up in the bow and the stern another small bulkhead is inserted, preserved in the Oseberg ship. In the Gokstad ship there is also a trace of it.

From top to top over each rib is a cross-beam. The top side is horizontally flat, while the underside forms a flat curve to give the maximum support to the tenth strake and the adjoining strakes in the planking. The ends are cut obliquely, flush with the lines of the ship at each rib. In the middle, the cross-beam is supported by a prop with the lower end cleft to sit astride the rib, and the upper end mortised into the cross-beam. There is no prop for the two ribs nearest the bow and stern, as the ship here is so narrow that no support for the cross-beam is needed. Midship there are no props, as the cross-beams here are supported in connection with the mast.

The cross-beams are the last of the main factors of construction below the water line. They complete the lateral reinforcement of the ship. At this point those parts of the structure which bear and secure the mast had to be put in. This is perhaps the most difficult problem to solve in a light and supple vessel. We know nothing of the past development of this part of the ship. All we know is that by the time of the Viking Era the structure had found a secure and regular form, obviously the result of a long process of trial and error by preceding generations. It is a pleasure indeed to see how this problem was solved in the Gokstad ship.

In the middle of the ship is placed a sturdy block of oak, resting on the keel and on 4 ribs (ribs 8—11 from the stern). The old term for this block was the *crone,* (a somewhat drastic image of its function in relation to the mast). It corresponds in function to the keelson of modern times. The *crone* in the Gokstad ship is 12'2" 3.75 m.) long, about 15¾" (40 cm.) high and 23½" (60 cm.) wide at the middle, tapering off toward the ends. It is not fastened to the keel. It is made fast to the 10th rib from the stern by two solid knees nailed on from each side, and by a knee on each side to the 8th and 11th rib. Right in front of the 10th rib, and forward of the socket for the mast that is cut into the *crone,* is a strong, vertically inclining arm, grown in one piece with the *crone.* The socket itself is formed with the bottom rounded forwards so that the foot of the mast may slip into place when the mast is raised, while aft it is cut square, to hold the mast securely when the ship is under sail: a detail contrived with remarkable skill in order to avoid the necessity of lifting the mast in and out when it was being hoisted or lowered, a frequently recurring task when the ship was under way.

The *crone* carries the weight of the mast, and holds it firmly in place. The mast partner is laid over the cross-beams, bracing the mast when it is in an upright position. The distance from the keel to the cross-beams is very short in relation to the total length of the mast, and the hold must be reinforced correspondingly to withstand the pressure on the mast when the ship is under sail. The mast partner is the largest single piece in the entire structure, an oak block 16' 4⅘" (5 m.) long, extending over 5 cross-beams (7th—12th from the stern). In the middle it is 3' 3⅖" (1 m.) wide and 16½" thick, with a steeply arched transverse section, sloping down towards the

e mast partner in the Gokstad p.

ends in a characteristic, fish-tail form. This detail explains the origin of the Norwegian expression «mast-*fish*» for the mast partner. Each end of the mast partner is mortised into a cross-beam, and the four intervening beams are fitted into grooves cut out from the under side of the mast partner. Under the mast partner there are no props supporting the cross-beams, but the cross-beam over the 9th rib is formed like an upended plank, supported by the rib and the *crone*. The cross-beam over the 10th rib is reinforced by the *crone's* vertical arm. Moreover, the mast partner is fastened to the cross-beams by knees nailed onto it from each side. The mast partner is thus firmly secured on all sides, and is in itself strong enough to withstand the greatest strain.

The hole for the mast in the mast partner corresponds naturally to the opening in the *crone,* and continues aft as a long, uniform opening extending to the 8th rib, so that the mast could be raised and taken down. When the mast was raised, the opening in the mast partner was closed by a solid plug, a flat block of oak with a rabbeted edge making a tight fit. Directly above the floor-boards, between the 7th and 8th rib from the stem, is a solid, pine block on each side of the deck. Each has two deep grooves, as if they were intended to support two rather sturdy posts at a slight incline with their ends braced against the planking. The puzzle of their purpose has been unsolved for a long time. Mr. Nicolaysen guessed that is was some kind of a windlass to aid in stepping the mast, but that seems hardly probable. The explanation of Mr. Fr. Johannessen seems more likely, *viz.* that they were supports for the sprits. It is well known that the square sail had to be stretched out with a spar on sailing into the wind or when the wind was abeam, and this spar had to be held firmly in place. The two pine blocks would fit this purpose very well, although it seems strange that there should be *two* grooves in each block. The two grooves are made so that the spar could be extended at different angles according to the direction of the wind, an arrangement which would be of great advantage to the ship, in the opinion of Mr. Johannessen. Not all the details can be accounted for, but everything points to the basic correctness of Mr. Johannessen's assumption.

We have now reviewed the structure of the ship up to the waterline, and shall proceed to examine the building of the topsides. The planking here has a different function. The purpose is no longer to keep the ship afloat, but to shield the inside of the ship against the waves, and to withstand the pressure of the sea when the ship heels over in the wind. To brace the ship inside, solid knees are placed at each cross-beam, one arm nailed to the upper side of the beam, and the other formed so that it corresponds to the curve of the planking at each rib. To these the strakes above the water-line are riveted. Above the water-line there is no need for the cumbersome construction with cleats and lashings used in the bottom of the ship. In the Gokstad ship the knees extend over four strakes above the cross-beam, but this is a particularly high-boarded vessel, with two more strakes nailed on to the top-ribs above the knees. These top-ribs are nailed to the three strakes immediately below them, one for every other knee. With that the ship was built to its full height.

The first three strakes of the boards are of the same thickness as the strakes below the water-line, *i.e.* 1" (2.6 cm). After them comes the 14th strake, counting from the keel, somewhat thicker, 1¼" (3.2 cm), as the oar-holes were placed here, and a stronger plank was called for. The Gokstad ship has 16 pairs of oars, one pair for each space between the ribs, except the last space fore and aft. We shall later return to the subject of the oars and the rowing; we shall only mention here that the oar-holes are closed on the inside by small, round shutters with a small hook aft, fitting over a nail in the planking. In the forward end there is a notch in the lower edge, fitting under another nail in the planking, so that the shutter will keep out the water. The shutter is opened by turning it forwards on the supporting nail. Even in this little detail everything is well thought out, practical and convenient. The two top strakes, fastened to the top-ribs, are particularly light, only 7/12" (1.60 cm.) thick, but along the upper edge, inboard, a special, rectangular gunnel has been added, measuring 4¼" by 3 3/32" (11 cm. × 8 cm.).

Below the gunnel there is an independent batten with rectangular openings (11 openings for each space between the ribs). Towards the ends of the ship, where the strakes curve sharply upwards, corresponding openings are cut in the gunnel itself. This is the shield rack, which in the old days was also the name for the entire upper strake. As implied by the name, this is where the shields were hung to adorn the side of the ship, a custom which is frequently mentioned in the sagas. When the Gokstad ship was found in the grave-mound it had 32 shields on each side, two for each oar-hole. The

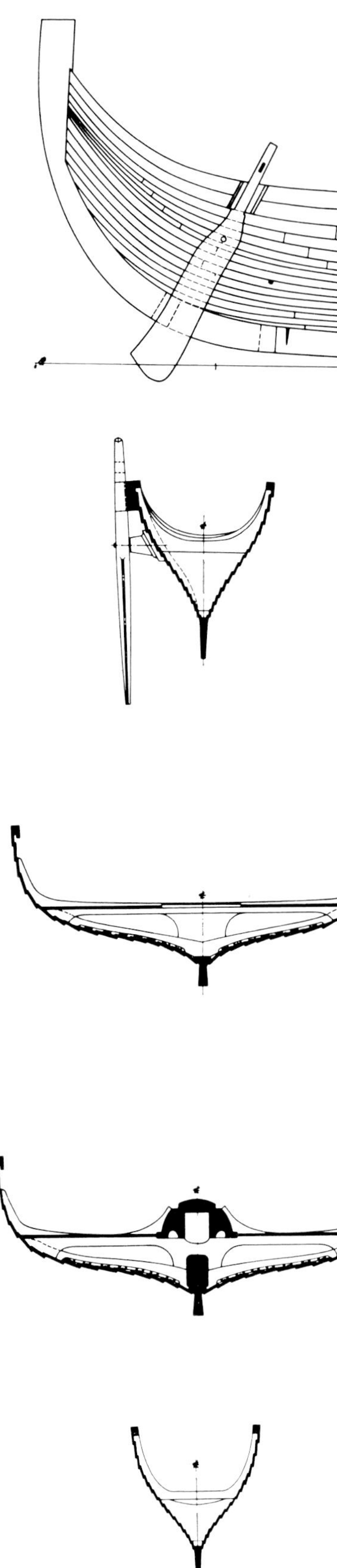

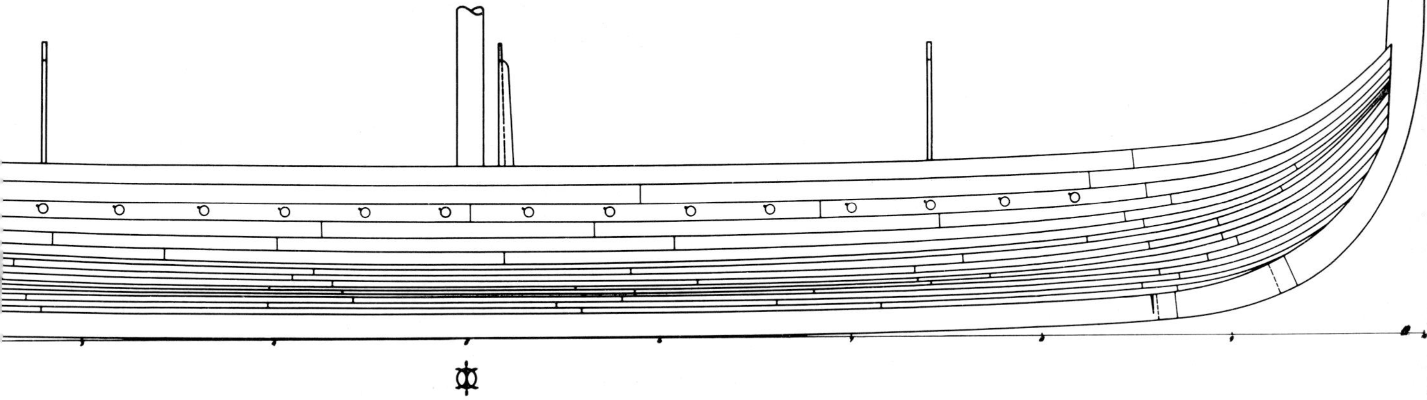

shields were hung externally along the gunnel, tied to the shield rack with thin bast cords drawn through the handles of the shields. The shields were hung so that each one half-way overlapped the one aft of it. They were painted yellow and black alternately, forming a continuous row from stem to stern. This corresponds to a stock phrase in the sagas: «The ship was completely *shielded* from stem to stern.» Naturally the shields could not hang there when the ship was under way, nor could they serve for defence; they were used solely when the ship was in port, and only for decorative purposes and to indicate the rank and honour of the ship. To sail with the shields hung out was at variance with proper conduct, or anyway a most unusual procedure; as we can see from the sagas when Bjørn, one of the early settlers of Iceland, came into Bjarnarfjord with the shields hung out; and bore the name of Skjaldabjørn (from skjold = shield) ever since.

The shield rack completed the height of the ship. After that, the *floor-boat* were placed over the cross-beams. That part of the knee which is nailed to the cross-beam is slightly narrower than the latter, so that a small ledge is left, serving as a support for the floor-boards. These are thin pine boards, held together on the under surface by narrow strips of oak. All the floor-boards are loose, so that the space underneath may be utilised. Nailed fast inboard are three cleats on each side of the stern, for sheets and other cordage from the sails. Finally, there is in the Gokstad ship a rather enigmatic contrivance consisting of three upright pine posts, each with a cross-bar on top and rising 7'8" (2.40 m.) above the floor-boards. One is mid-way between the mast and the bow, one mid-way between the mast and the stern and one right in front of the mast. The latter is fastened to the mast partner, and the two others are supported by an oak block on the keel and two small cleats at the level of the floor-boards. There has been some doubt as to what was the purpose of these posts, but there seems to be general agreement at the present time that they were used for stowing away the oars, sprits and other equipment when the ship was in port. The posts are slightly more than 13' (4 m.) apart and the oars are from 17' 2¾" (5.30 m.) to 19' ½" (5.85 m.) long. The cross bar is 7' 8" (2.40 m.) above the floor-boards, or well over the height of a man. When the ship was in harbour it

Longitudinal and transverse sections of the Gokstad ship.

would be quite essential to life on board that the deck should not be cluttered up with 32 large oars and other equipment. This problem is nicely and practically solved in the Gokstad ship. In the Oseberg ship the solution is somewhat different; here the oars were stowed away in four high gaffs fastened to the side of the ship, one on each side.

Finally we come to the *rudder,* one of the most important parts of the ship, and one which well deserves a closer examination. To the modern eye the Gokstad ship is furnished with a very curious arrangement for steering. The rudder itself is shaped like an oversized oar-blade, hanging outside to starboard, aft. It is cut from one piece of oak, 10' 8¾" (3.30 m.) high and 16½" (42 cm.) wide, with a slightly out-curving heel at the lower end. Fundamentally, it is thus a very large steering-oar. Originally, the rudder must have been just an oar, held against the side of the ship, as is done in small boats today, but with larger vessels such a rudder gets too heavy for one man to handle and keep in the correct position when the ship is under way. It must have been a very complicated problem to fasten the rudder so that it would cleave the water at a suitable depth, turn on its own axis and resist the pressure of heavy seas. We have seen how imperfectly this was arranged even at the time of the Nydam ship. In the viking ships a satisfactory solution has finally been found, the rudder being attached to the last rib aft, which is especially shaped for this purpose.

As mentioned earlier, the last rib is shaped like an upended, thick plank. On the starboard side a wide, solid board extends from this plank, pointing sternwards from the rib and lying against the ship's side, inboard, along the shield rack. The whole thing is made from the trunk of a large oak, and the rib is thus considerably reinforced so that it will withstand the pressure of the rudder against the side of the ship. Next to the gunnel there is, moreover, at this point a heavy plank, about 3¾" (10 cm.) thick and extending over two strakes, with an additional reinforcement where the neck of the rudder rests against the gunnel. Outboard, the rudder is kept in an upright position by a heavy oak block, rounded at one end and hence called *the wart.* This is secured by nails driven through the planking and the rudder rib. Here are also the actual fastenings for the rudder. A hole is made through the rudder, the wart, the planking and the rib, making room for a thick withy, with a knot in the outside end and made fast inboard through three holes in the upper end of the rudder rib. By this device the rudder is held to the side of the ship, while the pliant withy allows the rudder to turn on its vertical axis. The lower part of the rudder may be raised or lowered at will around the horizontal axis formed by the withy. When the rudder is adjusted properly, the end of the blade goes about 1' 6" (50 cm.) deeper than the keel, and this explains how the ship could be so well steered with such a narrow rudder.

To support the neck of the rudder and keep it in the right position, there is a broad band running through two slits in the gunnel, and tied inboard to the rudder rib. The band itself was not found in the Gokstad ship, it was probably made of rope and has rotted away. In the Oseberg ship there

king weapons found at Hol-
·inshov, Løten in Hedmark.

is a finely braided leather band, and here we can see how this detail was arranged. In one end of the band was an oval piece of wood, and in the other end a loop, shaped like a buttonhole. The band was passed through one of the slits, with the loop first, the wooden oval preventing the other end from slipping through, around the rudder neck, back through the other slit, and then the loop was slipped over a peg inboard. The band secures the rudder neck and keeps it in the right position against the gunnel. At the same time it is so arranged that the rudder neck could be loosened or made fast quite easily whenever the rudder had to be lowered or raised. This was done by means of a rope tied to a cramp on the lower aft end of the blade. This little cramp is still intact on the Gokstad ship.

The rudder neck goes up about 20" above the gunnel. Here is the hole for the tiller, a vertical slit made at right angles to the plane of the rudder so that the tiller projects horizontally across the gunnel. The tiller for the Gokstad ship was about 40" (1 m.) long, and the only part of the ship to be furnished with carved ornaments. When the ship was found the tiller was not in place, but stood near at hand, leaning against the stern.

The floor-board over the rudder rib forms the poop deck, slightly higher than the other parts of the deck. Directly behind the rudder stands the helmsman with the tiller in front of him at a convenient height to be grasped with both hands. The Norwegian newspaperman and seafarer, Captain Magnus Andersen, was very favourably impressed with the rudder when he sailed an exact copy of the Gokstad ship across the Atlantic in 1893. He regarded it as nothing short of brilliant for a ship of this type. Without the slightest difficulty a man could stand and steer the ship «with this little stick», in all kinds of weather and through the roughest seas. The fact that the rudder goes some 18" (50 cm.) deeper than the keel midship has also contributed greatly to the maneuverability of the ship. This too, is probably a result of the old experience with a loose steering oar. It was less important that they had to raise the rudder when they were in shallow waters, or when the ship was taken ashore, as it was a very simple procedure to loosen the band around the rudder neck and haul in the rope aft. The rudder was also usually raised when the ship rode at anchor, and in some cases when the sea was so rough that it threatened to tear the rudder off. This, however, was not mentioned by Captain Andersen, although he had some very rough weather on his voyage with the viking ship across the Atlantic. Otherwise he is full of interesting information about the rudder. He says that it does not matter whether the rudder is to windward or leeward, except that in the former case the band around the rudder neck has to be hauled taut. There is some pressure on the rope to the bottom of the rudder blade when the wind is to starboard, while on the other hand the withy to the gunnel is strained when the wind is to port.

The Gokstad ship was interred with the mast stepped, and when the ship was found, the mast projected through the roof of the grave chamber. This part had rotted away. The top of the mast had been cut off and placed on the posts in the stem. *The mast* is made of pine, 11⅚" (30 cm.) thick throughout the remaining part. We do not know the height, but according to an old rule the height of the mast should be equal to the *girth, i. e.* the circumference of the ship at the widest point.

When this is applied to the Gokstad ship we get a mast of some 42'7" (13 m.), which seems quite reasonable for a vessel of that size. The rigging consisted no doubt only of one large square sail; the three cleats aft for the sheets and braces have been mentioned before, but there is no trace of a cleat

Weapons from the Viking age.

for the halyard. In the opinion of Mr. Johannessen the halyard was fastened aft when the sail had been hoisted. In this way it also served to brace the mast. The yard was kept close to the mast by a wooden parrel similar to the ones still in use on old-fashioned craft on the west and north coast of Norway. A wooden hoop is needed, because rope would get stuck when the sail was being set or taken down. The parrel or hoop is missing from the Gokstad ship, but was found on the Oseberg ship. From the Gokstad ship we have, on the other hand, two strangely fashioned pieces of wood which very likely served as blocks for the sheets.

We know nothing more of the rigging, only that there are no traces of fastenings for shrouds or stays to brace the mast. It is doubtful whether any such things were needed on a vessel of this kind, with a comparatively low and very sturdy mast. Permanent stays or shrouds are furthermore impossible on a ship where the mast is to be stepped and lowered frequently, and even if they were only semi-permanent they would be highly impractical. In comparison we may remind the reader that the old boats from Hvaler had a relatively high rigging, but no stays or shrouds. Instead the mast was made stouter, especially near the mast partner. The pilots claimed that the boats sailed better without shrouds, as the mast then was more elastic. We have also seen that the mast partner in the Gokstad ship was extremely well reinforced, while the one in the Oseberg ship had been split, presumably because there were no shrouds to brace the mast. We must assume that the rigging on the Gokstad ship was very simple, probably with only the most necessary cordage for the sails. Sailing at that time was still quite elementary and unperfected.

The excavation of the ship supplied no certain information about the sail itself. A large heap of yellowish woollen cloth was found in the bow; originally it is supposed to have been white, with stripes of red cloth sewn on to it, and inside the heap were pieces of thin hemp rope. Mr. Nicolaysen maintains that this had been the tent, but one might just as well suppose that it was the remnants of the sail. The red stripes correspond very well to the colour-striped sails repeatedly referred to in the sagas. In the Saga of St. Olav there is *e. g.* a reference to «the sail as white as snow, with stripes of red and blue». In Old Norse the expression used to describe these stripes was always modified with the term «*með vendi*». According to Ivar Aasen, one of Norway's foremost philologists, this term implies that the stripes are woven obliquely into the sail-cloth. The appearance of the viking ships with the sails striped in this way is illustrated on contemporary Gotland sculptured stones. Here the ships are represented with narrow, diagonal stripes in a chequer-pattern of diamonds all over the sail. This pattern of multicoloured, narrow stripes forming diamond squares is quite different from the broad, vertical stripes in red and white which constitute the pattern formerly believed to have decorated the sails of the viking ships, and should be mentioned in a complete description of the Gokstad ship. We should, however, draw attention to the famous Bayeux tapestry, where the viking ships are depicted with broad vertical stripes in the sails; although this was about a hundred years later than the Gokstad ship, and by then things may have changed.

The strength of the Gokstad ship lay in its oar-power, as is evident from the shape of the hull. The long gunnel is parallel to the water-line almost all the way, so that oars may be used throughout the ship. Every feature of the ship is designed to facilitate the use of oars. She is strikingly slender, with one oar to each pair of ribs, and the distance between the ribs just right for an oar-stroke. The Gokstad ship is a direct descendant of the older type of vessel as known from the Nydam ship. This had only oars and no sails, but was otherwise quite similar in principle. By the Viking Era these principles had found a much more effective and practical expression.

All the *oars* of the Gokstad ship were found in the bow when the ship was excavated. They are of pine and range from 17' 4 3/4"—19' 1/5" (5.30—5.85 m.) in length, according to where they were used on the ship. (The oars used toward both ends had to be longer, as the gunnel here was higher above the water line.)

The blade was small and shaped like a lancet, with a slender loom tape-

Gotland sculptured stone showing the pattern of decoration in the sails of the viking ships.

ring off gradually towards the handle. To those accustomed to rowing only small boats these oars may seem rather peculiar. For their purpose, however, the oars are perfect, with the least possible weight and that maximum of efficiency which could only be obtained by a small blade on a long oar. The length of the oars is very well calculated in relation to the height above the water. The oars are 18 11/32" (48 cm.) above the water-line amidships, a little more towards the ends, and the oars are about 12 times as long, a very good proportion, as the oar is more powerful the longer it is in relation to the level of the oarhole.

There was plenty of room for the oars in the oar-holes, the latter being about 4¾" (12 cm.) wide. There is a small slit cut backwards and upwards from each oar-hole. This slit was for the blade of the oar, when the oars were put out from the inside. This was naturally more convenient than putting the whole oar out across the gunnel and then gripping the handle through the oar-hole and pulling it in. The slit is carefully made at that point in the circumference of the oar-hole which is least in contact with the oar during the normal process of rowing. This must have been done in order to avoid wear, as the opening of the slit might otherwise have chafed the oars severely. Protection of the oars outweighed the slight inconvenience of having the oars put out in an awkward position – front edge slanting down.

The oar-holes are about 15¾" (40 cm.) above the floor-boards, somewhat more towards the bow and stern, a good position for rowing with slightly less than a third of the oar inboard, asssuming that the oarsmen were seated. The handles of the oars would then be about 2'2" (65 cm.) above the floor-

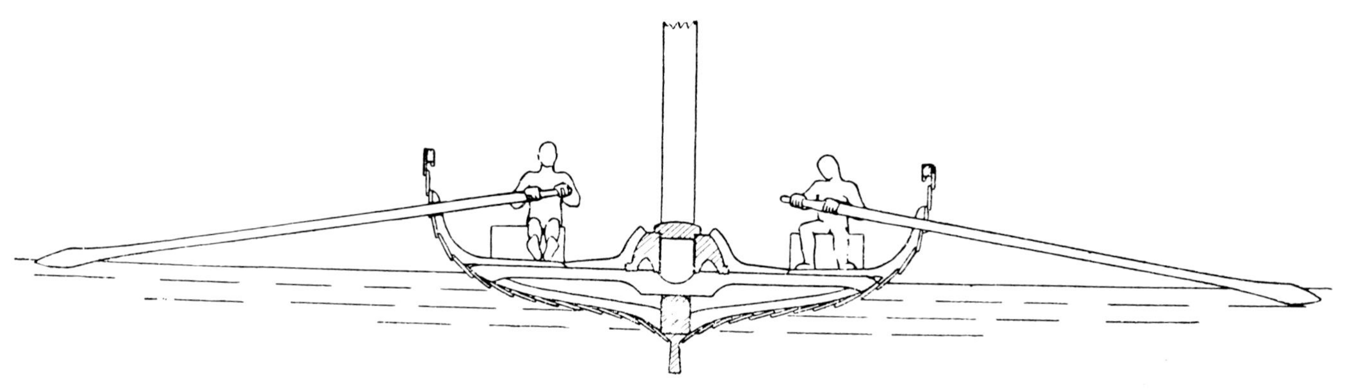

This is how we believe the oarsmen were seated.

boards, *i. e.* too low to allow a standing man to put full force into the stroke. How the oarsmen were seated remains an open question here as well as in the Oseberg ship. There are no thwarts, and no traces of any other permanent seating arrangement. We must consequently assume that the oarsmen had movable seats. This seems quite reasonable, as they may have used their sea-chests to sit on. The expression «half-room chests» occurs in the sagas, and a «half-room» correponds very well to the place allotted to each man while rowing, the interval between the ribs being called a «room». These chests would be brought on board by the crew when the ship was manned and that might well be the reason why no such chests were found in the grave-ships. Although the graves were sumptuously furnished, there would be none of the crew's personal effects.

We may be sure that the vikings contrived for an efficient use of oar-power in a ship which was so well planned in every other respect. Unfortunately, Captain Magnus Andersen had no opportunity to find out how well the replica of the ship rowed, as no practised crew could be assembled at short notice. Plans had been made for rowing the ship up to its berth in North River on arrival in New York. Extra hands were taken aboard, reportedly student volunteers and no doubt accomplished oarsmen, but they were unable to make much headway with the utterly unfamiliar vessel. Luckily, there was a favourable wind and the ship entered the harbour elegantly, under sail. The only mention Captain Andersen makes of rowing is on the arrival in Milwaukee, where Norwegian members of the Milwaukee Sailors Association asked permission to row the ship. Here «32 oars were set in motion at once as accurately as though every man had had a long experience on viking raids. The cheers of the spectators were boundless». There is no information as to the speed.

In the old days, with a crew of powerful men with years of practice at the oars in ships of this type, the Gokstad ship would dart forward like a racing boat when the chieftain bade the men pull hard.

Among other furnishings in the Gokstad ship we may mention the iron anchor, placed on the floor-boards forward of the mast, but so rusted that it fell apart at once. The stock, however, was intact, made of oak and 8'11" (2.75 m.) long. From this we may estimate that the anchor itself had been 3' 6 5/6" (1.10 m.) long, if the relation of anchor to stock was the same as in the Oseberg ship. To have a long stock is an advantage on a small anchor, as it makes the anchor grip the bottom more firmly. The anchor of the Oseberg ship is an exquisite little thing, so well preserved that one might think it had been newly wrought. In the top of the shank there is a ring for the rope, and in the other end, between the flukes, there is another ring for a second rope, so that the anchor might be more easily freed, if the flukes stuck too firmly. The anchor of the Oseberg ship is surprisingly light and small according to present standards, 3' 5" (1.02 m.) long and weighing only 21.5 lbs. (9.9 kg.). The anchor was not included to hold the ship by itself. The ships from Gokstad and Oseberg were built for voyages along the coast, and made fast ashore every night. The anchor was dropped from the stern in order to keep the ship clear of land. A gangplank had then to be put out to get ashore. The gangplank of the Gokstad ship was found outside the ship, along the planking near the bow; it is a spruce plank 24' ¾" (7.40 m.) long, with steps cut out of the upper surface and a square hole in one end, for making it fast on board. The plank is strong enough, but rather narrow for walking—for instance when the cook was taking the porridge pot ashore to make supper. No baler was found, but there must have been one, indispensable as it was. There is one on the Oseberg ship, a tremendous scoop essentially the same in shape as those of our day. Other equipment includes a large water cask, buckets and pails made of wood, a trough, trenchers, a very large copper cauldron, and an iron kettle with a hanger of the same material,—in fact all the utensils required for cooking and serving food.

There was always a ship's boat, or dinghy, to every ship. The Gokstad ship was very well supplied in this respect, as remnants have been found of no less than three boats. All three were in fragments, and parts are missing from them all, but Mr. Johannessen has succeeded in drawing reconstructions of them, showing that they measure respectively 31' 8½" (9.75 m.), 26' (8 m.) and 21' 5½" (6.60 m.), overall length. The biggest of them is a very fine boat with three pairs of oars, light and elegant with exquisite workmanship throughout. The others were smaller, with two pairs of oars each. All three have oar-locks mortised into the gunnel and then riveted. The rudder is on one side, aft. Apart from this latter aspect, the boats are strikingly similar to the old types of boats still in use on the western coast of Norway.

It is highly improbable that a vessel like the Gokstad ship would have three smaller boats as part of its standard equipment. Only the smallest of them can have been the regular dinghy, the two others being a part of the superabundant grave furnishings.

In the Viking and Saga Periods it was a matter of course that the ships had tents aboard, which could be pitched at night when the ship was in harbour; the ships were otherwise quite open, and had no quarters below deck. On the bigger vessels the tent was stretched over the ship itself as frequently mentioned in the sagas, but we also hear of tents being pitched ashore after the ship had been made fast for the night. Such land-tents were found on the Oseberg and Gokstad ships, and there is no sign of any fittings for stretching a tent over the ship itself. In the Gokstad ship only the verge-boards for the gables of the tent were left; two pairs of heavy planks ending in freehand carvings of animal heads. In the Oseberg ship, all the woodwork for two tents was intact, so that we may examine every detail of the structure. One tent covered an area of 17' 2³/₄" (5.30 m.) by 14' 7³/₄" (4.50 m.), the other slightly less. The height inside was respectively 11' 4³/₄" (3.50 m.) and 8' 9¹/₂" (2.70 m.). Both tents were thus very spacious. (The woodwork in the Gokstad ship is somewhat smaller than the corresponding parts of the big tent in the Oseberg ship). The woodwork of each tent consists of two pairs of verge-boards, a pole to form the ridge, a pole along the ground on the gable ends. Everything made of ash. Each end of the ridge-pole is mortised through the crossing of the verge-boards, and made secure externally by a plug, or key, through the pole. Likewise the long poles along the ground are mortised through the lower ends of the verge-boards, and through the ends of the boards along the ground in the gable ends. Altogether it forms a simple, but very sturdy framework. In both tents the ridge-pole is somewhat shorter than the poles along the ground, so that the gable ends of the tent slant inwards. The canvas was stretched over the ridge-pole and closed over the gables, so that the only bits of woodwork visible fron the outside were the animal heads on the verge-boards. This is aptly confirmed in the Flatøy book by the expression: «The heads stretching up from the land-tent were overlayed with gold.»

There was no gold on the animal heads belonging to the tent in the Gokstad ship, but they were quite handsome nonetheless—beautifully carved wild beasts with mouths open, baring their threatening fangs. Their features are emphasized by some simple strokes in black and yellow, the same colours as the shields along the ship's side. The form is strictly stylized, but yet conveys a grim and terrifying ferocity which affects us even today. This was done deliberately. The heads served another and more serious purpose than that of ornament, they were supposed to keep any intruder away from the sleepers inside. That the animal heads had some magic purpose of this nature is born out by the tents from the Oseberg ship. Here too, the verge-boards end in carved animal heads, and in addition there are various painted marks and symbols: a cross, a coiled serpent, a bearded male head, and three interlocking triangles. There can be no doubt that these were sacred symbols with a magical, protective power, and that they were painted to ward off evil spirits, just as people in later times painted a cross on their doors.

A similar power may also have been attributed to the animal heads themselves. This may be clarified by comparing them to the dragon-heads on the ships. These too were decorative heads, and they were carefully embellished to provide a fitting ornament for the ship. But that they had another purpose as well is evident from a paragraph in an old heathen law (Landnáma), stating that the dragon-heads should be detached before land was sighted, so as not to frighten the protecting spirits ashore. The animal heads on the tents had the same power to ward off evil spirits.

The existence of land-tents explains why *beds* were found on board. The

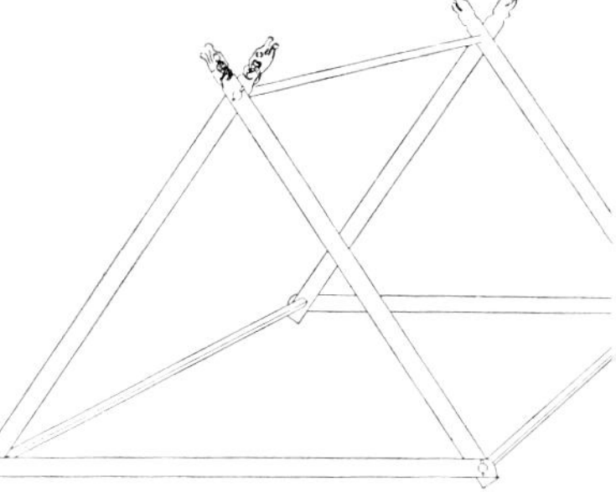

Simplified sketch of the framew… for the big tent in the Oseb… ship.

bols painted on the verge-rds of the tent in the Oseberg).

beds were needed for sleeping in the tents ashore, as it would not be practical to sleep in beds on such small vessels. Parts of a big splendid bed were found in the Gokstad ship. The head of the bed was flanked by two upright posts, ornamented at the top with carved animal heads. The sides of the frame are nailed to the posts, while the cross-pieces are mortised through and held in place on the outside by a plug which could easily be removed when the bed was to be stowed away. This bed stood in the bow. From the blue clay which had pushed up into the grave-chamber there was taken a loose fragment of a carved animal head, exactly matching those found on the bedposts. This is clear evidence that another bed of the same type had been in the grave originally. 6 simple beds were also found, partly in fragments, all so constructed that they could easily be taken apart, like camp-beds for travelling. It seems a little strange that there were so many beds and only one tent, but there may actually have been more tents with the ship. At any rate we can establish that the two state beds belong to the tent found in the ship, as the animal heads on the beds are very similar to those on the gables of the tent, no doubt cut by the same hand. We may also assume that both were made on the same occasion, as part of the furnishing of the Gokstad ship. They were regular equipment for a cruising ship of high class.

Similar furnishings were found on the Oseberg ship. In the fore part of the ship was a magnificent bed with carved animal heads, set up entire but without coverings, and inside the grave-chamber there was another bed, now ruined by looters, that had been spread with eiderdown quilts and blankets. In the bow of the ship two ordinary beds were found. Thus, the Oseberg ship also had two state beds, with animal heads which in all essentials correspond to the heads on the gables of the ship's smaller tent. This was evidently a set which it was common practice to have on board in those days, along with a luxurious supply of quilts and blankets. Remains of bedding were also found on the Gokstad ship.

The beds in themselves are clearly of great interest, as that kind of furniture from the Viking Era is extremely rare. The big beds are also impressive, monumental pieces, abundantly spacious, and with the animal heads raised menacingly over the bed-heads, splendid examples of the period's wood-carving and painting, but with a deeper significance than mere decoration. The bed-posts ranked almost as a sort of household god, as did the posts of the seat of honour. Their significance is confirmed when we hear of one of the early settlers of Iceland, Hástein Atleson, who, when land was sighted, threw his bed-posts overboard in accordance with an old custom, to bring luck.

As we have mentioned before, the value of a ship of the Gokstad type for sailing the high seas was demonstrated in 1893, when an exact copy of the Gokstad ship crossed the Atlantic for the Chicago Exhibition. This exploit deserves special mention in connection with the history of the ship. The Chicago Exhibition was held to commemorate the 400th anniversary of the discovery of America by Columbus, and Captain Magnus Andersen, editor of «Norsk Sjøfartstidende», proposed sending over a copy of the Gokstad ship as a reminder of the old Norse expeditions to «Vinland» (America).

The copy was to be exact in every particular, and be sailed to America as a proof that it had been possible for the vikings to cross the Atlantic in their ships. The idea was warmly acclaimed as excellent propaganda at the World Fair, while at det same time it was a fine opportunity to test the practicability of the Gokstad ship. The ship was built by commander Chr. Christensen in Sandefjord, entirely of Norwegian oak, except for the keel, which was in one piece. An oak plank of that size could not be found in Norway, but had to be imported from Canada. It was difficult also to find material for the mast partner, but this was finally obtained on a farm not very far from Gokstad. It was a huge oak, the trunk alone weighing 4 tons, and the wood was absolutely sound. The ship was launched on February 4th, 1893 from the Framnes shipyard at Sandefjord; a delightful sight, light and graceful as a bird, and trim as a toy compared to a modern, full-rigged ship.

There was no lack of grim warnings against risking lives on the open sea in a vessel like that; but Captain Magnus Andersen was an experienced sailor, and had no qualms about taking the ship across. He left Marstein, near Bergen, on April 30th, and landed at Newfoundland on May the 27th, after some rough weather, but no serious troble. This feat created a great stir in America, culminating in festivities and celebrations in New York and Chicago.

To us it is especially interesting to see what Mr. Andersen wrote of his experiences during the voyage. When they had become familiar with the ship he writes that «... we were able to watch the movements of the ship and her ability to weather storms more calmly and with less prejudice. The bottom of the ship was an object of primary interest. As will be remembered, it was fastened to the ribs with withy, below the crossbeams. The bottom as well as the keel could therefore yield to the movements of the ship, and in a heavy head sea it would rise and fall as much as three-quarters of an inch. But strangely enough the ship was watertight all the same. Its elasticity was apparent also in other ways. In a heavy sea the gunnel would twist up to 6" out of line. All this elasticity, combined with the fine lines, naturally made for speed, and we often had the pleasure of darting through the water at speeds of 10, and sometimes even 11, knots. This in spite of a primitive and relatively small rigging.»

«Whether the old Norsemen used their ships in the same way is hard to say, but it does not seem unlikely that they used the ships for all they were worth. It seems absolutely certain that in those days too they wished to travel as fast as possible, why else should they have taken the trouble to improve the structure until it was so perfect that not even the shipbuilders of our time can do better, as far as the ship's bottom is concerned. The fact is that the finest merchant-ships of our day, those regarded as the best sailers, have practically the same type of bottom as the viking ships.»

«The thing that attracted the greatest attention on board this ghost of a ship from the Viking era, was the side rudder. I have given this matter much thought, and have come to the conclusion that this rudder must be

he copy of the Gokstad ship, cal-
l «Viking», in the harbour of
ndefjord before the Atlantic
ossing in 1893.

regarded as one of the most striking proofs of the insight and experience of our ancestors in the arts of shipbuilding and seamanship. The rudder is nothing short of brilliant, and from the experience I have had, I consider it greatly preferable to a stern rudder for a ship of this kind. A stern rudder, in order to work as well as one on the side, would have to be very broad — owing to the shallow draught of the ship, and that would make it very vulnerable in its exposed position.» A further advantage of the side rudder is that it will keep in position to a much greater extent than a stern one, and likewise that it «turns around its own vertical axis, thus having a double effect ... A man has been standing at the helm hours in all kinds of weather without the slightest trouble, steering only with a small stick (the tiller).» The ship clove the water so well that there was practically no wake until the speed went up to 3—4 knots.

The Gokstad ship had been tested in a transatlantic voyage, and had also fulfilled its purpose in other respects. In the words of an after-dinner speaker, it had been sent over to commemorate the discovery of America by Leiv Eriksson, and had resulted in the Americans discovering Norway. After the World Fair, the ship was presented to the Field Columbian Museum in Chicago. It was never incorporated into the museum itself, however, and was neglected for 20 years, wrecked, and stripped of equipment and fixtures. Repeated complaints by the press had no effect, and only on the 25th anniversary of its transatlantic voyage was anything done. The Norwegian Womens' Organization of Chicago took the matter up, and collected funds to have the ship restored, a big, costly undertaking which was finished in 1919. Thereupon the ship was transferred to Lincoln Park in Chicago, where it is being maintained by the Park Commission. The ship does, indeed, merit preservation. A scientifically exact copy of the Gokstad ship, it is in itself an important historical document of great cultural value. Moreover it is to some extent a substitute for the original, should the latter be destroyed. Also it is of special significance to America, as a visible proof of the old viking expeditions. One might add that there is slight hope of the experiment ever being repeated by building another copy of the Gokstad ship, and still less of its ever being sailed across to the New World. The viking ship in Lincoln Park is the only one of its kind in the world, and will most likely remain so.

For a general characterization of the Gokstad ship, we can do no better than quote the words of Captain Magnus Andersen, a skilful, experienced sailor who had every reason to examine the ship carefully while preparing for his expedition to America in 1893. He wrote at the time: «It is amazing to see the degree of precision arrived at by our ancestors in constructing a ship of this nature, and no less admirable is the solidity and meticulousness with which the work was executed and the different materials joined. One is tempted to say that the construction of the ship equals the work of our modern shipyards in every respect, especially when the relatively primitive tools of the time are taken into account.» It was not the tools which determined the quality of the workmanship. As is often the case in a society of more primitive crafts, what mattered was the demand for a skilled and experienced hand, and even more; the demands the artisan himself made on his work. The Gokstad ship is throughout a splendid example of this ambitious craftsmanship. Every single piece of the structure is just as meticulously executed as it is perfect for its function in the ship. The extreme care taken in planning and construction, the choice and, in part, very sturdy materials as well as the elegant form, make of the Gokstad ship a masterpiece which must have been created under the personal supervision of a distinguished builder. He must have followed the building of the ship from day to day, just as the saga relates of Olav Trygvason when the «Long Serpent» was being built at Lade. Our unknown shipbuilder did not want the lavish ornamental wood-carving which we may see on the Oseberg ship; he meant his ship to appeal by its lines alone, those simple, clear lines which in themselves are a complete work of art.

Yet, the chieftain from Gokstad had at his disposal an excellent wood-carver who was responsible for the animal heads on the beds of the tents. The tiller is also a fine piece of workmanship, with a powerful, plastic animal head biting into the plug of the rudder neck, tapering off gracefully towards the other end, and terminating in an octagonal knob. Along the middle of the upper surface there is a row of tiny half spheres, like a string of beads, painted alternately black and yellow, and there is a similar trimming around the animal's neck, like a collar. The head itself is also painted yellow and black, with a dash of red around the edges of the ears and nostrils. Very likely the tiller was carved by the same hand that made the ornaments on the bed posts and the gables of the tent.

We notice that the choice of colours is the same as for the row of shields, that too was alternately yellow and black. It would seem that these were the distinguishing colours of the ship, or perhaps of the ship's owner. In any case, the colours give the ship an element of personal character.

The decoration of the ship itself is confined to a finely planed moulding along the edges of all the timbering in the entire ship, on big and small pieces alike, outboard and inboard and below the waterline. It has been very carefully done, for instance where the planking joins the bow and stern there are two lines cut into each plank parallel to the edges, indicating the end of the strake. Even in an inconspicuous detail like this great care has been taken in the execution. Furthermore there is a pattern of large, lightly traced circles on the floorboard. This must have been very attractive on a background of light, scoured wood. Some of the shutters for the oar-holes are also embellished with concentric circles, while others have ornamental crosses, both lightly traced on a flat surface. One gets the impression that the owner of the ship purposely rejected all plastic wood-carving in order to let the living, structural lines emerge as clearly as possible.

On the biggest of the dinghies the oar-locks are also decorated with elegant patterns in lines on a flat surface.

The bow of the Gokstad ship is completely void of ornamentation. The sides of both the bow and stern are quite smooth, and one particularly misses the usual decorations on the outside where the gunnel joins the bow and stern. Nor is there any trace of the ornamental pieces which should have been placed between the gunnels just before these run together in the bow. This part of the Gokstad ship had rotted away in the grave-mound. We may be certain, however, that the bow and stern had much more simple and sober lines than those of the Oseberg ship nor have they thrust so violently upwards. On the latter the bow lifts its dragon head in a double curve fully $16^{1}/_{2}$' (5 m.) above the water.

There is no way of knowing whether the Gokstad ship had a dragon-head at all. Nevertheless, it seems quite improbable that it should have been without one when we think of the tents and beds with their fine, carved heads, made as a part of the ship's outfit, and painted to match the shields along the side. It seems natural that the ship itself was furnished with bow and stern ornaments in the same style and colours, and with the same magical, protective power. Animal heads of the same type as those on the tent would be organically quite compatible with the forms of the bow and stern. But naturally, any concrete reconstruction would be wholly uncertain. Suffice it to say that there is some reason to believe the Gokstad ship had a dragon head proudly rising from the prow, as we should like to imagine.

As explained by Professor Brøgger, the Gokstad ship was built in the latter half of the 9th century, at the time of Halvdan the Black, and there are grounds for believing that it belonged to the King's kinsman, Olav of Geirstadir. We shall go further into this in another chapter.

The Tune Ship

The Gokstad ship is, and will remain, the classic example of a ship from the Viking Era, and it will in general be easy to overlook the attraction of the Tune ship, which is considerably smaller and, what is more important, far less perfectly preserved.

The ship is built of oak, except for the cross-beams and rudder, which are of pine; in all the essential features it is constructed just like the Gokstad ship. The keel, all in one piece, must have been approximately 45' 6 (14 m.) long, but is now incomplete forwards. The stern is complete, and here there are also parts of the transitional piece, which connects the keel to the stern, in addition to a stump of the stern itself measuring half a yard. If the missing parts are added in a reasonable proportion, the length of the entire ship outboard from bow to stern will be about 65', about 13' (4 m.) shorter than the Gokstad ship, the beam is 14' 1/2" (4.35 m.), and the depth from the gunnel to the underside of the keel 4' 5" (1.20 m.).

It is in every way a very solid vessel. The planking is only 3/4" thick, still thinner than that of the Gokstad ship. This was probably found sufficient for a smaller vessel. The aim was to make the planking as elastic as possible. The keel, though not as sharp and deep as in the Gokstad ship, is strong enough; the ribs are if anything stronger and have a highly arched transverse section. The cross-beams and knees are of good dimensions. There are no props under the cross-beams as found on other ships; but this was not required for a smaller vessel like the Tune ship.

A minor structural difference is that the ribs in the Tune ship only have one hole for the lashing to the cleat on each strake, while the cleats have two holes as usual.

The lashings themselves were bast cords. It appears that the different ship-builders had their peculiarities in such small matters.

The rudder and the rudder-rib are arranged exactly as they were described in the Gokstad ship, with the single difference that the rudder here is of pine. It is about 6½' long. In the back, at the end of the blade, are the remains of an iron cramp, to which a thin rope was fastened, used in lifting the rudder. When the rudder was in position it went deeper than the keel, which accounts for the fact that the rudder was removed and placed across the stern when the ship was buried. Had this not been done, it would not have been preserved by the blue clay which had penetrated into the grave. The structure of the foundation and support for the mast coincides throughout with the corresponding parts of the Gokstad ship, except that the «crone» and mast partner in the Tune ship are, if anything, heavier, more massive in relation to the ship, although very nicely proportioned to the somewhat smaller dimensions. The crone extends over 4 ribs, and the mast partner over five cross-beams, as against 6 in the Gokstad ship; it is made somewhat shorter, undoubtedly to leave more room on the deck behind the mast. The ship was burried with the mast stepped; a stump of the mast was found in place in the step when the ship was excavated.

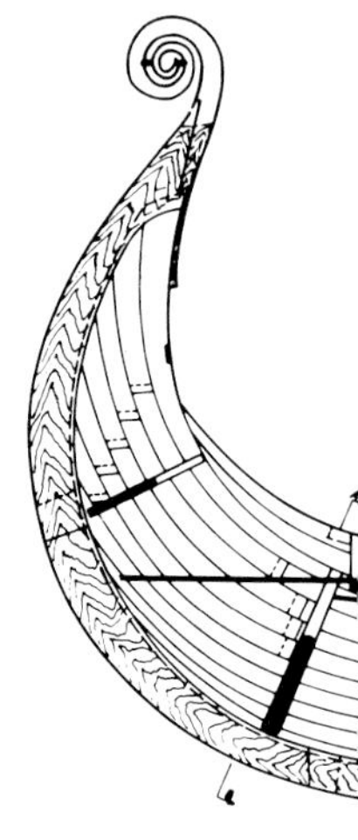

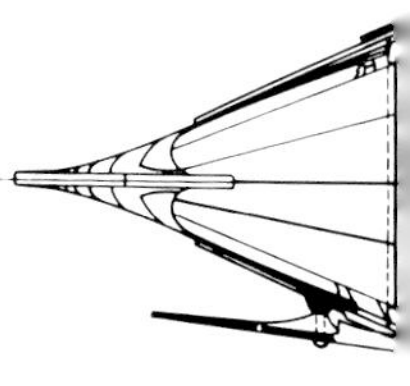

Skeleton drawings and transver[se] sections of the Oseberg ship.

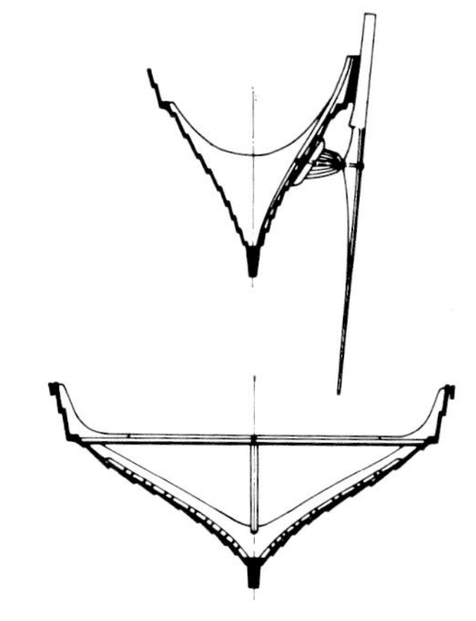

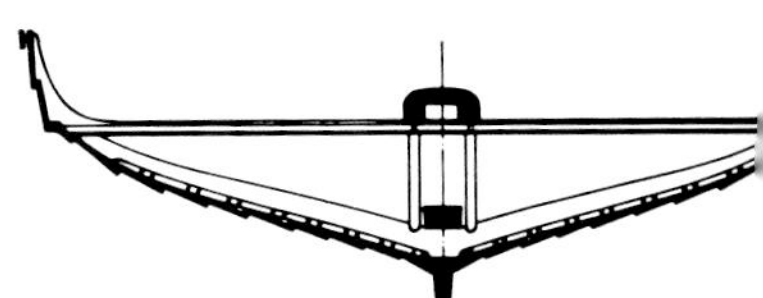

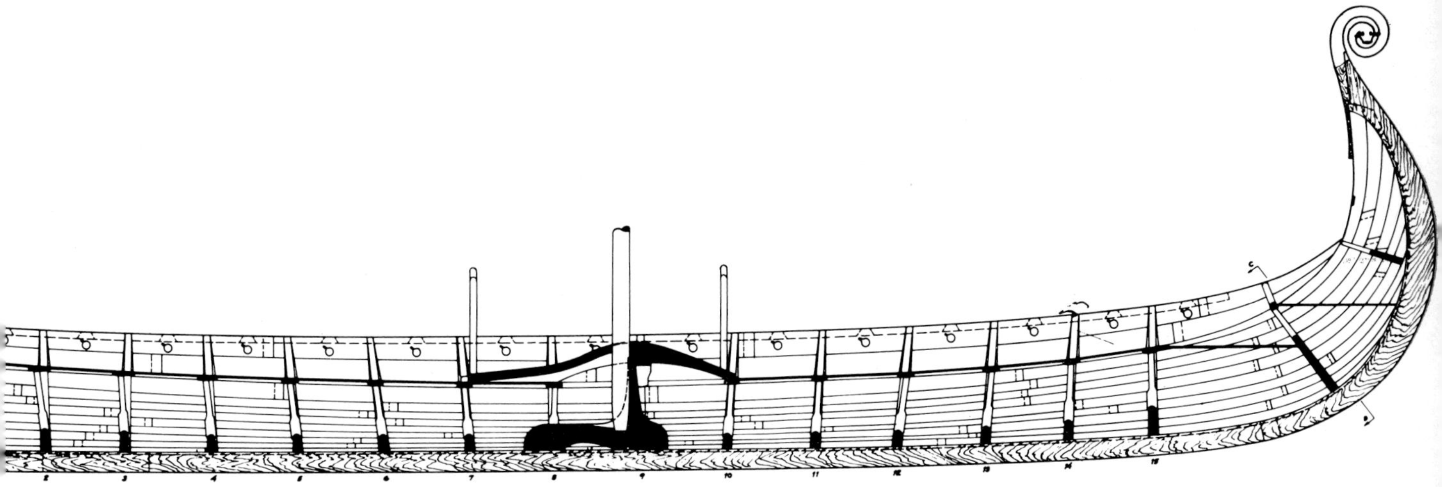

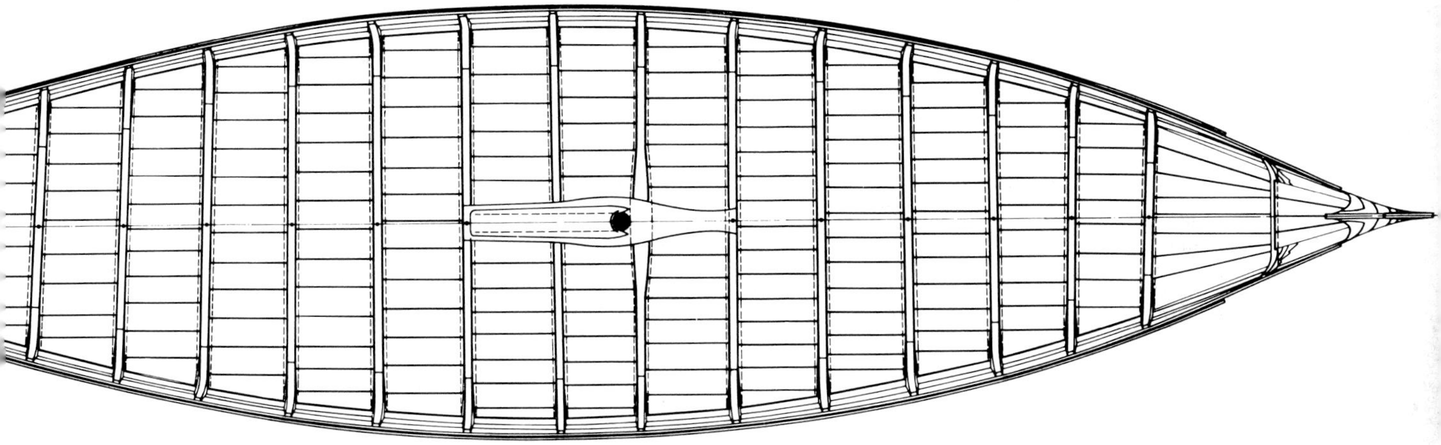

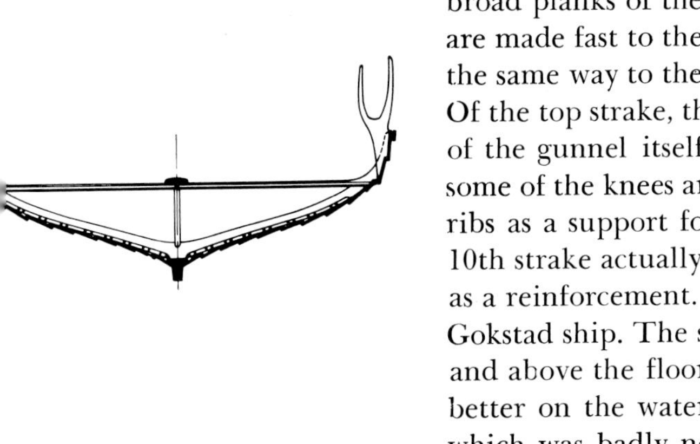

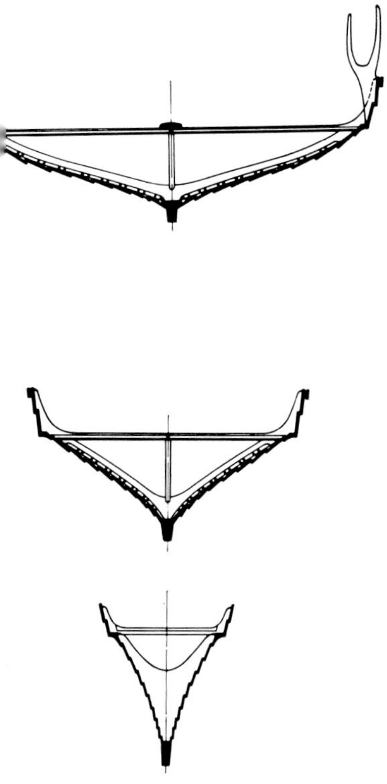

The ship's side has only two strakes above the water-line, but they are very broad planks of the same thickness as the planks in the ship's bottom. They are made fast to the knees with treenails, and the knees in turn are nailed in the same way to the upper surface of the cross-beams, one knee for every rib. Of the top strake, the 10th from the keel, only a few small fragments remain; of the gunnel itself there was nothing left whatsoever. On the other hand, some of the knees are preserved almost to the top, and there is no trace of top ribs as a support for further planking, so it can safely be assumed that the 10th strake actually is the last. The gunnel had presumably a heavy stringer as a reinforcement. There was probably also a shield-rack like the one in the Gokstad ship. The ship's side was thus remarkably low both above the water and above the floorboards, but it slanted heavily outward. In this way it lay better on the water, was better under sail and gave more room on board, which was badly needed when the oars were out. This feature shows that the method of construction in the Tune ship was especially adapted to the smaller dimensions which make the vessel rather narrow at the waterline.

The top strake was where the oar-holes were placed. There is no trace of oar-holes in the small fragments left of this strake, but it must be assumed

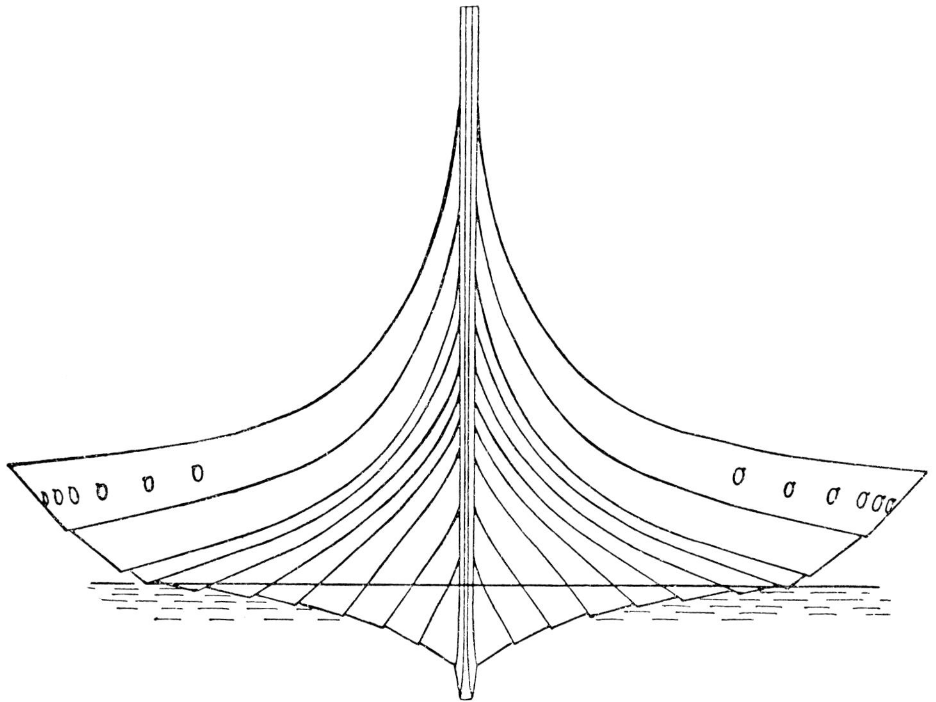

Drawing of the Tune ship seen from the bow.

that they were there, although the oars could hardly have been at a desirable height over the floor-boards in this position. There may, however, have been a way of regulating this in relation to the rowers' seats.

To get full force into the strokes, it is desirable that the rowers' position should be high in relation to the oars, though not so high that the loom strikes against the knees of the oarsmen when the blade is lifted. We may be sure that this matter received due consideration when the Tune ship was being built, and equally sure that there were oar-holes, not oar-locks, in a ship of this type. It had originally 11, or perhaps 12, pairs of oars, but there were none in the ship when it was buried.

The ship is characterized throughout by painstaking workmanship. Along the edges of all the timbering there is a planed bevel, with the same profile as in the Gokstad ship. There is one particularly beautiful detail; the ends of the knees are mortised into the cross-beam and cut in a point. This is further accentuated by the exceptionally fine treatment of the list on the edges of the timbering. Such features go to show that the work on the ship was executed meticulously down to the smallest detail, even though there are no signs of further embellishment. It is a good, stout ship for practical purposes.

The Tune ship is a very curious vessel; flat, low-sided and with shallow draught. The beam appears out of proportion to the draught, but the fine lines in the transition to the sharp prow and stern, give the ship a stately carriage. The surprising thing is that a sailing ship should have been built so low. The particularly sturdy construction of the mast-step shows that the ship was built for real sailing, not just for sailing in a favourable wind, as a

'he remains of the Tune ship, ow in the Viking Ships Museum Oslo.

supplement to the oar-power. The broad hull made it steady on the water, and the slanting sides helped to carry the ship over the sea. Taken altogether, the Tune ship may have been quite sea-worthy. She was easy to row with her shallow draught, and a good, steady sailing vessel.

It is curious to see how different the Tune ship is from the Gokstad ship, as a whole, although all parts of the construction are common to both. This method for building a ship was at that time common knowledge among skilled shipbuilders, something natural that was taken for granted. This did not, however, prevent each vessel from being individually formed for its purpose, according to the owner's wishes and tastes. It is quite possible that the Tune ship, as Mr. Johannessen imagines, was adapted for special local conditions, so that it could be taken up the Glomma river and stay afloat there in the shallow waters by Rolvsøy.

The Oseberg Ship

The Oseberg ship is actually the show piece among the ship-finds of the Viking Era. It is completely preserved, and it has been possible to restore the prow to its full height, with the serpent head at the top, so that at first glance, one gets a full and vivid impression of the ship as a whole. It strikes the eye immediately as a work of art – a harmony of form and lines, no doubt intentional, for esthetic purposes; but at the same time completely functional, with every part fully adapted to its purpose of practical utility. We may again call to mind the words of the great Norwegian sculptor, Gustav Vigeland, when he had seen the Oseberg ship, that it was worthy to be cast in bronze and set up in Oslo as a national monument. The Oseberg ship is 71' 6" (21.44 m.) long between the most extreme points fore and aft. That is slightly shorter than the Gokstad ship, but the two ships are almost equal in beam, the Oseberg ship 17' (5.10 m.) and the Gokstad ship 17' 6" (5.25 m.), amidships. The height from the bottom of the keel to the gunnel amidships is 33½" (85 cm). Draught: 29½" (75 cm.). The ship is built of oak throughout, and is in all respects of the same construction as the two ships we have just reviewed. Nevertheless, the Oseberg ship has its own individual character, as will be clearly seen from a comparison with the two other ships. The Oseberg ship is definitely of a weaker build, and is not intended for great strain. The keel is quite thin, and has a joint at the 5th rib from the stern. The stern itself is also joined out of two pieces. The planking is seriously pieced and very low, only two strakes over the cross-beams. The oar-holes in the sheer strake have no shutters to close them when the ship is under sail. The shield rack is a slender perforated list on the outside of the gunnel. We get the same impression from the structure of the entire ship. The bottom especially, with its broad, slanting planes coming up from the keel, and then joining the transition to the boards almost at right angles, at the thick plank in the water line, the latter standing out like a cornice. There is no attempt to achieve that full curve of the hull which we see in the Gokstad ship, nor the pointed profile of the bottom as it nears the keel.

A particularly salient feature is the weak foundation and support of the mast. Both the mast partner and the *crone* are exceptionally short (the crone extends over only 2 ribs as against 4 in the Gokstad ship), and the mast partner is also very slight. Even the considerably smaller Tune ship has much more massive pieces here. In order to counteract the weakness of these parts, the builder of the Oseberg ship let both the mast partner and the cross-beam nearest the mast form an arch over the deck, so that the mast should be supported a little higher over the floor boards, and from both sides. Nevertheless, the mast partner had cracked under sail, and had to be reinforced by two iron bands. There must have been some reason for the shipwright to make such a daring experiment, and abandon the conventional construction of the mast partner that was tried and safe, but took up considerably more room on the deck. There was probably a desire on the part of the ship's owner to have the greatest possible amount of free space on board.

There is also a characteristic peculiarity in the floor boards. In the Gokstad ship all the floor boards were loose, so that the space beneath could be used for storing equipment, provisions and all the other things needed on a voyage, and it was the same with the Tune ship. In the Oseberg ship, on the other hand, the only loose floor boards were those on each side of the mast, and the two nearest the stem and stern of the ship. Only in these places was it possible to get under the floor boards for various tasks, chiefly bailing. Throughout the rest of the ship the floor boards are nailed to the cross-beams with yewtree nails, forming a permanent deck in the more spacious parts of the ship. This may have been quite convenient in many ways, but it cut off access to the bilge. In planning the Oseberg ship there can have been no need to use the space under the floor boards, the ship was evidently not built for long voyages requiring large stores on board, still less designed to carry cargo. This feature shows clearly that the Oseberg ship was a pleasure boat where the arrangement on board was dictated by other than practical considerations.

The oar-power of the Oseberg ship was also inferior. There are 15 pairs of oars, but they are far too short for a vessel of this size. The oars are from 12' $1^{3}/_{5}$" (3.70 m.) to 13' (4 m.) long, as against those of the Gokstad ship with a maximum length of $19^{1}/_{2}$' (5.85 m.), the latter giving greater power to the oar strokes and being in a far better proportion to the level of the oar-holes above the water line. On the other hand, shorter oars naturally left more room on board when they were in use, again the same consideration as may have affected the mast partner. The oars are beautifully wrought, the blades ending in a graceful curve and having a finely beveled edge. Moreover, when they were found, several had traces of a painted pattern on the middle of the loom. The pattern consisted of two rings around the loom, a little square below the rings and an elongated, more complicated design above, all painted uniformly in black on the light, natural-coloured wood. When the oars were in use, the patterns would be just outside the oar-holes, obviously painted just for decoration. The oars are of pine.

All thirty oars were in the ship intact, and some were even in position in the oar-holes. These were the first three from the bow to starboard, and the third from the bow to port. About one third of the oar was inboard, a position wich seems natural for rowing. The other oars lay in various parts of the ship. The curious thing was that they were all quite new, seven or eight of them were not even finished, the handles being only roughly whittled, not completely shaped and smoothed like the others. The blade and the loom are finished and perfectly wrought on all the oars. None of them have been used; it is evident that they were made in all haste when the ship was to be buried. We may assume that the oars were made for this purpose, but as if for practical use – probably after the design of oars which had once belonged to the ship.

There is a similar circumstance in connection with the rudder. This is of oak, nicely wrought, and as it should be in all respects. The rudder neck is held to the gunnel by a broad leather band, artfully braided. The rudder itself is attached to the outboard block by a strong withy of pine roots, made fast inboard through three holes in the rudder rib. Everything is carefully prepared for use, only the tiller is missing. That might easily be explained as a mishap due to carousal at the funeral, but it is more conspicuous that the little iron cramp on the heel of the rudder also is missing. This served as a fastening for the rope with which the rudder was lifted, and was indispensable to the proper functioning of the ship. We are tempted to believe that the rudder, like the oars, was made expressly for the funeral. Yet it is not made as a mean substitute for the one that was lacking, but solid and dependable as though for real use. Here is a tangible expression of the profoundly serious thought which accompanied the furnishing of the graves.

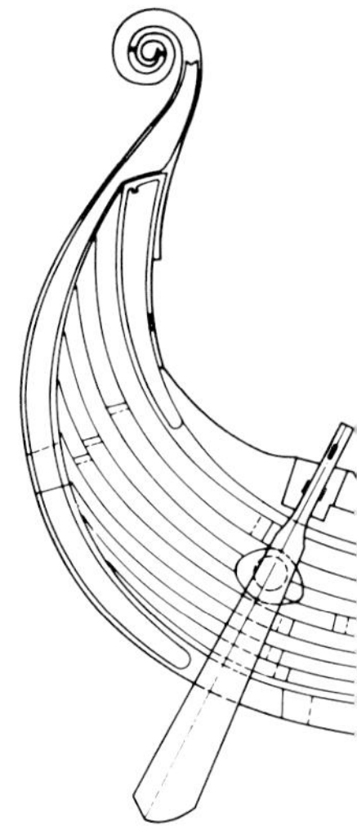

The missing oars and rudder which had to be remade in all haste for the burial, also throw light on the ship's earlier fate. The mast found in the ship did not seem to be the original either, that too was probably made for the occasion, and various pieces of fixed and loose equipment were also missing. In this respect we are in a position to make absolutely reliable observations, as not one piece of wood had rotted in the Oseberg ship, and the conditions under which the ship was found eliminate the possibility of anything being lost or overlooked during the excavation. Altogether we get the definite impression that the ship had been out of use and neglected for a fairly long time before it was buried. It had never been used much, perhaps only now and then, on special occasions. It was not suitable for practical everyday use, and as time went by lay half-forgotten in the boat-house. It was stripped. The oars and rudder and much else gradually disappeared; there was always a need for something when new ships were being equipped. At the same time it was natural that they should not care to demolish the fine little ship, once built for the pleasure of a high-born woman.

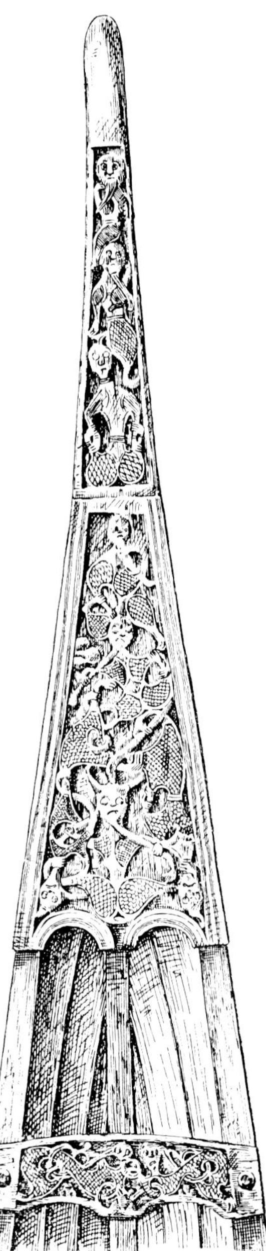

The Oseberg ship is a splendid piece of workmanship, both in form and in ornament. The long lines of the gunnels, low over the water on account of the oars, rise towards each end of the ship in a sharp curve to meet the prow and stern, which swing up in a daring arch fully 16' 4" (5 m.) above the water, to terminate in a slender spiral. There is a buoyant play in the silhouette of the ship, which shows how gracefully it could dart through the water, cleaving the crest of the waves. Its form is art of high order – the result of a genuine, creative imagination applied to the practical task of constructing a ship. All the ships of those days were created by the same process, all formed for their individual purpose and intent: the Gokstad ship with simple lines and a sturdy structure, a product of mainly practical considerations, and the Oseberg ship, a consummation of elegant, artistic form. The Oseberg ship was in no way unique at the time; we can see ships with similar furnishings on the Gotland sculptured stones of the Viking Era.

We also know that the graceful curves of the ship's lines were created deliberately and estimated with a critical eye, as when Olav Trygvason had the "Long Serpent" built, and we hear that the lines of the ship were much improved by a final stroke of the axe on the top strake, Torberg Skavhogg's master-stroke.

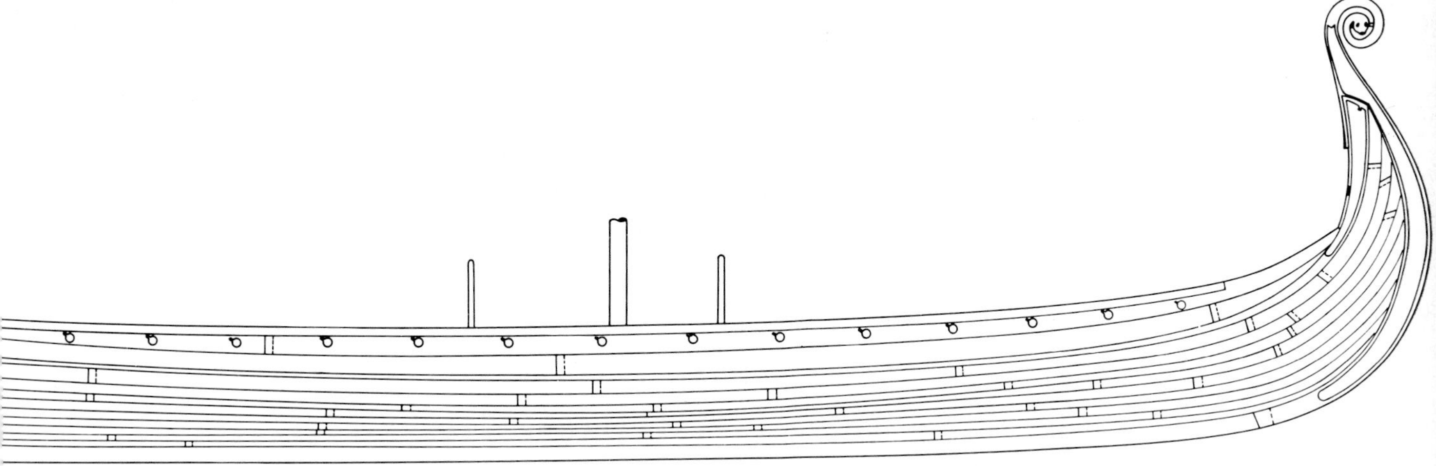

econstruction drawing of
e Oseberg ship.

The high stem and stern are of no practical importance, they are for decoration only. On the Oseberg ship they are furthermore lavishly embellished with woodcarving. The stem and stern themselves are carved on both sides – a frieze in deep relief, of stylized animals struggling up from the water line to the top like a vine. The top strake is also beautifully carved on both sides, near the stem and stern. Towards both ends of the ship, where the transition to the stem and stern begins, the gunnel is of beech-wood, the only part of the ship which is not oak. These beech-wood pieces are continuations of the 10th strake, and increase in breadth towards the top of the stem and stern. They carved with a frieze of stylized animals similar to those on the prow and stern themselves. The pieces are often referred to in literature as special, decorative elements (called *brander* in Old Norse, *i.e.* sword blades). In addition to these come two pieces inside, in the sharp angle formed by the «brander» as they approach the ends of the ship: a transverse board of oak near the bottom and an acute triangle of beech covering the point of the angle between the «brander». Both pieces are also carved with animal friezes in relief. In Old Norse these two pieces were called respectively *spán* and *tingel,* and they are frequently referred to both in the sagas and in the poetry of the time when beautiful ships are being described. We hear of King Harald's fleet in Hafrsfjord with «frightening heads and carved *tingels*» and of St. Olav who had sacred symbols cut into the *spán* of his ship.

Continuing the prow and stern, above the «brander», is the support for a large, freely projecting spiral ending in a serpent's head. The support is decorated like the other elements of the prow and stern, while the spirals themselves have only strong, simple lines suggesting the supple, undulating motions of a serpent. The serpent's head has the conventional, stylized form, well known in a profusion of other representations of the period, such as the snake pen on the Oseberg Cart, the Swedish sculptured stones and the Harald Bluetooth monument at Jellinge; a smooth head seen from above, a pointed snout and big, round eyes. This head is never seen on other animal-figures, but invariably in the same form, as the head of a snake. The

The decorative elements in the prow of the Oseberg ship. «Tingl» top) and «span» (bottom).

The stern of the Oseberg ship.

serpent on the stem and stern of the ships is a mascot to protect the ship and bring it luck, but naturally it is not conceived as the everyday viper or adder of our own animal world. In the folklore of the Viking Era the serpent was also a monstrous, mythical creature, akin to Favne guarding his golden treasure or the Lindworm keeping watch over Gudrun's bower. The dragon as such, the mighty serpent with wings, was actually not known in Norway in the early Viking Era, and was only introduced with Christianity and church art. The word itself, however, dragon or *dreki,* may have been used to describe kindred fabulous animals. In Hornklove's description of the battle of Hafrsfjord we hear of ships «with gaping heads and with grinning snouts», evidently two different types, as we can well imagine; heads like those on the posts in the Oseberg ship, and snouts like the serpent's head on the stem and stern. A poetic expression for an animal head is sometimes «*grima*», a menacing, distorted mask. The animal head on the ship was supposed to be menacing, we remember the paragraph in the heathen law on Iceland, ordering the animal heads to be removed before land was sighted, so that the protecting spirits ashore should not be frightened away.

The head on the ship is something else, as well. It expresses the conception of the ship as a living creature – a conception any child can understand as naturally as that every ship has a name. That the ship should then be imagined as a serpent, seems very natural when we think of Captain Andersen's experience with the copy of the Gokstad ship, when the light supple craft literally followed the waves with undulations throughout the hull, very much like a moving serpent. The bottom and the keel would rise and fall up to $^3/_8$" and the gunnels would twist as much as 6". For those on board it was strangely fascinating to feel the rhythm of the ship under way. It seemed to speed on of itself, with an inner life of its own. In a naive, imaginative mind the ships were given life and soul in forms drawn from the mythical world: a serpent, a bird or a dragon.

The dragon head was the proudest ornament of the ship, and is fondly described in poetry and sagas as a masterpiece of rich wood-carving with resplendent gilding. Here, as always, the saga is able to create a vivid, instantaneous image; we see the morning sun shine on the gilded dragon-heads. But gilding of that kind was hardly invented in the Viking Era, it smacks more of medieval style. Colours, on the other hand, were widely used, as seen on the gables of the tent in the Gokstad ship. The skald Valgard also tells of the prow and stern ornaments being coloured red. In the same poem Valgard has another beautiful image: «It was like fire in the mouth of the serpent, when we saw our ships coming from the South.» The serpent is of course the serpent of the ship's prow, just as when Tjodolv says: «The mane of the serpent glitters.» From the skalds' earliest mention of the dragon-ship it is compared to a serpent. In Thorbjørn's Glymdrápa, of about 900 A.D., we read that, «Ræsnadir (the speeding serpent) plunges on through the sea.»

It is, of course, the bow which bears the dragon-head, and the stern was shaped to correspond like the serpent's tail. This was only natural since the whole ship took the form of a fabulous animal in the imagination. We must assume that it was the rule in the Viking Era, at any rate, while the people still had a vivid belief in the magic power of the menacing animal head on the prow. Later, in the Middle Ages, it might happen that the ships had a head at each end, then undoubtedly for decoration only, without any deeper significance. There can be no doubt that the serpent's head in the Oseberg ship belonged to the prow, even though there was no proof of this in its position in the ship, as the grave had been disturbed by looters. It seems that the head had been taken off the prow and put in the grave-chamber when the burial took place. The stern had the serpent's tail, as on Raud the Strong's dragon ship, described by Snorre (the ship which later came into the possession of Olav Trygvason and was then called «The Serpent»): «On the prow was the dragon's head, but aft a hook ending in a tail.» In the same way we are told that St. Olav's ship «Visundr» had the head on the prow and the tail aft. On the Oseberg ship the top part of the stern was missing altogether.

The decorative wood-carving, on the prow and stern of the Oseberg ship, is art of high order in the style of the period. The high, narrow planes on the prow and stern and on the «brander» are covered with animated friezes of fantastically stylized animals, their bodies divided into two interlocking loops with a small head on a slender neck and thin legs and tails, the whole composed into a playfully braided pattern of carved planes and smooth bands. Yet the pattern is open and clear, easy to follow, as it ought to be in monumental ornaments intended to be seen from a distance. The individual animal figures are clearly drawn, each by itself, one row rising above the other, mostly equal in size, so that the repetition creates a rhythmical, undulating movement, organically alive, like a vine. At the same time the artist has been endlessly inventive in varying the details, so that no two animal figures are alike. There is a tension between rhythm and variation which is the secret of the vitality and freshness of the composition. The drawing is exquisite, and set off by a deep background, while the ornament as a whole is in one plane, without relief, so that the structural form of the prow is not disturbed. From a technical point of view the quality of the artistic wood-carving is first rate. In one place the work has not been finished, and here we get a glimpse of the craftsman's technique. There is a small part at the bottom of the stem to port where the decoration has been left incomplete. Here the outline of the figure is sketched in a fine surface-line with the point of a knife before the background was cut out and the details finished. The failure to complete this part of the decoration was probably an oversight, and is the only flaw that can be found. There is an unfortunate break in the composition in the middle of the stern, but this is not the fault of the wood-carver. The stern plank is joined here, and the overlapping butt prevents the ornament from being followed through smoothly and in full depth.

The *tingel* and the neck of the dragon head form a curious contrast to the style and elegance of the other decorations. Again the decorative theme consists of animal figures, but of quite a different order than the graceful designs on prow and stern; stout, ugly creatures with big, round faces and eyes like oversized spectacles, heavily rounded carvings in high relief. And yet all the carvings are done by the same craftsman. He has deliberately sought a sharp contrast to the elegant but somewhat anaemic linear designs on the prow, stern and «brander». We notice the same phenomenon in contemporary goldsmiths' art as a characteristic of a certain period in old Norwegian style history. The two decorative forms, both equally pronounced, are seen juxtaposed on the same trinket. On the prow and stern of the Oseberg ship we have the native Nordic style (the so-called later Vendel style, from the finds at Vendel in Uppland, Sweden) which was developed in the course of the two preceding centuries, while on the *tingel* we have a new, foreign style of ornament, attributed to the influence from Carolingian art industry. The latter style came into use side by side with the former around the beginning of the 9th century.

There is no place for a further exposition of style history. We should like to point out, however, that the Oseberg ship is the only known major work of decorative art from this period in the North. It is the work of a master craftsman in a clear and definite style, and the wood-carving gives us the information so important to our purpose; that the ship was built around the year 800 A.D.

It must have been a proud sight when the Oseberg ship was riding at anchor off shore in the morning sun, ready for a voyage; a symbol of luxury and high rank. Our examination of the ship in every detail has confirmed that she was a luxury craft. We have seen her weaknesses; she is severely pieced in the planking, the mast partner is frail and light, the gunnel is weak and the shield rack positively fragile. Moreover the ship is broad and open, low-built, and without shutters for the oar-holes. The unusually high prow

and stern must also have caught the wind in a most unfortunate manner, even without the serpent-head ornament.

Obviously, this ship was not built for real voyages on the high seas, hardly even for regular use on the fjords. Its character implies clearly that it was made for small trips in calm waters and fair weather, suitable for the personal use of a lady of high rank. For this purpose it is perfect: wide and spacious, with a large capacity and remarkably fine lines. At the same time it was wonderfully easy to row and sail. What a feast for the eyes to see the Queen's ship on a fine summer's day, either with the oars out or running before the breeze like a bird, under its magnificent sail.

As Brøgger has pointed out in several earlier works, there is much to favour the theory that the lady buried in the Oseberg ship was Queen Aasa, the mother of Halvdan the Black. There is naturally no conclusive evidence to this effect, but it is intrinsically probable. Furthermore, there seems to be an element of almost symbolic truth in the connection of the Oseberg ship with Queen Aasa, the most outstanding woman in the Saga of the Vestfold kings.

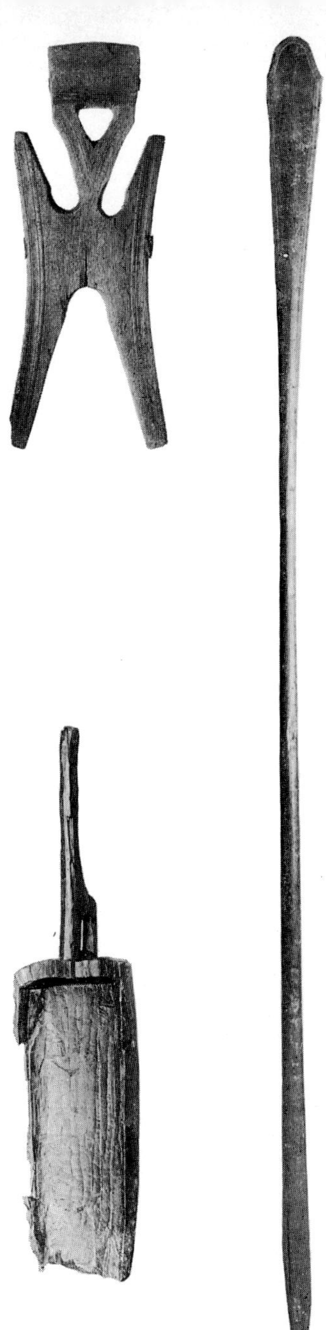

arious items of ships' equipment ›und with the viking ships. Left: 'he gangplank of the Gokstad ›ip, the rudder of one of the ›naller boats found with the Gokad ship. Right: A block from the ;okstad ship, a baler from the ›seberg ship and one of the oars f the Gokstad ship.

The Ships in the Saga of the Vestfold Kings

Naturally, the ships from Gokstad and Oseberg interest us primarily as cultural monuments, unique in themselves. Nevertheless, one must admit that it would also be rather thrilling to discover that they belonged to personalities we know in history. We have no hope of finding the owner of the Tune ship, as there is no historical information about Østfold in this period. In Vestfold we are more fortunate. The Sagas of the Kings relate of the 9th century Kings of Vestfold, the ancestors of Harald Fairhair, and here we are justified in looking into the question, in trying to find out whether the buried ships can reasonably be connected with specific names encountered in the Ynglinga Saga. The graves themselves show quite clearly that we are concerned with people of more than ordinary means and importance. They are few in number, sumptuously furnished and covered by tremendous mounds. One has every right to call them royal tombs. They may be dated, archaeologically within a margin of 20 years, an accuracy which allows us to compare them within the line of kings in the same period. Although this limits the range of choice considerably, we still have to look for evidence of some kind pointing to a specific name. The historical records of these times available in the sagas are extremely imperfect, and it is quite possible that other members of the royal family besides the King, were buried in ship-graves. Later tradition and the writers of the sagas may also have added names which actually did not belong among the Vestfold kings. We shall here give a brief account of our reasons for believing that Aasa, the wife of Gudrød the Hunter, was buried in the Oseberg ship, and that the Gokstad ship was the tomb of Olav Geirstada-Alv.

That Aasa was a person of actual, historical identity must be considered beyond doubt. She is mentioned in Tjodolf's Ynglingatal, a contemporary poem praising the Vestfold kings, in the stanza which tells us how Gudrød the Hunter lost his life by treason, when:

«The King in drink at Stivlesund was stabbed to death
As Aasa's blackguard her vengeance wreaked by stealth.»

Snorre tells us the reason for Aasa's revenge. She was the daughter of Harald Granraude, King of Agder. When Gudrød's first wife died, he asked Aasa's father for his daughter's hand but was refused. Shortly after this Gudrød and his men arrived in force, killed Aasa's father and brother, and carried her off. Gudrød married her, and later she gave birth to a son, Halvdan. Next autumn, when Halvdan was six months old, Gudrød was staying in Stivlesund with his ship. Drinking was heavy, and the King was in his cups. After dark the King left the ship, but as he went ashore a man rushed at him and stabbed him with a spear. The man was killed on the spot, and in the morning he was identified, according to Snorre, as the queen's «lackey». The poem uses a term which suggests an armed groom. That is all we know of Aasa, but thanks to Snorre's masterly description it is enough. A proud, strong-willed woman who slew her husband to avenge the murder of her father and brother and pay back in full the outrage she had suffered when she was forcibly made Gudrød's wife.

In the Saga of Halvdan the Black Snorre goes on to relate that Aasa later returned with her son to her father's lands in Agder. Here Halvdan grew up. When he was 18 he ascended the throne, and shortly afterwards he went to Vestfold to take over his share in that kingdom from his brother Olav, Gudrød's son by his first queen. Olav was some 20 years older than Halvdan, and had ruled Vestfold since the death of his father. We hear no more of Aasa, but we should like to think that her counsel helped Halvdan to secure his heritage in two kingdoms.

When the Oseberg ship was found, there was a natural urge to establish the identity of the person buried there, all the more as this person had pas-

ragment of a tapestry found in
e Oseberg ship.
eft a reconstruction drawing.

sed on to us a unique treasure of viking art. At first conjecture hit on Øistein, the son of Halvdan Whiteleg. This theory fell apart, however, when it became evident that the person buried had been a woman. The news that a woman had been buried in a magnificently furnished ship created quite a stir at the time and the sensation naturally increased the desire to find out who she was. Notes were found in the papers left by Professor Gustafson, showing that the problem had occupied him, but that he never found a satisfactory solution.

A. W. Brøgger was the first to offer an answer to the question. He found the key to the mystery in the name of the farm where the ship was found, *Oseberg*. This name had in its original form – Aasuberg – been found by Professor Oluf Rygh to contain the feminine name *Aasa*. Rygh's interpretation was especially weighty as it had come forth at a time when no one had any idea of the existence of the Oseberg ship-grave. With this in mind it seemed justifiable to concentrate attention on Queen Aasa, well known from the Ynglingatal, a reliable and practically contemporary source of information. The poem was written in honour of Ragnvald the Glorious, Gudrød the Hunter's grandson. Here the skald is not referring to an old saga, but to a tragedy which had occurred in the family a short time ago, still fresh in the memory of the people to whom the poem was recited. The lines are replete with bitterness against her who brought the murder about: It was a «revenge by stealth», doubly false because it had been carried out while the victim was honestly drunk. Both Aasa's name and her deed are thus historically confirmed, and the murder was no doubt common talk in Vestfold for a long time afterwards. It is quite possible that a verbal version of the story reached even Snorre.

Halvdan the Black was about 20 years old when he became king, and his mother's age at the time must have been around 40. Her grandson, Harald Fairhair, won the battle of Hafrsfjord while he was still quite young, according to tradition in the year 872, in the light of modern critical research possibly some 20 years later. The Oseberg tomb is dated by the decorative wood-carvings to about 850 A.D., maybe a little later; a period that could quite well tally with the death of Queen Aasa. Aasa was probably

Sledge from the Oseberg find.

born during the first decade of the 9th century, but apart from that our chronology is rather vague. The only demonstrable fact is that the battle of Hafrsfjord took place a little before the year 900. In his works Brøgger has used the chronology of the Norwegian historian Gustav Storm, whose dates tend to be a little ahead of those given here. This is however of minor importance to our present purpose; nor is it possible for a chronology based on art styles to be precise within a year or two.

In summing up his investigations Brøgger writes accordingly: «A supposition of this nature cannot be ultimately proven, but up to a point, in the sense that one can draw conclusions on wholly reasonable grounds it must

Detail from one of the sledges the Oseberg find.

be said that a genuine conclusion has been reached. No lesser person than the mighty Queen Aasa could have been buried in the Oseberg ship.» Brøgger's idea was immediately acclaimed by the public, and the Oseberg ship was given a central place in early Norwegian history, apart from being an invaluable contribution to our knowledge of art and culture in the Viking *ɔnt piece of one of the sledges ·m the Oseberg find.*

Era. The story of Queen Aasa's grave has, so to speak, become the property of the people, and it would be very hard to change.

Let it be said here that no conclusive evidence has been found, and that Brøgger's findings have not passed unchallenged. Professor O. Rygh later suggested that the name Oseberg might also have been constructed from the word *osar,* the plural of an old Norse word for a rivermouth or estuary.

According to another historian, Sophus Bugge, it might also come from the word *aesir,* meaning gods. Both these explanations seem rather artificial, while the alternative of Aasa seems to be the only natural and simple one. On the other hand one may say that the farm of Oseberg is not an estate of the consequence one might expect for a Queen Mother. There have more over been certain difficulties in reconciling the theory with the anatomical evidence on the age of the two women buried in the ship. The most recent survey of the case in all its aspects is by Professor Gutorm Gjessing (in the journal *Viking,* 1943) who comes to the conclusion that the woman in the Oseberg ship cannot be Queen Aasa. But he, too, lacks a final, decisive argument to settle the question for good, and as long as it is left open we should prefer to have in mind the proud queen, the only woman whose name is mentioned in the Ynglingatal poem. The furnishings of the grave belong precisely to her lifetime, they give at any rate a true image of the luxury surrounding a woman of her rank in those days.

We are on safer ground in naming King Olav Geirstada-Alv as the owner of the Gokstad ship. He was the son of Gudrød the Hunter and his first queen, the elder half-brother of Halvdan the Black and father of Ragnvald, in whose honour the Ynglingatal was composed. All we know from the Ynglingatal is that he ruled over Vestmarr, died of an infection in the foot, and was buried at Geirstadir. Snorre adds that he was twenty years old when his father was murdered. «He was a mighty man and a great warrior; he was of all men the handsomest and strongest and large of stature.» When Snorre calls him a great warrior we are reminded that it was during Olav's youth in 843 that vikings from Vestfold plundered Nantes on the Loire. It is quite possible that Olav himself took part in the viking raids on Western Europe. The chieftain who was found in the Gokstad ship had certainly played a part in such raids; in his grave was found a peacock, then an extreme rarity in Norway but highly fashionable with the aristocracy of Charlemagne's France. According to the chronology of the Ynglinga Saga, Olav's death seems to have taken place towards the end of the 9th century, when he was between 50 and 70 years of age.

The eminent Norwegian archaeologist N. Nicolaysen pointed out as far back as 1882 that the chieftain buried in the Gokstad ship must be Olav Geirstada-Alv. The grave can be dated archaeologically to the end of the 9th century. The chieftain's skeleton is that of a man well over 50, powerfully built and unusually tall. He has been suffering markedly from chronic arthritis and muscular rheumatism. The anatomical diagnosis is a vivid illustration of the skald's statement that King Olav died of «pains in the feet». The only flaw is that Olav's tomb is said to be a Geirstadir, while the ship-grave was found at Gokstad. However, next to Gokstad is a farm called Gjekstad, and it has been established that Gjekstad is a corruption of Geirstadir. Furthermore, Brøgger has shown that the site where the grave was discovered originally belonged to Geirstadir (Gjekstad). All Gjekstad lies to the east of a small river, and all Gokstad to the west, except for that small piece of land where the grave was found. This land is on the east side of the river, but it now belongs to Gokstad. All in all there can be little doubt that the Gokstad ship belonged to Olav Geirstada-Alv.

In this connection we should also like to mention the third of the ship-graves found in Vestfold. This grave was discovered in 1852, when gravel was being taken from one of the grave-mounds at Borre, near Horten. Inside the mound was found a superbly furnished grave, and a ship of about the same size as the other grave-ships. Unfortunately only a few things have been preserved. Among them a set of gilded bronze ornaments for a harness, corresponding exactly to a set found in the Gokstad ship. The two graves are thus of the same period, one might even be tempted to think that the buried persons were connected in some way, as the ornaments for their harnesses were made in the same workshop. On the other hand, the Borre grave is linked with the royal family of Vestfold, through the information found in the Ynglingatal that the elder King Halvdan (the Mild and Stingy), father of Gudrød the Hunter, was buried at Borre. Snorre adds that the grave of

Iron-bound chest from the Oseberg ship.

Halvdan's father was also placed here. Therefore we must connect the Borre grave with a younger generation of the royal line, probably at the time of Halvdan the Black at the end of the 8th century. We might even reasonably believe it is the grave of Halvdan the Black himself, but for the fact that his grave has been fixed by tradition at Stein in Ringerike, and Snorre even relates that the King was buried in four parts, in four separate grave-mounds, so that each of the four kingdoms he had ruled should be blessed. Brøgger is right in saying that this smacks a little to strongly of the saint-worship of the Christian Middle Ages. There may, however, have been cenotaphs, grave-mounds without a grave, dedicated to the memory of a beloved king to secure his favour even after death. The king's body was probably buried in only one place. There are unequivocal examples of such viking cenotaphs at Seim near Tønsberg and at Gunnarshaug on Karmøy. This gives us a most reasonable explanation of the Halvdan-mound at Stein and at Tingelstad Church in Hadeland. Both these mounds are in existence today, but they are in no way inconsistent with the theory that Halvdan the Black was buried at Borre, near the graves of his immediate ancestors.

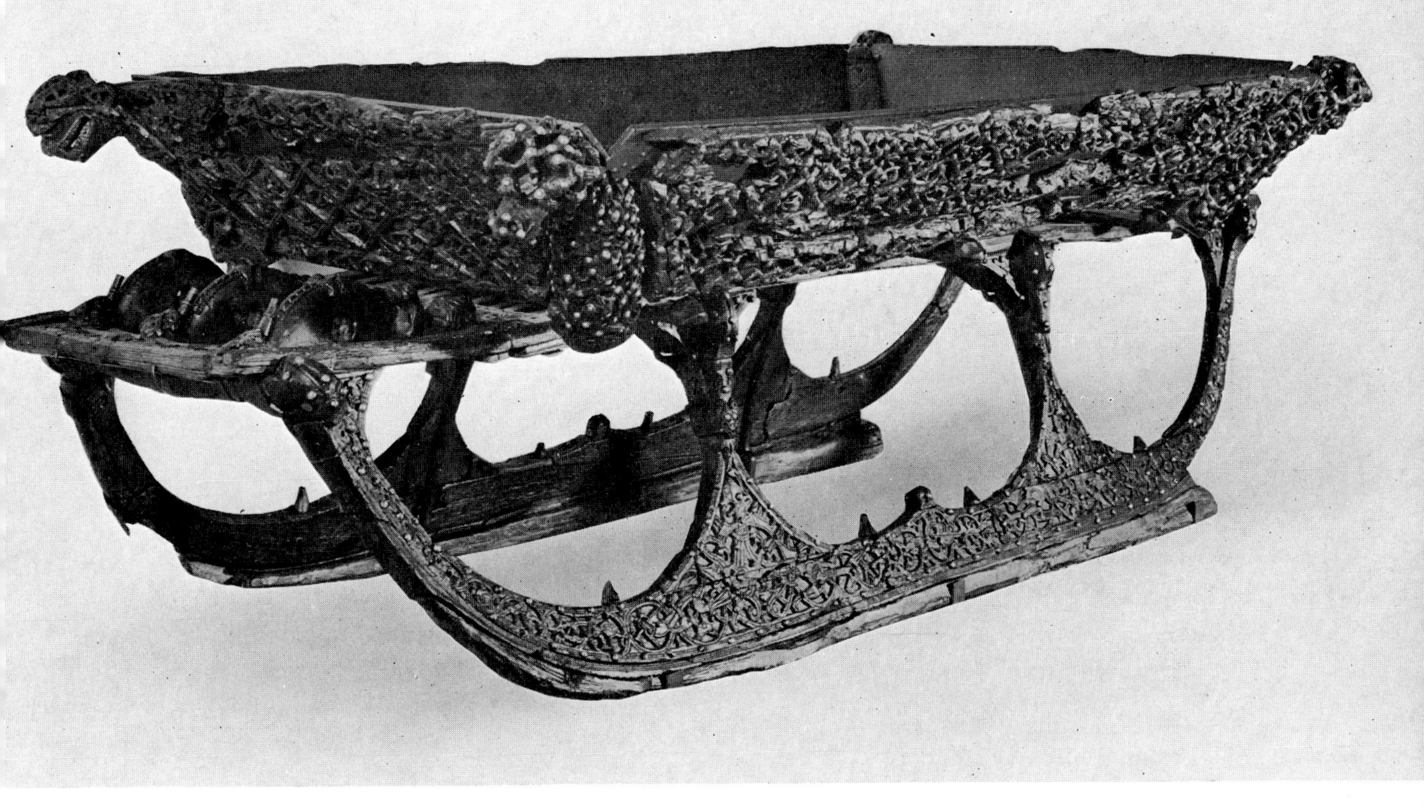

Kings of the Ynglinga Line in Vestfold:

Halvdan Whiteleg, about the year 700.
Øystein, after 700.
Halvdan the Mild and Stingy, up to 800 (approx.).
Gudrød the Hunter, about 800.
consort 1 Alvhild:
Olav Geirstada-Alv
Ragnvald the Glorious.
consort 2 Aasa:
Halvdan the Black
Harald Fairhair.

sledge from the Oseberg find.
·ft a detail from the rear part
owing the rich wood carving.

The various Types of Ships

Of the excavated ships of the Viking Era, only the three mentioned above – the Gokstad, Tune and Oseberg ships, are sufficiently well preserved to allow us to study them in detail, so as to form a clear and complete picture of the ship as a whole. The three ships are of about the same dimensions, and by and large of the same type: a type which today hardly would earn the name of *ship*. It is a very large open boat, with floor-boards over the bilge, but without a real deck and with no quarters below deck. At the time, these things were not necessary conditions for calling the vessel a ship; the «longships» and dragon ships (fast ships for war), both much bigger than the ships found in the grave- mounds, were built in the same way, like open boats on a vastly exaggerated scale. The difference between a ship and a boat in viking terminology was solely one of size, without any definite line of distinction. The biggest vessel to be called a boat was as a rule the «twelve», with six pairs of oars, but the expression «twelve-oar ship» or even «six-oar-ship» was by no means unusual.

A vessel with more than twelve oars was never called a boat. That was a ship. The size of the big ships was given by the number of thwarts or spaces between the ribs of the ship, in both cases equivalent to the number of pairs of oars. The number of oars is in other words twice the number of thwarts, and this is clearly stated from time to time in the poems and sagas of the day. Of the ship «Ormen Skamme» with 30 thwarts, it is said that «60 oars played from her sides». Harald Hardrade's ship had 35 thwarts, and is

The front of the sledge.

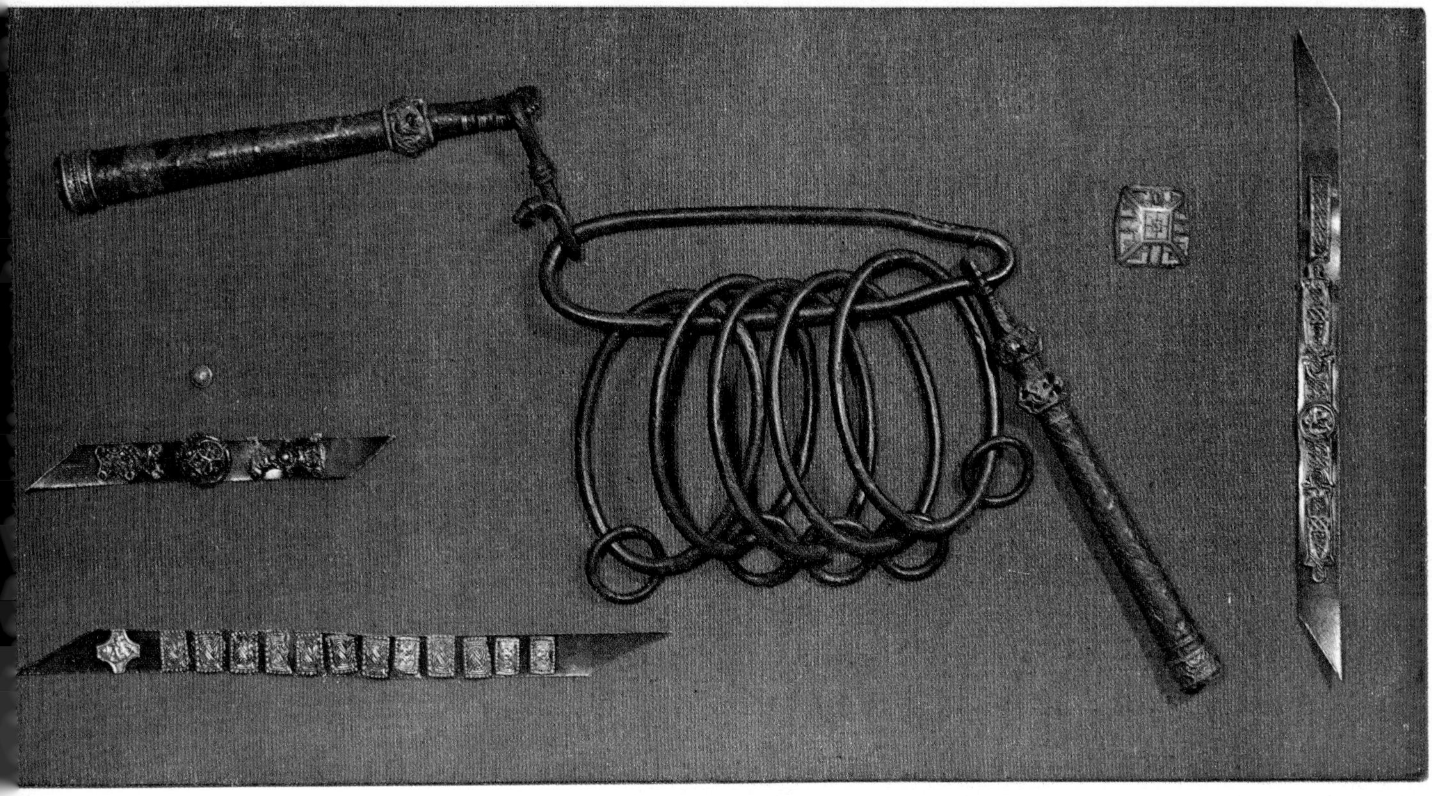

’arts of golden bracelets and a attle with golden ornaments from he Oseberg find.

A bucket of yew-wood with brass fittings of Irish origin found in the Oseberg ship.

One of the five animal-head pos
found in the Oseberg ship.

described by the skald Tjodolv Arnessøn as having 70 oars stretched out «like the wings of an eagle». The ships furnished by the peasants for defence were normally of 20 or 25 thwarts, with twice that number of oars. The ships of kings and chieftains were larger, Earl Haakon is reported to have had a ship of 40 thwarts. Smaller vessels might also occasionally be referred to as «longships», the smallest ship thus classified seem to be one of 15

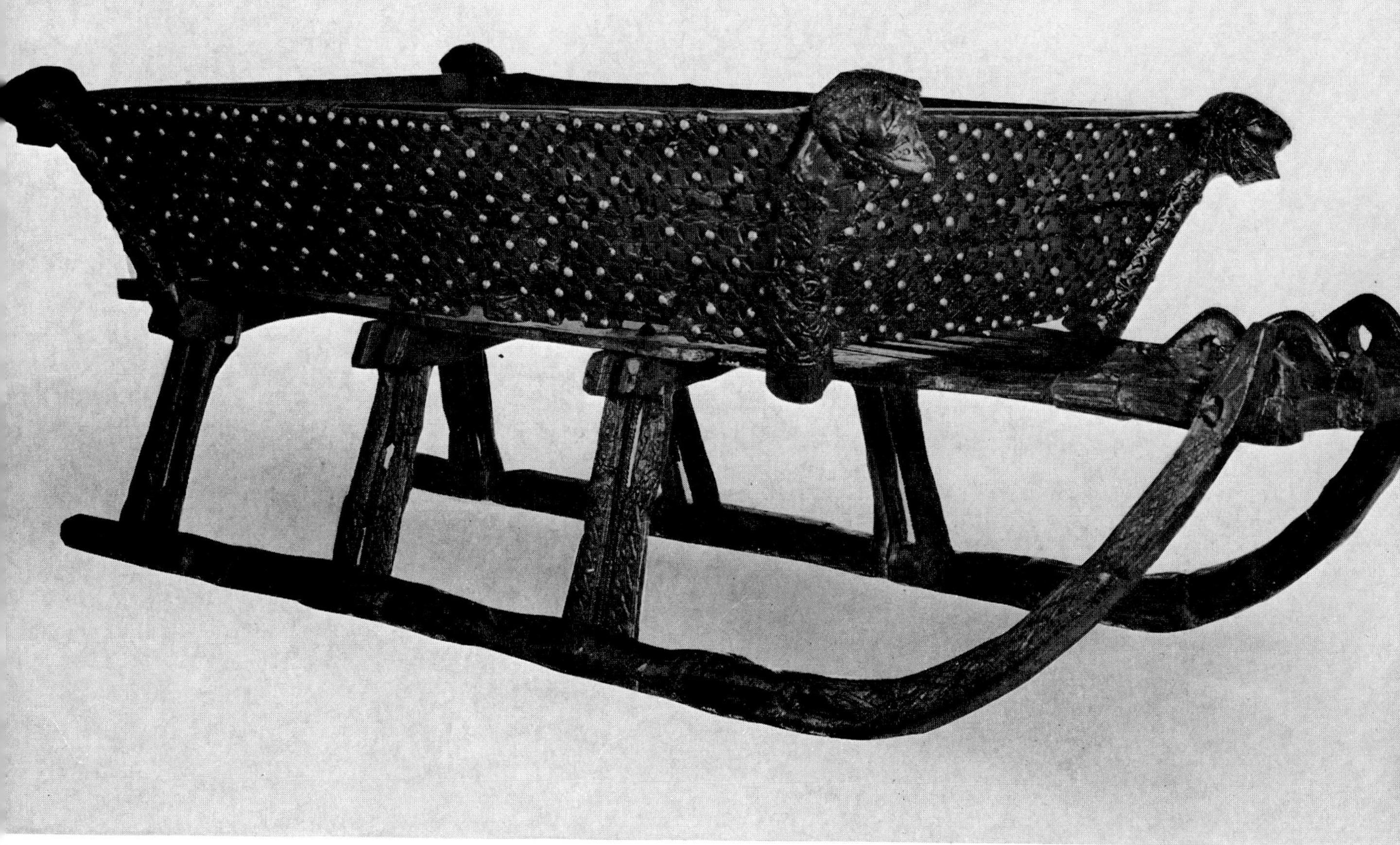

ledge from the Oseberg find.

thwarts, but the expression should not be taken too literally, as it occurs only in passing in the course of the sagas, and not in order to classify the ships. One may be reasonably certain, at all events, that the viking ships found in the grave-mounds are not in the «longship» category. Professor Hj. Falk is undoubtedly right in pointing out that the graveships represent a special type of smaller vessel, referred to in old writings as a *karve* (Old Norse: karfi). When this is mentioned in literature it is always with the distinguishing feature that its size is expressed not by the number of oars, as in the smaller vessels, nor by the number of thwarts, as in the longships, but by the number of rowers on each side. Thus: « . . . rowed at the board 12 or 13 men.» Clearly a very characteristic expression based on some special feature of the vessel itself. If the *longships* could be measured by the number of thwarts, it was because they had stationary seats where the men were placed while rowing. Thwarts are also mentioned for instance on the «Long Serpent» in Tord Kolbeinsson's poem on the battle of Svolder: «There fought helmeted men on bloody thwarts.»

If a somewhat artificial expression was required to indicate the size of a *karve,* it can only have been because there were no stationary thwarts or seats for the oarsmen. The size of smaller vessels is never given by thwarts, this was done only where the really big ships were concerned. In the course of our study of the Gokstad ship, it was emphasized as a particularly remarkable feature that there were no thwarts, nor any fixed seats for the oarsmen at all. This feature must therefore have been characteristic of the *karve*. The *karve* and the graveships are also in the same class as to size. The biggest *karve* mentioned is in Gretti's Saga: « . . . he set out a large karve that he owned; 16 men rowed at the board.» The smallest *karve* is in Egil's Saga, with only six men at the board. The Gokstad ship with 16, and the Oseberg ship with 15 pairs of oars are of the biggest type of *karve* known to us in literature. The Tune ship with its 11 or 12 pairs of oars comes very close to another *karve* mentioned in Egil's Saga, where «12 or 13 men rowed at the board». The boat from Bø on Karmøy had 8 oars on each side. It was a very nice little boat with oar-holes in the board, a certain indication that it had been built as a *karve* proper, for an ordinary 12-oar boat row-locks would certainly have sufficed. The boat from Holmedal in Sundfjord with 6 oars on each side may have been a *karve,* but just as likely an ordinary 12-oar boat. It is hard to draw the distinction as there were few remains of the hull itself. The same appplies to a boat about 40' (12 m.) long found at Mardal in Brønnøy, Nordland. One must remember that the small *karve* mentioned in Egil's Saga, with only 6 pairs of oars, belonged to a child, the boy Ragnvald, one of the sons of Erik Bloodaxe. The boat was probably built more as a pleasure craft than anything else, fine and delicate in structure, and nicely painted in bright colours. The saga relates how Ragnvald set out in his boat one night on a pleasure trip from the royal estate at Herdla, and came to a tragic end when he was run down and killed by Egil Skallagrimsson.

The word *karve* comes from the Greek word *karabos* used by Byzantine writers to designate the Russian ships in the Byzantine Navy. The Russian form of the word, *korabi* is found in many accounts of the Varangians' expeditions from the Dnieper to Constantinople. These boats must have been a type of light craft well suited for voyages on the Russian rivers and for being drawn past the rapids at Yekaterinoslav on the Dnieper. In Norway too, we are told on several occasions that a *karve* could be moved a short distance over land. Thus the Greek word has come to be used in the North for the same type of craft, although it is only known to exist in Old Norse literature, not in Danish or Swedish. Nevertheless, it no doubt came to us from the Baltic countries. We are told in Egil's Saga that Bjørn and Torolf Kveldulvsson had a fine *karve* they had taken «on (a) viking (raid) in Austerveg», i. e. to the East. The first time we encounter the word *karve* is in a stanza by Egil Skallagrimsson in the year 934, and the word was in current use as late as the 14th century, when we hear that Bishop Haakon of Bergen had a *karve* made for his personal use (1340). A document of 1381 makes mention of a *karve* belonging to a member of the chapter at Nidaros Cathedral. That is the last time the word occurs.

From the mention of the *karves* in old writings it is evident that they correspond very closely to the boats found in the grave-mounds. Like them they were light boats with a relatively small crew. It is apparent from the

ails from the carriage of the berg find showing the rich ornentation.

literature that the «karves» were mostly private boats kept by wealthy people for trips along the coast and on the lakes. We are told, for instance, that King Olav Trygvason gave Haarek of Tjøtta such a ship for his voyage home from Nidaros, and that it was a good ship where «10 or 12 men rowed at the side», and there were 30 men aboard. Snorre tells us this to show that Haarek was given a conveyance in keeping with his rank of chieftain. In token of gratitude for his help at the battle of Nesjar, Ketil of Ringanes was given a *karve* by King Olav. Ketil took the boat up the river Glomma, past the rapids at Sarpsborg, to the lake of Mjøsa where he kept it at his estate of Ottestad in Hedmark. No doubt it was customary for a chieftain to have his own ship built for voyages, and he would attach the greatest importance to having choice materials and first-class workmanship. Naturally a vessel of this kind would be chosen when the dead were to be buried in a ship.

On this background we get the proper understanding of the ships from Tune, Gokstad and Oseberg. They were ships built by persons of high rank according to their own wishes and needs: ships of one type, but with individual variations in each case, as becomes strikingly apparent on a comparison between the Gokstad and Oseberg ships. At the same time it is safe to assume that these ships, for their purpose, represent the highest level of shipbuilding in the Viking Era, and as we have seen, they were perfect vessels in their way. It is a little misleading, however, that they should be populary called viking ships, a term which carries the suggestion of viking raids to foreign shores. The ships in the grave-mounds were not built for warfare, nor for voyages on the high seas, they were intended for travel along the coast, where one could reach port every night. Then a tent would be raised for the owners ashore. It would be inconceivable to go on a long voyage with vessels like the Tune ship or the Oseberg ship. The Gokstad ship with its broad hull and high boards, was altogether more seaworthy, but it lacked all the equipment which would be needed on a voyage to foreign waters.

Ocean-going craft such as those used on the viking raids were undoubtedly built on the same lines as the Gokstad ship, but most likely they were of a broader and heavier type, designed primarily as sailing-craft to cover great distances, and with less regard for the use of oars. On the whole, the ocean-going vessels were rather like the «jekter», the coastal vessels used until ca. 1900 in North Norway, with the difference that the viking ships had a high, pointed stern and the rudder on the starboard side. But the viking ships of the 9th century were also light craft which in an emergency could be drawn a short distance over land, as was done after the siege of Paris in 884, when the ships had to be taken around the city in order to continue up the river. The viking ships were not built as warships; they served to transport the forces which set out to raid foreign shores, and only very rarely do we hear that ship fought against ship at sea.

We happen to know of one encounter between Norwegian ships in the waters between Scotland and Ireland, described by the Irishman Findan who was a prisoner on one of the ships, but the whole thing was just a brief skirmish, the result of a private feud, not a regular sea battle. We are only

Carved head supporting the body of the Oseberg carriage.

once told of a regular battle at sea, and that was during the struggle between Norwegian and Danish vikings in Ireland, in 851. A Norwegian fleet of 70 ships, under the chieftains Stein and Jerkne fought the Danish fleet under Orm. Such loss of life at sea had never been heard of before, says the Irish

Detail from one of the Oseberg sledges.

chronicle. But apart from that both sides preferred to fight ashore, and the outcome of the struggle was decided on land.

During the first century of the Viking Era the vikings had no need for actual warships, as the countries of Western Europe were almost defenceless at sea. An effective watch for pirates was being maintained both in England and in the lands of Charlemagne, but the defence did not begin until land forces had been mustered, and as a rule the vikings could disembark in peace. In Scotland and Ireland there was no effectively organized defence at all. We see, indeed, that the great army of Danish vikings which conquered more than half of King Alfred's England had quite small ships of little more than 30 oars. Their fleets were all the larger when the armies crossed from the Continent. In the last invasion, in 892, the army from the Seine area reached Kent in 250 ships. Hasting came from the Loire with 80 ships, and

Earl Sigfred from the north with 140 ships. In England the viking ships were called *asks* (from the anglo-saxon *aesc*), hence the term *Askmen* meaning vikings. We remember in the sagas the giant Alv Askman who served with the sons of Erik Bloodaxe. The asks of those days must have been of about the same dimensions as the Gokstad ship.

With an eye to the future, King Alfred organized a more powerful sea-defence during the last war with the vikings. The chronicle relates that he built warships almost twice the size, of the *asks,* some with 60 oars and some with more, and they were faster, bigger and higher, and were neither of Frisian nor Danish design, but such as the King thought would best serve their purpose.

Thus King Alfred had created a new type of vessel built for war at sea, in order to keep the vikings away from the coast. This fleet was the foundation of a sea power which was kept up by the later kings of England. By the middle of the next century it was stated that the fleet had 3,600 ships and that it was ordered out each year for manoeuvres.

King Alfred's vessels were not, properly speaking, viking ships; on the contrary, they were a fleet used for coastal defence against the vikings. But this is the first we hear in Western Europe of a type of ship which in Norse terminology would be called a longship – in this case a ship of 30 thwarts or rather more. Later even bigger ships were built, to keep up with the powerful ships sent to England by Svein Forkbeard. After King Ethelred's reorganization of the defence in 1008, the ships were built with 43 thwarts. Thus we know that the first longships in Western Europe were used in England, during King Alfred's struggle against the vikings. It is another question whether he was also the first to build such ships and these were later copied in the North, or whether he had possibly modelled his ships on Nordic longships which might already have existed, even if they were not yet in regular use on viking raids. The longships were never very suitable for use on the high seas.

A battle at sea between two fleets was not altogether unusual in Norway in the 9th century. The skaldic poems in the Saga of Harald Fairhair give us at least three instances of this. In a verse by Hornklove on the battle of Solskel we are told that the men fell before the King in the bow, and he says of the battle of Hafrsfjord that the wounded were thrown down under the thwarts, their heads against the keel. In both cases there was unmistakably fighting on board, from ship to ship. We must make a similar assumption when Eyvind Skaldaspiller says of the battle of Stavnes that the waters of the bay were mingled with the blood of men. But we have no idea how big the ships were, neither Harald Fairhair's nor those of his adversaries. It proves nothing that the sagas tell us of longships and dragon ships at the time of Harald Fairhair as when Snorre says that King Harald had a large dragon ship built in the winter at Lade, or Egil's Saga relates that Torolv Kveldulvsson had a large longship built, with a dragonhead on it. The sagas were written several centuries later, and were inevitably coloured by their own times. The only slight hint we have on the type of ship used in the 9th century may be that Hornklove refers to the enemy ships in the battle of Hafrsfjord as «*knarrs* with grinning heads and carved ornaments». A «knarr» is usually an ocean-going craft, mostly a merchant ship; but we should not stress the interpretation of a single word *too* much in a poem of this nature. The demands of rhyme and metre often decide the choice of words.

From the English side we have some sparse but reliable information on this subject. The chronicler William of Malmesbury tells us that Harald Fairhair sent as a gift to King Aethelstan a ship with a golden prow and purple sails, and a serried row of shields inlaid with gold along the sides. The envoys were Hallgrim and Osfrid, they were royally received in York and rewarded with gifts. As we know from Snorre, Aethelstan sent Harald a sword with gold ornaments on hilt and handle, obviously a worthy gift. From archaeological finds of the same period it is apparent that English swords were at that time highly treasured by the Norwegians as superb weapons. Thus we can assume that a Norwegian-built ship was likewise a mark of high quality, a Norwegian specialty suitable for an exchange of gifts between kings. A gift of this nature was also intended to throw lustre on King Harald himself.

Now that we know the Gokstad ship, a vessel which was buried about the same time as the battle of Hafrsfjord, and was the property of a chieftain closely related to the kings of Vestfold, we know that King Harald had every reason to be proud of Norwegian shipbuilding at that time. The same pride is apparent in the Song of Harald, which was written by Hornklove in the King's honour. Here the ships are mentioned as the first instance of King Harald's power:

Methinks you know the King?
Dwells at «Kvinne»
Head of the Norsemen
Master of deep keels
and scarlet shields
tarred oars
and spray-drenched boards.

In the imagery of the skald the ships are here a symbol of the King's might in war, and there is no doubt that warships are referred to. From the way they are introduced into the poem it is apparent that Harald was eminently equipped in this respect, even if we cannot know how big the ships were. At any rate, it is a genuine contemporary statement, and we may be sure that whoever built a ship of the Gokstad type could build a bigger vessel of a similar type. It is quite possible that the Norwegian chieftains of the time kept ships for battles in home waters which were bigger than those used in the viking raids.

Evidently the development in shipbuilding which was to lead to the appearance of longships of great size in the Saga Period had now begun. Under Haakon the Good 20 thwarts became the normal size of a warship in the western waters, and with the Saga of Olav Trygvason the big royal ships

'he carriage seen from the front ·de.

come into the foreground as symbols of national feeling, and as models for the great ships of later years. We know from Snorre that when Harald Hardruler was arming for the expedition against Denmark he had a ship built on the lines of Olav Trygvason's «Long Serpent», and he also mentions a ship which was built for Øystein Magnusson shortly before he died, «in size and build just like the Long Serpent». It is characteristic that just from the time of Olav Trygvason, from about 1000 onwards, the sagas begin to describe the shipbuilding of the kings, mentioning the finest ships by name.

In the next chapter Brøgger will discuss the ships of the Saga Period and the Middle Ages. We shall see that the Gokstad ship, in its form and construction, gives us a key to the understanding of later developments.

SAGA AND MIDDLE AGES

All through the first section of this book, – the boat and ship down from the Stone Age to the Viking Age, – we could really almost confine ourselves to writing a description and history of the boat and ship, and not least, a history of boat-building itself.

Now, as we pass on to the Saga Period and the Middle Ages, the sources are of such a nature that we might easily be tempted to write a history of seafaring, and interlard it with snatches both small and great of Norwegian history in general. This alluring little pitfall we must try to avoid.

From the preceding chapters of the book we shall retain an almost fantastic impression of how deep a mark this boat and ship theme gradually comes

The state carriage from the Oseberg find.

to set on the Norse communities. Right down from Merovingian times to the close of the Middle Ages, most of the heroic legends and sagas are interwoven with stories about ships and voyages. The sea invades the mental life of the Norse, both individual and racial, and the boat and the ship with it.

Naturally we hear little or nothing of all the labours connected with boat and ship, hunting and fishing, lading and carrying. It is the «higher sphere» of social life which predominates. Our sagas for more than four hundred years, from Harald Fairhair to Magnus Law-Mender, are one long story of ships and boats, of building and adornment, of pride and not a little bragging over these grand ships, of the delight of skalds and storytellers in ships that plough the waves, rejoicing like living creatures in the sea which foams round their bow, and in the pitching swell, and the bellying of sails in breeze and storm.

This ship-delight recurs in the pictorial arts. The ship invades the church, both in the stone-church wall paintings, and in the Christian symbol itself, the ship hung up in the church roof. In tapestries, in paintings on shields and panelling, in carvings on wood and bone, they play with ship-stems and strakes. And in the seals of towns, and signets of the great, we meet their lines afresh.

Higher and higher soared this ship-delight and ship-worship. The *Boglungasogur* relates what ships each of the chieftains built in one winter and spring, and tells their names and what they looked like.

Saga and legend are so meticulous in their accounts of these ships throughout four centuries, that we can actually reconstruct a fragment of a shipping register, including a great number of the ships built in Norway during this period, with class and owner, and details of the vessel's history.

But of all these ships, we possess not so much as a nail or a chip of board. We have not even a picture of such great ships as Olav Trygvason's *Long Serpent,* Olav the Saint's *Visunden* (the Ox), King Sverre's *Mariasuden* (the Ship of Mary), Håkon Håkonssønn's *Olavssuden* and *Kristsuden* (the Olav and the *Christ),* Earl Skule's *Good Friday,* or any other of the great ships of the high Middle Ages.

In our account of the early history of the ship we went from one ship-find to another. On the basis of the archaeological material, we could depict the history of boat-building for a thousand years, down to the great ships of the Viking Age, and with the Gokstad ship as climax, as Shetelig has done in the last chapter.

The literary source-material is truly large and comprehensive. But in the nature of the case, it gives a monstrously one-sided picture. For all the saga-writers, skalds and so on, interest is centred first and last upon the brilliant warships. When King Olav in his evil days (1028) was trying to gather ships in the east, he sent a summons out from Tunsberg, but, says the saga, he got nothing but «the peasants' boats.» It is the *longships* we are told of, and this collective name will here be used as comprehending every type of war craft. Of all the manifold prosaic boats — merchant ships, freighters, ferry boats and all the rest — we learn extremely little. But here the fixed traditions going right back to the Middle Ages take one a long way. While all the proud royal ships have wholly vanished and survive only in literary tradition, the *jekter* of Nordland, Sogn and some few other places still give us a clear picture of the ordinary coastal freighters, with their lines, rigging and equipment. And in the small boats of the west and north there lived on into our own day a miniature constructive model of the old viking ships.

Ships in the Saga Age (800—1300)

Somewhere in the saga of Håkon Håkonssønn we read: «They said it was the Norsemen's wont to take to their ships when they would be at strife.»

There is some justice in this observation. Throughout these saga centuries, unrest and war in Norway are bound up with the ships. Battles and wars on land are on the whole an unknown phenomenon. This does not change until the late Middle Ages, with its new battle-methods and formations. No doubt it will be objected that we have, for instance, Stiklestad, Kalvskinnet and Ilevollene. But they do not affect the main point. Into the bargain, all these land engagements also depend on the ships, indeed are frequently about the ships. At Stiklestad the ships of the peasant army, in Værdalsøren, were a fixed point. And what Sverre won at Ilevollene was King Magnus' entire fleet.

So all the rich material we possess gives us not merely something of the history of boat and ship-building, but also a segment of the history of Norway. For four hundred years the ship is the vital thread in the story of Norwegian unification. It is much more a history of naval warfare than of politics and diplomacy. Everything from the battle of Hafrsfjord to the battle of Largs (1263) — the last of the old Norse empire — has its base and background in the ship.

«From this have come all our distresses,» says King Sverre in his speech to the burghers of Nidaros in 1181, «that we lost all our ships.»

And before the battle of Norefjord, three years later, he says, adressing his crews, «And if I now lose these ships, never again will I seek to gather ships in Norway.»

A king of Norway without ships was a pretty helpless being. That is why the ships of war, the longships, came to play such a leading role in the sagas.

The Longships

In this description we shall rather break with chronology, despite the fact that there are undoubtedly many different phases, some of them sharply defined. Nevertheless, we shall get at least as good a view of what really counts by trying to straighten out the main individual factors for the whole period of these four centuries.

Longship is the basic term throughout for ship of war. It means what it says, a ship which is long and narrow in proportion, to make it a fast-rowing vessel. It has many nuances, many varying characteristics. But these are once

«Brandar» and «tingel», decorati[ve] elements in the prow of the Os[e]berg ship.

for all its essential features, the earliest development of which we saw in the Gokstad ship.

The sources for a history of the ship of war, the longship, are of highly unequal value. It goes without saying that the descriptions of the skalds are almost worthless, when it comes to precise information about the ships, though otherwise they can be splendid enough, and broadly graphic. Most of

the skalds, by virtue of their whole upbringing, were very knowledgeable about ships and the sea.

With Snorre there is a fairly sharp dividing-line in the 1160's. What he has to say of ships before that is often both vague and incorrect, and not infrequently rather conventional. But in sections where tradition was positive and good — for instance, in his stories of the *Long Serpent, Ox,* etc. — he gives many valuable details. For some reason on which we shall not enter here, all his information after that date is much more trustworthy and ample. But the most reliable sources when it comes to ships and shipbuilding, sea-fights and seamen and all the rest of it, are the sagas of Sverre and of Håkon Håkonssønn. Nor is that strange. They are contemporaneous with the events described, they have first-hand knowledge, and the writers — most of them, at any rate — are well up in all that has to do with ships, the sea, and naval warfare. There they are on home ground.

The Classes of Ship.

When Olav Trygvason set out from Nidaros on that far-famed voyage which ended in his death at Svolder, the saga has it that he sailed out with «eleven great ships, as well as ships of twenty thwarts and some smaller craft.» This vital source, indeed, may possibly be a throwback from Snorre's own time. But it is much more probably traditional. And in those days, when the great age of seamanship had dawned, they held the nautical in mind perhaps more clearly than many other things.

Which means, again, that by about the year 1000 they had already reached the fairly precise classification of their warships which we meet in this statement, with three main classes — the great ships, the twenty-thwarters and the smaller class.

From the Viking Age onwards, probably still earlier, the measure of a ship was how many «rooms» it had — that is, the number of spaces between the cross-beams. Each «room» corresponds to one pair of oars. Thus the whole system is derived from the rowing-craft. By each oar there is a seat — a thwart — and thus a twenty-twarter has forty oars. The Gokstad ship has 16 rooms, and it has 32 oars. That rooms and oars correspond is definitely confirmed by a passage in the saga of Harald Hardruler, which says that the King's battleship (built at Nidaros during the winter of 1061—62) was of 35 rooms and had 70 oars.

This designation by rooms and thwarts goes on right through the Middle Ages, and echoes of it may be heard long after that. In the 13th century a different measure for the size of ships is making its way, this time from quite a differnt quarter. The ship is measured in *lasts,* by loading-capacity.

These terms, as it is easy to see, contain a piece of history. The first derives from the age of rowing-ships, the second from the time when mast and sailing had acquired prime importance, and the oars were subordinate.

However, this does not mean that for example, a thirty-thwarter is automatically twice the size of a fifteen-thwarter (Oseberg). It is not as simple as that. What follows will provide a number of instances here and there which throw some light. It may well be a question of the length from stem to stern. We have a statement from an Icelandic source which seems very reliable on the length of certain sizes of ship, expressed in feet, but here converted into meters, so that we may compare them with Oseberg and Gokstad, where the measurements were checked by Fr. Johannessen.

Oseberg 15 thwarts . . . . 22 metres
Gokstad 16 thwarts . . . . 24 »

The measurements in the Flatøy Book:

A 13-thwarter . . . . 18,5 »
A 20-thwarter . . . . 28 »
A 30-thwarter . . . . 52 »

But for comparison it must be stated that the levy ships, most of which had to be of twenty thwarts, were allowed to be much shorter in proportion — about 15 meters. There is a difference of no less than 12 meters. Yet the ship was to have twenty pairs of oars. This must have meant a very considerable diminution in the size of the rooms. And there may have been various adjustments apart from that, to bring the ship up to standard. Later, incidentally, the size of the muster-ships was reduced still further for certain districts, but then it was a genuine reduction, as far as we can make out.

But to return to the old grouping in three classes. With the development of war at sea this became somewhat more differentiated, but the king's navy usually kept nominally to the old grouping. In time the largest class came to predominate — the ships of 30 rooms and over.

It received the official name of *thirty-thwart,* and to begin with this class probably included ships of *over* 30 rooms. The biggest ever built in Norway was of 37 rooms. As technique evolved, it was essentially this class which came to dominate all sea-fights. These were the big battleships of the age, resembling the *Hood, Nelson, Roosevelt* and *Bismarck* of our own day. When King Olav built the *Long Serpent* with 34 rooms, and King Harald his big ship of 35, a designation was added for this new class: the *thirty-five.*

Before the battle of Fimreite (Sogn) in 1184, King Magnus says in a speech to his men: «Methinks that all the ships are won, if *the great ship* is won.» What he means is Sverre's big new battleship *Mariasuden.*

The second class was very effective in its own way, and according to its structure and equipment: these were the ships of 25 rooms and thereabouts. They were called *twenty-fives,* and became very popular. We know a great number of them. They were easier to manoeuvre, and what they lacked in height they could make up in sundry other advantages which the huge and heavy thirties did not possess.

However, in any sea battle there was also a need for smaller ships, preferably numerous, of under 20 rooms — about the size of the Gokstad ship. These could be very useful to their own side and do a lot of harm to the enemy. Indeed the majority of the ships in sea battles were of this type.

The Oseberg ship's kettle, with a collapsible tripod, is Norway's oldest piece of «camping gear».

Craft smaller still, though not of much less than 13 thwarts, were also used in sea-fighting. They had another task as well. Since they were comparatively light and not large, they were used as small warships on Norwegian lakes, having the inestimable advantage that they could be drawn for long stretches overland, from lake to lake.

Here we have named the three battle-classes which gradually established themselves in Norse naval architecture, and which were to become the most important. Of course the fleet also had attached to it a crowd of freighters with food and cargo, tools and reserves, which always went along on its incredible and restless flittings. They are mentioned now and again.

By pure chance we also learn that the royal fleet — and presumably its enemies would do the like — when it lay off Bergen in 1239, had two small craft, exceptionally fast, lying one in Sognesjøen, the other at Hellen (now Bergen), for the speediest possible liaison. They had no telephones or wireless in those days. Of the *Sprite,* which lay at Hellen, we are told that it was decidedly the fastest of all ships.

A fuller account of the great *battleships* which were being built from 999 (the *Long Serpent)* down to 1262 (King Håkon's *Kristsuden)* is much needed. In accordance with the arms technique of those days, the specific object was to build them as high as possible, so that the crews might stand by the top strake and shoot their arrows down into the enemy ship; secondly, to try to obviate all boarding by the enemy; and in the third place, by this superiority in size, to make it possible to board a hostile ship from above, and prevent fighting aboard the big battleship. From the battles we know of in which the great ships took part, it can be seen that they achieved the first aim in a high degree; their lofty gunnels gave the bowmen an amazing advantage. Of one of the biggest ever built in Norway, King Håkon Håkonssønn's *Kross-suden* (the *Cross*) (1252–53) we hear that when it was berthed among the other ships its sides were level with the tent-ridge on the *Olavssuden* (of at least 35 rooms) and had at least 5.6 metres freeboard. Apart from that, however, it seems pretty clear that these floating fortresses did not always answer their purpose. It might be put like this: technique was not in all respects advanced enough to be applied to that kind of ship. When the huge *Kross-suden* itself was newly built and had been on the Danish expedition of 1253, it was sailing northward off Bohuslän with the King's son Magnus aboard as admiral. It reached the Øker Isles, put into harbour and cast anchor. As the cable was running out, fire broke out in the windlass.

Because they were so famous and admired, we have more knowledge of these battleships than of the other craft. Actually there are not so very many of them. We give a list of those that are known, in chronological order. The biggest we know of is Håkon Håkonssønn's *Kristsuden,* which had 37 rooms. King Håkon's *Kross-suden,* built ten years earlier, *may* have been larger still but the number of rooms is not given. According to the saga, when this ship was in port in the Øker Isles off Bohuslän, it was said to be the biggest of the ships lying there, and yet old folk declared that they had never seen so many great ships in a single muster.

There was certainly nothing to prevent them from building even bigger ships than the *Kross-suden* and the *Kristsuden.* But all the technical chances are that they would then lose many of the qualities, which the longships chiefly owed their pre-eminence, as the finest type of medieval craft in North and West Europe. With ships of over 37 rooms — at least of this structural type — such problems as the keel, the strakes and the stem and sternpost become very difficult. And rowing, rigging and steering all demand quite different solutions. Taking into account all that has yet to be stated in this chapter, I think one may say that increasing the number of rooms up to 37 did not repay the great exertions, labour and expense involved.

urial chamber from the Gokstad nd.

Register of known great ships of over 30 rooms.

Name	When and where built	For whom	Rooms
1. Tranen	Nidaros 995	Olav Trygvason	30
2. Ormen Korte	Salten before 999	Raud the Strong	30
3. Ormen Lange	Nidaros 999—1000	Olav Trygvason	34
4. Anon.	Rogaland before 1020	Erling Skjalgssønn	30
5. Visunden	Nidaros 1026	Olav the Saint	30
6. «Bussen»	Nidaros 1061—62	Harald Hardruler	35

Name	When and where built	For Whom	Rooms
7. Mariasuden I	Nidaros 1182–83	King Sverre	30
8. Ognabranden	Nidaros 1199	King Sverre	32
9. Anon.	Nidaros 1206–7	King Inge	36
10. Anon.	Nidaros 1206–7	Earl Håkon	32
11. Anon.	Nidaros 1206–7	Peter Støyper	32
12. Olavssuden	Unknown	Birchlegs	31
13. Langfredag	Nidaros 1232–33	Earl Skule	36
14. Kross-suden	Orust 1252–53	Håkon Håkonssønn	35
15. Mariasuden II	Bergen 1256–57	Håkon Håkonssønn	30
16. Kristsuden	Bergen 1262–63	Håkon Håkonssønn	37

It looks as though the natural level for the great ships was the class of 20 to 25 rooms.

But it is not the less interesting to look a little closer at the battleships class, the ships of 30 rooms and upwards. The chronological register above, which is certainly complete according to the sources we have, shows that there were never many of them. Of course there may have been more than are included here. But as a sample view of probabilities, the list does roughly correspond to how things were.

One further detail should be given. During the heavy period of rearmament after 1206, when, for instance, King Inge built his 36-room ship at Nidaros, the Baglers started arming feverishly in the east. The saga tells, and on this point it should be reliable, that in Tunsberg King Erling Stonewall, Reidar the Messenger and Philip commissioned three great ships, «far bigger than had yet been built in Norway.» Well, there is nothing very strange in that. The strange thing is that we have heard nothing of the type before, and seem to hear nothing afterwards. «They had *two rows of oar-holes between the well-rooms, and among them there were 24 oars in the lower bank and 48 in the upper.* The oars in the upper bank were 20 ells long (that is 11 meters!).» There must have been several men to each oar. It is difficult to say how all this should be understood, and it is made no easier by the statement that these duplicated oar-holes were only between the well-rooms. The meaning must be that in the lower bank there were 12 oars on each side, and in the upper 24. We are told also that in each half-room there were to be 8 men. The usual number in the great ships was three or four. I wonder if the correct interpretation may not be that the ship was a 24-thwart with this curious arrangement of the oars, very high-built, and doubtless very heavy-rowing and inefficient. Perhaps it was an experiment, inspired by ancient literature, and certainly quite stillborn. We read that only the tallest seamen, standing on the ribs could reach up to the deck with a broad-axe. For the tent they used 25 ells across – nearly 14 meters!

These ships were not tried in war. I assume they go no further than the experiment.

In the earliest times the name for a great ship of this first class was *dragon;* others are added later. It is highly probably that the dragon Harald Fair-

tchen utensils found in the Ose-
g ship.

hair built on the west coast had 30 rooms: which means that in the west at any rate, the evolution to bigger vessels than the Gokstad ship occurred long before 900. At least it would seem that the term dragon is reserved mainly for the class of over 30 rooms. And if so, probably a few more should have been added to our register.

But if we take it as it stands, the great ships of the battleship class are 16 in number. This gives us, on a liberal reckoning, only an average of one great ship in twenty years. But on a closer study of the list, one cannot help noticing that they are bunched together. They belong to the exceptionally troubled periods, the 1160s and the time of Sverre, and above all the grim years of civil war from 1207 to 1217. The last little group derives from quite a different period, that of Håkon Håkonssønn's expeditions to Denmark, and lastly his ill-fated Scottish expedition.

And after 1263 comes an abrupt end. Therefore in broad outline we may say that the list gives a little picture of the course of Norwegian history from 800 to 1300. However, we are not in pursuit of history, but of shipbuilding and all connected with it. Therefore we shall begin by glancing at what we know of these battleships.

As has been said already, all linguistic usage warrants the assumption that Harald Fairhair's dragon was of about 30 rooms. What we see here is his encounter with the old ship-culture of West Norway. But there is another thing that strikes us in this list: two of the earliest of the great ships were built and owned by great landholders, Raud the Strong and Erling Skjalgssønn. This is certainly no accident. While national consolidation of the kingly power was still incomplete, there was no one to prevent a great landholder from building as many big longships as he pleased. Though we have no hint of a statute to that effect, the list seems to suggest that the building of thirties and thirty-fives was later reserved to the Crown. This is the beginning of a war policy.

Of Raud the Strong of Salten, landholder, owner of rookeries and much else, we know little more than that he owned a great ship which filled King Olav with envy and enthusiasm, when he came sailing up Saltenfjord on his great missionary cruise to North Norway in the summer of 999. The King himself had the *Crane,* «the biggest ship», as he believed, which means it had 30 rooms, but Raud's ship was at least as big. In the saga it is called a dragon. «It was a much bigger and fairer ship than the *Crane,*» says the saga. To be on the safe side it is entered on the register with 30 rooms.

We have no particulars to guide us, and may therefore assume that King Olav Trygvason was building on traditions going right back to King Harald's time, when in 995 he fitted out this *Crane,* a ship of 30 rooms, at Nidaros. The name *Crane,* which sounds so odd, is pretty obviously linked with what we read in the saga, that it had a lofty stem and stern, and yet was not large in proportion. Thus the stem and stern would rise high into the air, like the neck of a bird, and this simile would enter the Kings mind.

It is more than a century from the Gokstad ship to the *Crane* and Raud's great ship. The evolution which begins with Harald Fairhair has chiefly tended to an increase in the ships' length and size, which means again a deeper study and improvement of the keel, stem, stern and hull. The cause is the increase in naval warfare.

Then, in 999, King Olav sails northward with the *Crane,* which he and his followers believe to be the proudest ship yet built in Norway. But when they reach Salten and see Raud's great ship, they are both astonished and impressed. Therefore these northerners had the lead in shipbuilding and had solved all problems, so as to impress even a sea-king. King Olav took the ship away with him, after having disposed of Raud in what seems to us rather a disgusting fashion, because he would not be christened. But that was the way of the age. We may be sure that Raud himself felt no great surprise at the King's line of conduct.

The most interesting point in this whole connection is that it was Raud's great ship, the *Nordlander* – later the King renamed it the *Short Serpent* – which established a tradition for the royal ships and warships of medieval Norway, as a model first for the *Long Serpent,* and through that for the royal ships of several centuries. The tradition was developed and maintained at Nidaros, in the royal dockyards at Øren and under Ladehammeren, where

Animal-head post from the Oseberg find.

for some hundreds of years the shipbuilders preserved the «chief measures» of the *Long Serpent.*

The *Long Serpent* was built in the winter of 999—1000, for the great expedition King Olav was planning to «Wendland». The slips where laid down under Ladehammeren outside Nidaros. As is well known, the name of the shipbuilder is very seldom recorded in the saga. When it does occur, it is because the building brought forth something unusual. And so it was with the *Long Serpent.* «There were many shipwrights there,» relates Snorre, «some cutting out the strakes, some riveting, while others carried timber to the site.» We know the names for some of the most important groups. The man in charge was called the shipwright. Under him were several important craftsmen, including the prowwright, whose task was perhaps the most vital and difficult of all — that of connecting the lines of the boat fore and aft, the transition from the keel and strakes on to the stem and stern. On this in very great measure it depends whether the ship is to be well fitted for its purpose, sailing and war.

Torberg was the prowwright's name. Here we shall not repeat Snorre's account of what took place, but merely give an interpretation of the main result, as I believe it must be understood from Snorre's narrative in general, which is not quite clear. The whole ship had been planked while Torberg was away at home on a personal errand. When he got back this work was finished, and all were of the opinion that the ship was matchless in build. The King thought so too. When Torberg saw it he thought differently. According to tradition he went out to it by night and cut new joints in the stem and stern posts, to get more play in both from the strakes upwards. At first the King was furious, and all the other shipwrights were horribly affronted. But when Torberg had shown the King what he meant, he was allowed to carry out this radical change, and then all agreed that the ship was now much better at every point. And the King made Torberg master-builder for the whole ship, and he completed it in his own way. After that he was called Torberg *Skavhogg* (he who cuts smoothly with the axe).

Naturally the shipwright proper has the main credit for the *Long Serpent.* It was something of a feat in itself to construct a ship of 34 rooms on the model of a 30-roomer. But he must share the honour with Torberg, the prow-cutter. Torberg did not lengthen the ship, or try in any way to alter its main lines. But he improved it at a vitally important point, by a new development within the prow and stern.

One of the state beds from the Oseberg find.

The *Long Serpent* was not, indeed, to have a long life. But it was all the more long-lived in story. It was King Olav's great ship at the battle of Svolder, and afterwards, as far as we know, passed to the victor, Earl Eirik. But he cannot have had it at the battle of Nesjar, or the fact would surely have come down to us. What is beyond doubt is that it acquired a legendary halo as Norway's most famous ship.

The *Long Serpent* was a genuine great ship, the first in Norway. We learn from the Flatøy Book that the keel measured 72 ells — that is, about 39 meters (the old Norse ell = 0.55 m.).

How big a part was played by the treatment of the prow and stern areas, from the keel and strakes to the prow, emerged in 1926 in a longish discussion which sprang up over the joinings fore and aft in the Oseberg ship. In reply to one of my contributions, Johan Anker, on April 26th, 1926, pronounced the following opinion:

«I do not believe the joins in the strakes of the Oseberg ship fore and aft can have been placed as they are on purpose. It was undoubtedly the size and availability of the materials which obliged the builder to dispose these joins in their present position.

«For it must be noted that the strakes run down towards the stem in a straight line, or sometimes an inverted curve, and then they have to rise again, in something like a semicircle. To obtain trees which have a natural bend from straight to semicircular is next to impossible, even in our own day. Of course in modern boat-building the wood can be boiled and bent into the desired shape. But that was certainly not known to any wide extent at that period.

«On the other hand, it is much easier to procure timber in which a shortish section has a uniform bend throughout. And so the shipbuilder, on account of his material, will naturally join all the strakes as near as possible to the beginning of the curve. And that, as may be seen from the disposal of the joins, is what was done here; all the strakes are joined approximately one above the other, just at the lowest point of the transition from the straight line to the rising curve.»

In his description of the *Long Serpent* Snorre says that «this of all the ships in Norway was the best made, and at the greatest cost.» But here we have undeniably something of convention, of the eulogistic phraseology which was accorded to so many kings and chiefs.

It was not till 1026 that Olav the Saint built his great ship of 30 rooms and called it *Visunden,* the *Ox*. That also was built at Nidaros, but the saga tells us little of the building. It could not steal the fame of the *Long Serpent*. It passed to Olav's son King Magnus, who took it on a Danish expedition. We have unquestionably gorgeous, but – from the point of view of building technique – vague pictures of this *Ox* in poems by Sigvat Skald and Arnor Tordarson. In his elegy on King Olav, Sigvat calls the *Long Serpent* the «Heather-Fish» (which just means serpent), and depicts the Ox washing his horns in the sea.

«Bold was thy use of the longships, battle-mighty King,» says Tjodolv Arnorssønn in his *Magnusflokk* (v. 4). The crews steered 70 ships to the east. Southwards rushed the ships' sides. The sail sang in the stays, the ship of the long strakes cut its way through the water, the Ox plunged into the sea.

No less playful are the images of Arnor Tordarson in his *Magnusdrapa,* where he describes the King's voyage in the *Ox* from Nidaros to Denmark. «The *Ox* sailed out of the north with men in Gallic helms at the oars. The foaming waves drove into the poop and the rudder trembled. The wind bent the strong ship, shining with red gold. Thou didst steer the mighty stems out of the north, past Stavanger to the realm of the Danes. The sea-currents trembled and the mastheads shone like glowing fire.» And in another verse: «Thou hast the art, O King, of sailing stormy seas and living long under the sea-sprayed tent. The *Ox* bears thee, glorious friend, like the keen hawk, in its poop. Never will sail a fairer ship with a more splendid king.»

Of course these stanzas do not tell us very much about the ship and its build. But then they are not meant to. They present graphic images, and express the delight of a whole age in a well-built ship at sea, and in the glorious life on board. That Magnus was a great shipmaster, on the other hand, is pretty clearly nonsense; he was hardly that. But the king is a symbol, he must be showered with praise. This is very natural.

One technical peculiarity in the royal skalds' mention of the ship should be referred to. They both call it the *pine* – *fura* in old Norse. This, however, probably does not imply that the *Ox* or any other of the royal ships was built of pine. The word occurs here in the same sense as when in early times they used the word *eiki* (oak) for the boat. Both *eiki* and *fura* are simply generic names for the boat or ship. A third word is also to be met with, but more rarely — *ask* (elm).

But still one cannot exclude the possibility that the *Ox* was built of pine. In North Norway, where oak was not to be had, they used pine for their boats. And it may very well be that at the moment when the *Ox* was building, it was rather hard to procure good oak timber, so they had to be content with pine. Both in the north and in Iceland — to which North Norway often supplied ships — the ship was most commonly called pine. In *Sigurdsbolken* (1140) Ivar Ingimundsson calls it the *northern pine,* skimming along under full sails. And the Icelandic law-book grágás speaks of the floating pine = the ship. Ivar, incidentally, also rates that this pine was a *sinew-bound* ship — thus that the strakes were not riveted, but sewn together just as in the Halsnøy boat. In Nordland they kept this up for a long time, and Gjessing sees it as an archaic and very «backward» feature. But that can hardly be the case. If anyone could build boats it was the men of North Norway. And Ivar actually relates of this ship that it sailed faster than any other. (v. 26).

It was no less than 35 years before a great ship was again built, this time a larger one than any yet built in Norway. This was the heavy «galeas» (Busse) of 35 rooms built by King Harald Hardruler at Nidaros in the winter of 1061—62 for his expedition against Denmark. This ship also was constructed «on the measure of the *Long Serpent.*» The King himself saw to a careful choice of all equipment — of sails and ropes, anchors and cables. Tjodolv Skald has given us glimpses of this ship and of the crucial part it came to play at the battle of Laholmsbukt in Halland. He rejoices to see the long hull lying on the water, «the serpent's mane gleams yellow-green against the deck», its neck is of burnt gold. He describes the throng on shore watching the «Serpent» glide down from the town — «the ship's side groans as 70 oars take it down to sea, before the army ply their oars in the ocean. As Norsemen row the Serpent, the riveted, down the icy stream, it is like a sight of eagle's wings.»

Not till 120 years later was yet another great ship built in Norway. This was King Sverre's famous *Mariasuden.* After Harald Hardruler there had long been relatively peaceful days in the land, and great ships were not needed on Magnus Barefoot's western expedition of 1103. Then came the season of unrest in the 12th century, and from the 1160s to the fall of Skule in 1240 there was incessant fighting for many years on end. In these years a number of great ships were built, whose names and destinies we know, sometimes pretty well.

After alternations of success and failure, mostly the latter, King Sverre realised that ships were the only means of winning and keeping power in Norway. And after his defeat at Nidaros in 1181 he made a start by building *Mariasuden,* in the winter of 1182—83. It was built «above the town». At the same time he raised several ships of the «middle class», those of 20 to 24 rooms. It was now a question of rearmament.

ass ornament probably of Irish gin on a bucket found in the eberg ship.

The ship was finished by the autumn. It was of 32 rooms, but bigger than it looked. As has been said, it was built *above the town,* and thus a long way from the sea (for reasons of security?); and naturally enough people were telling each other that it would hardly be possible to get this ship launched without pulling houses down. They said the King had overreached himself in his arrogance, and many augured ill for the ship. They turned out to be right. But it was managed; and as the ship was running down the slipway to the river it gave at the seams.

The cause of this, according to the saga, was that King Sverre had spent part of the winter at Møre, and meanwhile they had got as far as laying nine rounds of the planking. When the King saw the ship, he said it was going to be much smaller than he wished, and demanded that it should be cut in two and the keel lengthened amidships by twelve ells — that is, over six metres.

The master-builder spoke against this; he is not named. But the King would have his way — another incident showing that he was not much of a judge of ships. And therefore things went wrong.

As a result the ship had been pieced, both in the keel and obviously too much in the strakes. And that was where it gave and creaked on launching. It was what boat-builders in the west call *samskaret,* with the joints close together in a bunch amidships. A frail ship, highly vulnerable on the sea.

The King, however, was expecting much of this ship. When it was launched he stood in it and made a speech:

«Thank be to God, the blessed Virgin Mary and the blessed king Olav, that this ship has come happily upon the water and to no man's hurt, as many prophesied. – God forgive them all the unkind words they threw at us for that. Now I may trust that few here have seen a bigger longship, and it will greatly serve to ward the land against our enemies if this proves a lucky ship. I give it into the protection of the blessed Mary, naming it *Mariasuden,* and I pray the blessed Virgin to keep watch and ward over this ship. In testimony I will give Mary her own such things as most belong to divine service. Vestments that would be fine enough for even the archbishop though he wore them on high days. And in return I expect that she will remember all these gifts and give aid and luck both to the ship and all who fare in it.»

There are several indications that this rather elaborate ship-christening was not the first in early history. The idea was not simply to give the ship a name, but to devote it to the protection of higher powers. That this particular baptism had its political significance – the appeal to the Church and the Archbishop – is a question apart.

The King made good his promise in a high degree. He had sacred relics let into the crossbeams behind the stem and sternpost. And he shared out the vestments; St. Mary's Church got the chasuble, Elgeseter the cope, Nonneseter at Bakke all the other things.

With ineffable sincerity the saga adds: «*Mariasuden* was no fair ship. Everything was less towards the bow and stern than amidships. That was because she had been pieced.»

In the spring of 1184 King Sverre once again had a good navy, with *Mariasuden* at its head. The ship had then a crew of 320, which is to say it was well manned. For in those days they reckoned three men to a «half-room», but as *Mariasuden* was a 32-roomer it worked out at five men to a half-room. – The saga relates as a strange interlude that when the fleet was to sail the King had four chests carried out to the ship, and it took four men to carry each chest. Nobody could make out what this was for.

The ship sailed out of Nidaros and then southward. Off Stadtlandet they ran into rain and storm, so that it was not an unmixed pleasure to be in the prow. *Mariasuden* gave more than was right – of course a good ship ought to give a little in the sea, but this was evidently something else. Therefore the King turned into Ulvesund. And there the crew found out what the queer heavy sea-chests were intended for. They were ship's rivets. The King dealt out a quantity of rivets to each halfroom, and told the men to use them as they were needed under sail.

When the fleet reached Sogn it steered into Sognefjord. While there it was surprised in Norefjord by King Magnus with a superior force, but none the less the battle ended in a victory for King Sverre.

Mariasuden played a leading part in the battle after all. To that extent Sverre really had shown foresight in building a great ship like this, if only

ronze strap-embellishments from e Gokstad find. Representations naturalistic as this lion and orseman are rare in Viking art, id animals in Viking ornaments in seldom be identified with iown species.

the building had been a proper seamanlike job. Its later fortunes are soon told. From the battle of Norefjord Sverre sailed to Bergen with his own ships and his prizes. There he beached *Mariasuden* on Holmen and built a roof over it. It never took the water again.

When the Kuvlungs entered Bergen in the autumn of 1185 they wanted to relaunch *Mariasuden.* All the common citizens were called out to give a hand. But the ship would not budge. At last there was such a shuddering and straining that the prowtimbers snapped. Then they set fire to it and burnt it up. So its active lifetime had been only a few weeks, from the day it set sail from Nidaros in April 1184 till it reached Bergen via the battle of Norefjord and was laid up, in June of the same year.

Struggles in the latter part of King Sverre's life produced more seafights here and there, and led to several fresh periods of shipbuilding. But these are events which it is easier to pass over quickly. The new factions which sprang up against him took care of that. He even lost his ships again and finally was left empty-handed.

It was in the 1190s that these events took place and he had to start shipbuilding afresh. The biggest ship built in this period was *Ognabranden,* which was of 30 rooms and was the eighth great ship in Norway (se register on p. 147—148) as far as we know. Among other big ships we may single out *Hugroen,* which had probably about 26 rooms and must have been a very well-built ship. Its life was to be long; Sverre's grandson King Håkon Håkonssønn still had it in Bergen in 1239. Among the others may be mentioned *Vidsjåen* and *Hjalpen,* both of 26 rooms.

When Håkon Sverressønn died in 1204 there began a fresh period of trouble with incessant clashes on a small or large scale, which lasted practically till 1217. Almost all the fighting took place at sea, so that shipbuilding again comes into the foreground. In no single brief period of early history were so many ships built as for example in 1206-07 and several times later. The ship King Inge built at Nidaros in 1206-07 was also the largest yet built in Norway, with 36 rooms. At the same time, also at Nidaros, there were built two ships of 32 rooms. Here we have two essential phases. The first is what might be called the great rearmament period after 1206, when both the leading parties among the combatants were engaged in an almost feverish shipbuilding which in the long run simply tended to impoverish the country in many ways. The second follows on the naval agreement of Kvitsøy in 1209. As a third factor of importance we may include the lake warfare which in itself forms a fantastic chapter in the history of war and shipbuilding.

This perpetual armament race cost more than the factions and the people – especially the peasants – could afford in the long run. Harsh necessity compelled the parties to negotiate. It is said to have been Bishop Nicholas who arranged the first of these meetings. They took place at Kvitsøy in 1207, and did not lead to very much as regards armament, but a number of other questions were settled. Finally, at a fresh meeting at Kvitsøy in 1209 where King Inge and Philip came to terms, it was agreed that no party should use or command ships of more than 15 rooms, and no one should be allowed to muster more than 15 ships. This is a genuine parallel to the Washington agreement in the 1920s. Naturally the agreement was soon broken again. But for the moment it was a great relief to the peasantry who bore the burdens.

Party conflicts did flare up now and again, with great activity all along the line, and a certain amount of looting, skirmishing and so forth. But naval warfare in the old style was largely at an end. Indeed the only naval battle was the one which developed accidentally at Oslo in 1240. However, it had no significance.

Land engagements, on the other hand, begin to play a greater part than before. But here we shall not enter on the reason for this state of things.

And now it may be said that the large-scale, often completely pointless shipbuilding was over. For some time it had been a plague to the whole nation. Nothing remains to tell of it but snatches from the last chapter, the conflict between Skule and King Håkon Håkonssønn. In the winter of 1232–33 Skule was already much engaged in shipbuilding, which culminated in the spring of 1233 when he fitted out at Nidaros the biggest ship so far built in Norway. It was of 36 rooms, but even larger in proportion than King Inge's ship, nominally of the same size. This great ship Skule retained to the last. He called it *Good Friday*.

King Håkon had no real need to worry about it. His navy was now strong enough and under reliable command, with many great ships. The fact that he had a new great ship built at Tunsberg in the spring of 1234 – the second *Olavssuden,* of 29 rooms – need not be interpreted as a countermove to Skule's shipbuilding.

With the fall of Skule in 1240, the demand for the building of war craft dwindles yet more and very rapidly. Great ships were no longer raised in Norway. The sole exception is the novel call for great ships produced by King Håkon's Danish musters and his expedition to Scotland. For these three great ships were built, which broke all previous Norwegian records.

The *Kross-suden* was built to King Håkon's order in the winter of 1252–53, by Gunnar King's-blood of Ravnsholt in Orust, Bohuslän. We do not know the size, but judging by descriptions it cannot have had less than 35 rooms. The King attended the launching and made a fine speech. The saga says that never before had such a big ship been built in Norway. It was so high-built that when it was berthed among the other ships in harbour the top strake came level with the *Olavssuden* and it had a freeboard of nine ells, or five metres — which is fantastic if one thinks of the first longships, the Gokstad ship with a freeboard of just over a meter.

The King had *Mariasuden II* built at Bergen in the winter of 1256—57, again in view of his Danish muster. It was of 30 rooms. This ship left the country, when in 1258 King Håkon sent it as a gift and pledge of their peace treaty to King Christopher of Denmark.

Finally the *Kristsuden,* the biggest ship built in Norway in the Middle Ages. It was raised at Bergen in the winter of 1262—63, expressly to be the royal flagship on the Scottish expedition. It had no less than *37 rooms,* and even so was very large in proportion. In this ship Håkon Håkonssøn's body was brought home from Orkney to Norway in the spring of 1264.

And that is the end of the *great* shipbuilding in Norway. There were to be no more ships like the *Kristsuden,* nor yet like the *Long Serpent.* It is typical enough in itself that the period should end with a violent climax, a bang. It is a mirror of history.

We have viewed these huge great ships, the ships of over 30 rooms, with considerable doubt, perhaps unjustly. It may not be quite fair to say that they never won a battle. That they were the exception in shipbuilding is certain. They were enormously expensive to build, and when in use required a great number of hands, together with equipment and provisions on a large scale.

So it is probable that the second class of great ships, *the ships* of *20 to 30 rooms,* counted for most. Especially it looks as if the middle class, those of 25 rooms (the *twenty-fives)* were the most suitable and most effective. And we know a good deal about these ships. We are rather more in the dark over the smaller class, the ships of 15—20 rooms. But even in wartime they were of great importance. These too were the franklins' ships, as appears from the saga of Håkon Håkonssønn.

A few ships may be singled out of this whole category; they will throw light on the position of the *magnate class,* as the «battleships» did for the kings.

Of Erling Skjalgsønn we are told that besides his big ship of 30 rooms he had also ships of 20 and 22 rooms. His sons had ships of 20 rooms. Erling used his 22-thwart in a *muster,* and it had then a crew of 200, that is, about five men to a half-room. It was in this ship that Erling afterwards sailed to England, when he had fallen out with Olav the Saint.

From some more casual references it appears that just at the time of King Olav the 20-thwart was the magnate's ship.

However, as demands increase we see the most skilful boatbuilders in the country, as well as the military experts, fixing on the 25 or 26-thwart as the best and most effective size of longship. Accordingly, the standard sizes for the muster-ships are 20 and 25 thwarts. This seems to become established in the 11th—12th centuries.

In this period it was the ships of the «25-class» that made a name and grew especially popular with all real judges. We know a good many of them — the history of their building, the part they played in the sea-battles and their various destinies. A few of the most famous and typical may be discussed here. Let us, for example, mention two of those which took a lead in the sea-fighting of King Sverre's time — one from each camp, the *Olavssuden I* and the *Beard*.

When the *Olavssuden* was built is rather incertain; it was built by Erling Skakke and called after Olav the Saint. After the battle of Ilevollene in 1179 King Sverre took it from King Magnus. It was of 25 rooms, and was then the biggest ship in Sverre's navy. In the battle of Nordnes near Bergen (1181) it played the chief part in Sverre's fleet, and became the real focus of the conflict, as King Magnus' *Bear* did in his fleet in the same battle.

In this naval engagement off Nordnes Sverre had 16 ships and King Magnus double the number. Here it was demonstrated that the deciding factor was neither the number of ships nor their size, but their manoeuvring. And this was clearly shown to be more elastic and effective with 20—25 thwarts than in the later battles with the bigger ships as a rallying-point. In King Sverre's fleet some of the steersmen must have manoeuvred superbly.

That same autumn, however, King Magnus carried off the victory in the sea-battle of Nidaros, and captured the whole of King Sverre's fleet, including the *Olavssuden* — 33 ships in all. Such an accession to his own navy was more than he had means to equip. He kept the *Olavssuden* and a number of others, and the rest were burnt.

The *Beard* was of 26 rooms. Again, the place and year of building are unknown. King Magnus had it when he reached Saltøysund (Bohuslän) from Denmark in May 1181. After changing owners as described above, it returned to King Magnus, who had it at the battle of Norefjord in June 1184. Its name comes from the decoration on the prow, a bearded male head. (Cf. the *Carl's Head*, the *Head* etc.).

To add one or two more examples, it may be mentioned that Sverre had several ships of this «25-class» built at Nidaros in the winter of 1183—84. And he had others built by some of his «great men» (whom their contemporaries can scarcely have regarded in that light!). For instance, Ulf of Lauvnes built the *Vidsjåen* (the ship one must beware of) of 26 rooms, and Torolv Rympel the *Help* of the same size. That winter Eirik Kingsson had *Oskmøyen* (the *Valkyrie*), which was of 25 rooms. It may be mentioned also that in the same year Sverre had taken from its owner, Vidkunn Erlingssøn of Bjarkøy, a 20-thwart named the *Goldenbreast*. This was originally built at Nidaros for Archbishop Eystein; it must have been an uncommonly well-built and successful ship, and won great fame. It also had a long life. We meet it now and again, for the last time in 1239, when it belonged to King Håkon, and was at least 56 years old!

Håkon Håkonssøn also built several ships of the «25-class.» One of them

The Oseberg ship seen from th bow in the Viking Ships Museur in Oslo.

we know well. He called it simply the *Dragon;* when it was built is not quite certain. This was another ship which won great fame as a successful craft. In 1226 the King sailed it south to Viken, and this cruise made it known as one of the best sailers in the royal fleet. It left all the other ships behind, and also gained a name for uncommon beauty. Later, in 1249 — 23 years afterwards — Håkon the Younger had this ship on his expedition from Oslo against the Swedes. And in 1253 he commanded the *Dragon* in the big levy against Denmark. At that time it cannot have been less than a generation old.

When large-scale conflict had died down and the King acquired naval authority throughout the whole country, it looks as though he came to prefer that the magnates should be content with ships of the 13 to 15-room class. The ships in «class II», the 25-room type, had indeed been built in many of the war years by the King's nobles. But they were in the King's service, and they repaid the profits of it by building these expensive ships for the King's navy, naturally in return for privileges which made it worth their while. We must certainly regard his new decision as a link in the policy of national kingship. Håkon had too much experience of ship-building by the «magnate class» which might be used in party struggles with the Crown. The line he now took must be accounted a judicious step towards pacifying the country, and making an end of party strife and squabbling. We cannot see that the King placed any direct veto on the building of big ships. But then there can have been no need. The magnates were certainly not displeased to be spared this immense outlay on great ships. The «realm», the state (not in our sense) acquired a healthier balance.

During his conflict with the Church in the 1190s King Sverre had embarked on a similar policy, when he took care that the Archbishop of Nidaros should have no ship above a twenty-thwart, with a crew of 90 at the most.

Much of the purely technical side has been discussed already in different places. Here we shall deal with it only in certain aspects. which touch on social conditions, labour conditions, or anything that may throw a little light on what it meant that the people of this country for more than four hundred years, willingly or unwillingly, devoted such enormous efforts to all this building of ships. Even though it was well suited to the economic outlook of the coastal population, still it must gradually have burst the bounds at more points than one.

However, there is one thing that seems clear from all the sources we have. Even in the worst building periods, shipbuilding was carried on only in winter. It was *seasonal work for the winter half-year,* when it was easier to procure what mattered most of all, labour. All the farm work was over then, so they could get going in the autumn. Of course it was a presupposition that all timber and other materials should be conveyed to the building site well in advance, and that the keel should be laid before winter came.

This trait that much of boat-building was winter work persisted in all Norwegian coastal districts down to our own time. Gunvor Ingstad relates of Helgeland (1924) that in the living room there were two beams running lengthwise to shore up the walls. Against these beams the boat-builder

ver coins (now lost) depicting ps with serpent head, sail, stays, ouds and shield-rack. From out 900 A.D. Found at Spanger-, Vest-Agder. Drawings from Archaeological Museum, Oslo iversity.

lengthwise would brace the ship's prow when he was plying his craft indoors of a winter evening.

From all the sources we have consulted it appears that all the ships whose building we know about were completed in the course of one winter and spring. And at a pinch, if need arose, even big ships could be begun and finished in the three months from Christmas to Easter. We have no example of a ship, however big, whose building «stood over» from one season to the next.

In this connection it is natural to say something of the actual *timber supply,* whether this was pine as in the north, or oak as was most common elsewhere. We may assume that in the south and west they took it as a matter of course that the «bearing» material, the keel, prow, stern and strakes, should be of oak. But also in the big shipyards at Nidaros, which for centuries can be regarded as the royal dockyards, they must in general have wanted oak for the bearing parts of the ship. It goes without saying that prime oak timber could not be found straight off on the building sites, either under Ladehammeren or on Øren at Nidaros, or at Bergen or Tunsberg. It had to be sought out in the forest at least a year before the building was to start, then felled and transported to the building site. Moreover, botanical authorities are positive that no oak suitable for shipbuilding grew either in Trøndelag or North Norway in the Viking Period or the Middle Ages. On the other hand, no doubt suitable oak was to be found in Rogaland-Hordaland, and it cannot have been an insuperable task to transport the materials northward up the coast.

From the earlier ships of Oseberg, Gokstad and Tune we have learnt a good deal about the actual timber question. Granted that oak was much more plentiful in those days than it is now, the bulk demand for it was very great, especially as the ships increased in size.

It has been said, undoubtedly with perfect justice, that the English oak woods were pretty thoroughly reduced by all the naval shipbuilding of the 16th and 17th centuries. It may be that the four centuries of large-scale shipbuilding we are discussing here had something of the same effect on the oak forests of Norway.

In the case of our preserved viking ships we have exact timber measures to go by. For instance, as Shetelig has described, the keel of the Gokstad ship is of magnificent, straight-growing oak, the longest piece measuring 56 feet (about 17.6 meters). According to information for which we are indebted to Professor Erling Eide, the oak from which this piece of keel was cut had a trunk diameter of 44.5 cm. This would give roughly a diameter at breast height of about 70 cm. and a total height of at least 25 meters. It would be practically impossible to find such an oak in Norway today. Only in Vestfold there would be a chance. Eide mentions that in Treschow-Fritzøe's woods near Hallevann, as late as 1920, there was a handsome oak which at a height of 11 meters, where the crown began, measured 90 cm. across. «There are still big, handsome oaks in Vestfold and both the Agder provinces. Most ancient oaks, which are protected now, are free-growing, with a

Section of the Bayeux tapestr with viking ships (11th century

large circumference, but *low in height* and often hollow-trunked. In tracts of denser forest one may occasionally light on oaks which have a well-formed trunk and a great height, and would be suited for exacting technical objects.»

What this consumption of oak timber in these four centuries implied, not least for the big ships, was faintly indicated in 1892—93, when Christensen of Sandefjord undertook the copy of the Gokstad ship which was to sail to America in 1893. As has been said (p. 100), it proved impossible to find an oak-log in this country from which the keel could be made. It was difficult also to find a piece of timber which would do for the mast-partner, though in the end it turned out that a famous old oak growing not far from where the Gokstad ship was found would serve the purpose.

It should be said that the mast-partner of the Tune ship is even more massive than that of the Gokstad ship.

And finally one must remember that these two ships are of the smallest class among the hundreds and hundreds of ships which were built in medieval Norway before 1300.

This picture illustrates the vast consumption of oak timber alone which was demanded by the shipbuilding of these centuries. Then we must add the great, incalculable multitude of freighters which were being built for the carrying trade right through the Middle Ages. But here we have no means of tracing what the numbers were. In a great many of these ships the timbering was pine.

Today these rich resources of oak forest are only a legend. The Viking Period and Middle Ages must have borne pretty hard on them, and later, in the 17th and 18th centuries, came the English and Dutch demands on the Norwegian forests, for ship's timber and for poles on which the Dutch towns were built.

One other small point must be mentioned here — the frightful way material was squandered by the old technique. With the means at their command, the axe, right down from the migrations to the Middle Ages, they never

got more than two planks out of the same tree. The process, as must be quite well known, was to begin by splitting the log length-wise down the middle. From the two half-logs thus obtained they cut away all the outer wood, till they had prepared two thin boards which could be used as planking for the ship. And of course the aim — at any rate in the longships — was to get the strakes as thin as possible. All the material thus cut away was in fact mainly wasted. Anders Sandvig has shown that it was much the same with house-building. Only the water-saw was to correct this extravagance.

Here we have kept solely to the materials required for the small ships from Tune, Oseberg and Gokstad. As early as King Harald's time demands began to mount, on a progressive scale. Think only of the shipbuilding of 1206—07, when something like fifty ships must have been built in the same spring, the great majority much bigger than the one at Gokstad. A ship like *Kristsuden* must have required, in wood and timber alone, more than five times the material of the Gokstad ship.

As I began by saying, few valuable particulars about the ships are to be found in the skalds or sagas, as regards form, equipment and technical detail. Of the skalds we could hardly expect more. Theirs is only the florid language of enthusiasm for the ship at sea, cleaving the billows and pitching in the swell, for the prow-carvings in their golden dress, the beauty and power of the taut sails. The sagas really mention only three things: the size of the ships, the prow-ornaments, and now and then the sails.

The size of the ships is often quite precisely stated, in rooms (number of oars) and thwarts. The immediate impression of a rather bragging tone — «the fairest ship» etc. — turns out, however, on closer scrutiny to arise from some misjudgment on our own part. On the contrary, we must say that the sagas are more apt to contain a fairly precise estimate of what a ship is worth, whether good, successful, or not so good. If a ship was not a complete success according to the taste and judgment of connoisseurs, the fact was by no means hushed up — cf. Sverre's *Mariasuden*. There is far less bragging in the sagas than one might think in advance. Of course that is because in Norway there were too many people who could judge and estimate a ship. Here fulsome praise would have been vain.

With the *prow-ornaments* we enter on two themes: love of beauty, and magic. They are more or less inseparable, and tell us a good deal about the psychology of this race of shiploving men.

The Oseberg serpent is like a palpable dedication to this chapter in the history of the Nordic spirit. And its reality is confirmed by the Gotland reliefs. A couple of hundred years later, the snake becomes, through the *Long Serpent,* the most enduring and famous symbol in the Norse folk-psyche.

In ancient magic as we know it, at any rate from the beginning of the Viking Age, the snake plays a great part, as Shetelig has described above more fully. And then it passes over into Christian magic, which is really nothing but an obviously ineradicable prolongation of heathenism. Perhaps our best example is the crosier from Bishop Absalon's grave. Everything goes to show that the snake is no less ancient in the symbolism of Christian magic than in Nordic paganism. Indeed, for that matter, it is infinitely older than the Christianity which came to influence Nordic communities from the west and south. Among us, and probably no less in the communities of North and West Germany, it is mixed up with a number of ideas which, in a manner often unaccountable, are woven into legend and history.

They also called it *drekahofud,* the dragon-head, and this becomes the name for the ship itself, a *dragon.* In the saga of Olav Trygvason its meaning is explained in a highly ingenuous and very rationalistic way. The King, as related above, had been on that missionary cruise to North Norway which ended in his seizing Raud the Strong's proud ship and sailing it down to Nidaros. On the prow, we are told, it had a dragon-head, and at the stern a tail; prow, stern and necks were laid with gold. And as the King stood looking at the ship under sail, it was as though the sail were *the dragon's wing.* Here we have a complete picture, which in itself may be «true» enough. The word dragon, moreover, may have been originally a joint name for snake and animal head. Later it becomes specialized into the fabulous winged creature of the Middle Ages — animal body and snake's head.

Both archaeological and literary sources give us information on the serpent's role and significance. It is at once a protective, guardian power and a threat to enemies. There is no doubt that these inseparable themes played a leading part in the mound-breaking at Oseberg — where the Serpent lay in the burial-chamber and the spoilers cut it to pieces, so that it should neither protect nor threaten any more.

We remember the oldest law in Iceland (quoted in *Landnáma*), that the serpent was to be taken down from the ship's prow when they were steering shoreward, so as not to frighten the land-spirits with its gaping head.

In this magic, serpent and dragon gradually merge into one. When the very Christian King Sverre baptizes one of his great ships the *Portast,* the enemy's warning to beware, it is certainly a belated echo of the power in this magic. Neither serpent nor dragon has its root in so-called reality. Probably *he crosier of the Danish archshop Absalon. (12th century).*

they had a snake in mind, its outward form at any rate, though an adder has very little in common with the Oseberg serpent. But nobody has seen a dragon. It is a visionary shape, emerging from the rich and strange abyss of popular fantasy, rather like the monster Grendel in *Beowulf*. It becomes a magic dream-figure from the underworld of these men, the world which we call unreal, but which to them was far more real than reality. Its might was great. In the sagas it survives for hundreds of years, from the Nibelung legends to the carvings on the doors of our Norwegian stave-churches in the Middle Ages.

In the Oseberg find we see the serpent with *man's head and cross,* painted, for instance, on one of the verge-boards. This combination of man's head, serpent and cross recurs in many places, as for example on coins from Dorestad, of about the same period as Oseberg. In a Viking-Age grave at Nordfjord there was a charming set of bronze pendants with the serpent and man's head. And in the rich 9th-century treasure-find at Hon in Eker (above Drammen) there was a beautifully executed little serpent of pure gold. Shetelig not long ago reported on a find in a 10th-century boatgrave at Haram in Sunnmøre, with a serpent carved in jet, of really outstanding workmanship. And a silver serpent of the same type as in the Hon find, attached to a necklace, has been discovered in a Viking-Age grave in Granvin, Hardanger.

Danish finds of the same period also show that the serpent, «the snake's head with the two eyes», as Lis Jacobsen calls it, had special virtue as a protective charm.

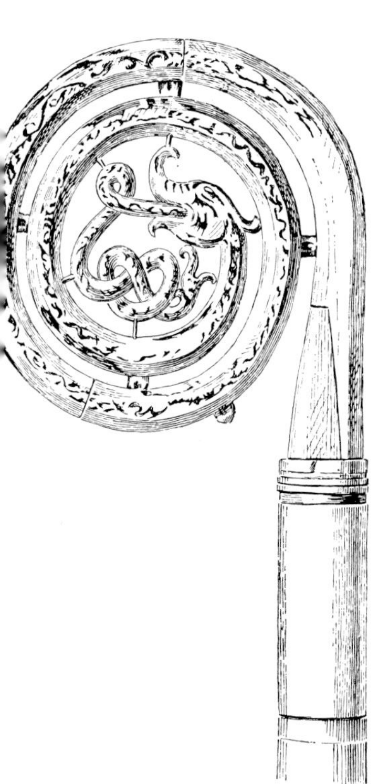

The serpent or dragon became a leading motif for the ships of both Norway and Denmark in the Viking Era and throughout the Middle Ages. The first we hear of is King Harald's *dragon* in the 870s; it had both a serpent-dragon at the prow and a tail at the stern. And they were all equipped in this way, from the *Long Serpent* down to the great ships of King Håkon Håkonssøn's time. It is possible that in those days they had forgotten or had only a vague idea of what was meant, but even of the last of the great ships, the *Krossuden, Mariasuden* and *Kristsuden,* we are told that they had gay dragon-heads, the *Kristsuden* both fore and aft, and all laid with gold.

Now where did they get the other idea, of adorning the prow with a *man's head?* There must obviously be a connection with the magical designs which have come down to us from the early Viking Age, combining serpent and man's head. The first time we hear of such a prow-carving is in the account of the battle of Nesjar (1016), where Olav the Saint's ship is named the *Carl's head.* Because, says the saga, the prow was adorned with a man's head, which King Olav had carved himself. «And this head,» the saga adds, «was borne long after on the ships commanded by chieftains.» This is a rationalisation. It has naturally a deeper source, though we can no longer work it out. In later days as well, it turns up mostly on royal ships. In 1202, King Sverre has a ship called *Hovdebussen,* the ship with the man's head. And King Magnus has *Skjeggen* — the *Beard* — which comes to the same thing.

A rather uncertain, but very plausible detail is given on Earl Eirik's ship *Barden* (at the battle of Svolder). We are told that on the prow it had an

Shipbuilding. Scene from the Bayeux tapestry.

image of Thor, and this was afterwards replaced by a *cross.* – This *Barden* of Earl Eirik's is incidentally a ship apart. As described by the saga, it had a thick iron plate «below», a military detail, whose exact function is very difficult to make out. It can have served no purpose *below* the waterline, but at least may have had some point if it was mounted at the prow from the waterline upwards, as a kind of defence against grappling and boarding. And this is how Snorre appears to understand it, when he says that from the neck right down to the water lay this thick iron plate. According to Gustav Storm, the name *Barden* was synonymous with *Skjeggen.*

Yet another magical theme recurs in the prow-ornament; this is the *ox.* King Olav called his only great ship the *Ox;* on the prow it had a gold-embellished ox-head and at the stern a tail. Both these, together with the «neck», were gilded all over. In the ballad on King Olav his ship is called the *Ox.* Several ships have that name. The last we know of is King Håkon Håkonssøn's *Ox,* which was not a great ship. Later the name of ox is extended to the merchant ships. In the English customs-registers of 1304 there are no less than four Norwegian ships called the *Ox.* Other ships in these English customs-registers are called the *Beard,* the *Help* and the *Heartsease.*

In the saga of Sigurd the Crusader we are told that when the King was leaving Miklagard (Byzantium) he gave all his ships to the Emperor as a parting gift. On the ship the King had sailed there were golden heads, and these were placed in St. Peter's Church. We are not told what kind of heads they were.

Finally the *sails*. These were of course the most conspicuous feature and made the greatest show. As Shetelig has mentioned, (p. 157) it seems likely that we possess some remnants of the sail from the Gokstad ship, but they give no reliable idea of it. And the saga descriptions are vague and rather tritely boastful, as in the story of Sigurd the Crusader's voyage to Byzantium. When his fleet was to sail north he kept it lying a fortnight off Cape Malea, the most south-easterly point in Greece, to get the wind that would display his sails at their finest. There was a fair enough wind for the north, but King Sigurd wanted it directly abeam, so as to cut a figure. The account is vague, though the tradition must be accurate enough since it includes such a definite place-name as Cape Malea. The only thing is that from there up to the Dardanelles would mean at least forty-eight hours at sea, so it was at any rate a queer place to lie waiting. His object was to have the sails as taut as possible so that the fleet should be conspicuous from land. All the sails were canopied on both sides. And none on board, whether in the fore or after part of the ship, wished to see «less fair sails».

In an account of King Håkon Håkonssøn's *Mariasuden* (1256) the sail is said to have been embroidered with *fair pictures*. We should have liked to hear rather more of those!

The many terms for ships used by the sagas and the skalds — *snekke, skute, drake, skeid, busse, sud, brand* and many more — do not really serve to «classify» them by size or equipment. Often they are used merely in a transferred sense as indistinct imagery. And one must also bear in mind that the choice of words in skaldic verse was strictly controlled by the demands of metre and rhyme. A philological interpretation of these names with the idea of classifying the nautical type is of no great value. It may, for instance, be true enough in itself that *sud* and *skeid* gradually attach to the great ships. But on observing, for example, the fairly radical evolution of a term like *busse,* which in the end has quite a different meaning from the one it started out with, one gladly gives up the attempt to unravel the threads.

It is different with *the names of the ships themselves.* These form a chapter in the history of the ship which is by no means immaterial, but on the contrary very rich and full of interest. It is too comprehensive to be treated here. There are only one or two points on which we should like to throw some light in passing.

How old the custom of «christening» a ship may be we have unfortunately no means of finding out. It looks as though they were content at first simply to call them the *Serpent,* the *Dragon,* the *Ox,* the *Carl's head,* after the prow-ornament. Olav Trygvason calls his great ship the *Crane.* We imagine this was because the elevation of the prow gave it the apperance of a long-necked bird, a crane. Indeed Snorre says as much: The *Crane* was called so from its lofty prow. The name becomes part of the ship's destiny, a piece of magic which is supposed to give it power to fulfil its task. Several times we have related how the king *baptised* the ship, gave it a name and made a speech to secure its protection through the name. Remember King Sverre's speech when he was christening *Mariasuden.* The christening is always connected with the launching, both in King Sverre's and King Håkon's time. It is no casual act, but a profoundly earnest and sacred ceremony.

Names which are something more than a contemporary impression of the ships (the *Reindeer, Help, Well-Bedight* etc.) do not really crop up until the civil war, from the 1150s onwards. And here we can distinguish, through the choice of names, a change of style and period which shows the Church and kingship in evolution. This naming of ships in the century between Erling Wryneck and Magnus Lawmender contains a large slice of history.

It begins in 1170, when Erling (nominally of course his son King Magnus) christened his great ship *Olavssuden,* after Olav the Saint. This christening was an unequivocal and public expression of Erling Wryneck's policy.He wished to shape a national course by an appeal to history. On the chaos which began with all the sons of Magnus Barefoot and their successors he was trying to impose a certain order. Since Olav the Quiet, honoured by his contemporaries as Olav the Peasant, the name and political mission of the royal saint had been somewhat obscured. Certainly there was an Olav (d. 1115) after Magnus Barefoot, but neither he nor his circle had created any firm ground. Erling Wryneck had the vision and the will to do so.

Now comes the significant point of the affair: in 1182 King Sverre christens his great ship *Mariasuden* and makes his dedication speech at the launching. Thus, while Erling Wryneck appeals to national history and seeks to build on Olav's groundwork, Sverre turns to the Church, to the blessed Mary — the Church with which he is later to be hard at war.

The whole of this little interlude is like a symbol – even the ship drawn into political history, its nomenclature a programme and propaganda feature.

Something of the sort recurs in 1233–34, but this time with the position of the parties reversed. Sverre's grandson King Håkon builds a new great ship at Tunsberg and christens it *Olavssuden,* the name that Erling Wryneck had once annexed in the political struggle. This might of course be understood, if the old *Olavssuden* of King Magnus' time had passed into Sverre's hands. But this does not seem to have been the case, although we do not know what became of it. The last we hear of it is that Magnus, who had lost it at Nordnes in 1181, won it back the same year at Nidaros. And it was not in his last battle at Norefjord (1184).

And now we have a repetition of this curious propaganda game. In the same winter, Håkon's opponent Skule builds his great ship at Nidaros, and calls it *Good Friday.* No doubt his reason for striking this ecclesiastical note was that he had great need of the Church's support at Nidaros.

After Skule's death in 1240, when the union of patriotic and ecclesiastical policy had been accomplished by the absolute victory of the Birchlegs, King Håkon, in his later building of great ships, could allow himself the generosity of giving them religious names: *Kross-suden* (1253), *Mariasuden* (1257) and *Kristsuden* (1263). At this period, moreover, it became the fashion to give ships Christian names of different kinds. We have, for instance, *Postolasuden, Katrinarsuden, Sunnifusuden,* and *Torlakssuden.*

It would take us far beyond our proper subject to give a general view of the names and their story, interesting as it might be. It would present a fragment of psychological history, but a wide departure from the history of the ship and shipbuilding. Only a few names which are not merely designations tell us a little about the ship itself. We have, for example, *Hrefna* (*May* 1181). *Hrefn* is the fifth plank in the strakes of the twenty-thwarts. But why the ship was named for such a technical detail I cannot explain. Reindeer is used once or twice as a ship's name. This seems to be a very ancient paraphrase for ship, derived from skaldic idiom as far back as the 9th century. It has its source in a magical idea of making the ship fly like the reindeer. There is less significance in the fact that for a shortish period the word *brand* was used as the last part of the name; this begins in Sverre's time. *Brand* means that part of the ship which mediates the transition from the strakes to the prow and stern. Here again, it is impossible to say why they selected just this feature and turned it into the ship's name. Most probably it was a case of *pars pro toto.*

A highly exclusive little detail is the name of one of Bishop Nicholas's ships, the *Redside,* which can scarcely have any other meaning than that the hull was painted red. *Goldenbreast,* on the other hand, refers only to the gilded prow.

The Sea Battles

We have heard something of these in the foregoing account. Here they will be discussed more fully, as far as they throw light on the history of the ship and shipbuilding. The most interesting points to work out in this connection are: What form did these sea battles take in Norway, how many ships and men might they involve, what part was played by individual ships of the various classes which have been described above?

By way of preface it must be said at once that these sea battles were not at all what we understand by a naval battle in the centuries from about 1600 to 1850. There, if we stick to the *age of sail,* the point in an engagement was to *manoeuvre on the open sea,* to «take the wind out of the enemy's sails», and get into battle-order so that the guns could be used. This is what happens in the classic naval engagements in the waters of North and West Europe.

In modern times, owing to the development of engines and artillery, another quite new period opened up. It reached its extreme stage during the last world war, when naval battles were fought out between enemies who did not even see a speck of one another's ships at all.

The old technique of naval battle which goes back to Hafrsfjord has nothing in common with either of these phases. The battles *were not fought under sail.* We have plenty of evidence in the sagas that the mast was lowered during a fight. They were simply contests between floating fortresses moved to the scene of action, where manoeuvring before and during the battle depended first and foremost on the *oars* and rowers, and therefore on the steersman. As is well known, the aim was to manoeuvre in such a way as to afford a chance of *grappling* the ships together for close fighting. Or to express it rather paradoxically: to grapple them together so that they became a fenced arena for hand-to-hand fighting, a boxing ring! In other words, we have three stages in the «battle». First the manoeuvring to get the ships into the most favourable position; this is where the steersman's highly exacting task comes in. The second stage, which may well open during the manoeuvring itself, is the «range-finding», first with arrows and later with all kinds of iron and stone missiles. And finally the third stage – grappling, hand-to-hand fighting, the decision.

The place chosen for all these naval battles add their own tale. One need not even make a geographic list of them to see the main point: Not one of these engagements was fought out on the open sea. That would have been pretty hopeless with these light ships, and even more so under sail, when the captain would have lost the complete picture, and the deck, like a rocking floor, would have decreased the chance of fairly accurate marksmanship. All the sea battles were fought in enclosed waters, where they were tolerably certain of being able to manoeuvre and shoot in peace and quiet – in fjords and sounds, a bay or the lee of an island. It is highly symbolical that the history of naval battles should open with Hafrsfjord, where they had first to pass through narrow sounds in order to close. Therefore it is easy to understand that all the preliminaries gave the captain a momentous task. He acts as *steersman* in battle; his job is of a military, almost more than of a navigational character. Steering a ship under sail or on the open sea was no great art; probably almost everyone could do it. But to be steersman in battle was another thing. We know a number of them by name, back to the days of Olav Trygvason. They were very rarely the kings themselves, but mostly talented naval leaders of the chieftain class — though tradition has it that King Olav «steered» the *Long Serpent* in person at the battle of Svolder. A typical example is King Sverre's «admiral» Tord Finngeirsbror, who commanded *Mariasuden* in the decisive battle of Norefjord (1184) and *Heartsease* at the battle of Strindsjøen fifteen years later. Under the levy system it became the task of the district sheriff to appoint these steersmen. That would more or less correspond to royal appointment of the higher-ranking naval officers in our own day.

The captain's first duty as a prelude to battle is of especial moment and responsibility. He must be all eyes as he directs the oarsmen so as to exploit the smallest chance of getting a better position than the enemy ships; not least, he must observe the movements of the latter with intense care. The various details of manoeuvre at the battle of Norefjord serve admirably to illustrate this knife-sharp «struggle for position». We learn from this account that the whole prelude was characterised by mobility, vigilance, the question of military intelligence and judgment. Mobility continued to be an important factor in the battle itself.

All this, indeed, looks simple enough. But it can hardly have been child's play. These conditions, furthermore, serve to explain why the kings and their leading military advisers were at pains to build the great ships as high as possible. We might say of these latter, which we have examined fairly thoroughly above, that «the navy is experimenting.» Of one of the biggest warships built in Norway, King Håkon's *Kross-suden,* we learnt that it was so highbuilt that when it lay in harbour, its gunnel came up to the tentridges of the *Olavssuden,* which itself was no pigmy. Here we see the whole evolution in perspective. It would not be easy to board a ship like that, however effectively an enemy ship might get the range. It must have been rather like trying to climb a sheer fortress wall.

Here another aspect of the technical evolution comes into view. One of the most vital qualities of the longship as created and perfected in the Viking Age was that it should lie as low as possible, for the advantage of speed at sea and ease in handling. Thus Shetelig has pointed out that in the Gokstad ship, the carved keel with its deepest point amidships gave a capital power of manoeuvre. With ships like Sverre's *Mariasuden* and Håkon's *Kross-suden* we are far from that. When they had to turn *Mariasuden* during the battle of Norefjord, it was so heavy that it swung out and came broadside on, and that at a fairly crucial moment in the battle.

From various expressions in the sagas of Sverre and Håkon Håkonssøn we see that this was one of the problems of shipbuilding at this period, when longships had to conform increasingly to naval requirement. They did not find it easy to reconcile these two distinct objects. One was attained at the expense of the other. With a ship like *Kross-suden,* whose fate, however, we do not know, it looks as if the breaking-point was reached. As for the even larger battleship, the *Kristsuden,* built by King Håkon for his expedition across the North Sea, we do not know whether it proved of much use as a warship. But it seems unlikely. I do not believe it was an accident that after *Kristsuden* these heavy ships ceased to be built.

The question *how many ships* took part in the naval battles has been partly answered in what goes before. Here we can only glance at one small point. There is a great gulf between the details given in the earlier sagas and those we owe to the sagas of Sverre and Håkon. Take for example the battle of Hjørungavåg, where Snorre tells us that Earl Håkon had 60 ships, Earl Eirik had 60 and Ragnvald of Ervik (Stadt) had 60—180 ships in all, against the 180 of the Jomsvikings. One need not go on to prove that this is a mere fable. It is quite different with the information given, for example, on the battle of Norefjord. King Sverre had 20 ships, King Magnus 26. Such a report is true. There would be no great interest in a detailed account of particulars on the other naval battles.

In the heyday of the royal navy, under King Håkon, it occasionally happened that he sailed with 40 ships (1239).

Again, we need say little more about the *manning* of the ships on war service than has been stated already at different times. According to the levy regulations, the normal standard was 3 men to a half-room, but much of our information gces to show that in the bigger and the biggest ships the number varied from 3 to 5, and even 8 men to a half-room. There seems to have been no fixed rule; it was determined by the numbers available, and not least by the time of year.

The crew consisted above all of oarsmen. It seems probable that it was their regular duty to take a fighting part in the battle itself, and thus that they are to be included among the combatants. But even within this group we must allow for specially well-trained units. In big ships the command would have to form a separate group, but there was no reason why it should be very numerous. The steersman whom we have already mentioned not only had the chief command in battle, but was undoubtedly in charge of the helm during the fight. The technique of battle made this a highly responsible task.

We get some gleams of information on the «soldiers» and their arms in sagas and skaldic verse. But for the normal standard, *levy regulations* are the best source.

As far, then, as we can make out, the classic period of sea battles in home waters never involved a great mass of naval units; the maximum was about 30 ships on each side. This lies almost in the nature of the case, in the geographical character of the arenas just mentioned. It is certain that the figures given in the earlier sagas do not agree with the facts.

The death of Skule (1240) brought to an end the everlasting naval battles off the coast and on the lakes of Norway. Henceforth we begin to hear rather more of *naval musters for use abroad.* In this connection, since we are not

Mountings and ornament of iron on a church door in Stillingfleet, Yorkshire.

writing general history, the only point that need engage us is: How many ships took part in these expeditions? Here as usual, early sources of information are very often patently fantastic. They are perhaps worst when reporting the number of Danish, Swedish or English ships. The Danish Gold-Harald levies an army and had 600 ships. Canute the Great crosses the North Sea with 600 ships. The Swedish king Anund Jacob has 350 ships, while Olav the Saint has 60. And so on. Of course the underlying idea is to convey the fearful superiority these enemy forces constantly enjoyed, and thus bring out the courage and audacity of the Norse against the innumerable foreigners. There is good reason to believe that these estimates are fabulous.

The first overseas expedition we know of must be that of Olav Trygvason to Wendland, which ended at Svolder. Here we are told with some plausibility that the King had 11 great ships, with a number of 20-thwarts and smaller ships, when he set sail from Nidaros. But then it is added that when he left the country he had gathered 60 ships in all. The same number is credited to Olav the Saint when he left Norway for Helgå in the summer. On this occasion, incidentally, the saga has preserved a tradition that many peasants (with their muster-ships) turned back at the frontier. The naval muster was created for home defence, not to be used abroad. Magnus the Good had 70 ships on his expedition to (not against) Denmark.

For the great English expedition of 1066, avowedly designed for war and conquest, Harald Hardruler, according to the saga, gathered 200 ships in all, *besides* small craft and freighters with all kinds of provisions. This does not sound wholly improbable. A genuine *army of invasion* was involved, the only one we know of in our entire history. So it would have to take supplies of every kind for the first period of operations. Here, by the way, we have a curious little introductory scene — the fleet assembled off Solund (just outside Sognefjord), the place of departure. The ships put out to sea, and some, including King Harald's own, arrived at Hjaltland, while others got to Orkney. This was doubtless no very uncommon incident in navigation. They would be sure to find each other later on!

No accounts of Magnus Barefoot's western expeditions give any figures for the ships.

Sigurd the Crusader made one expedition, against Denmark — though it was wound up without a battle. We are told that it consisted of 360 ships, a figure which is hard to swallow. The full muster, which incidentally was never levied, was of 310 ships at most.

More plausible, though once again on the extreme side, is the statement that King Sigurd had 60 ships on his voyage to the Holy Land.

King Sverre and King Magnus never took a fleet abroad. They had enough to do at home. Only with King Håkon do expeditions to the western isles and Scotland start afresh. His saga mentions with a kind of pride that he made at least six expeditions, four of them to Denmark, one to the Hebrides, and one, the last, to Scotland. Of one of the levies against Denmark (1256) we are told that the King had *360 ships*. And in the third (1257) he had *375*. I cannot repress a doubt. Norse sea power reached its zenith in this period, when we learn, for instance, that at the time of his expedition of 1253 King Håkon wielded such authority over the Norse empire that he could oblige King Jon and King Dugal of the Hebrides to go along.

How many ships King Håkon had on the Scottish expedition of 1263 is not mentioned. There must at any rate have been a large number, in this last great levy. The political and military aspects of the expedition cannot be discussed here. There is no doubt that it was competent enough on the administrative side. But militarily it was ill-conducted, with no breadth of outlook and no proper plan. The event which is quite wrongly called the «battle of Largs» was not a «battle», but the outcome of military blunders for which the King himself bears the responsibility. It was the rather discordant swan song of the «Great Age.» And the sickness which a couple of months later, in Orkney, ended King Håkon's life was at root unquestionably psychic, though it took the form of physical exhaustion.

Once more a muster was called out; it was King Magnus Lawmender's only one, and against Denmark. And the saga says that it consisted of 140 ships.

There is no reason to believe the longships were originally designed only for war and combat. At first they were built just as much for peaceful *cruising,* but as the security measures of the age were not socially organised, every ship had to be designed for combat as well. It is early related that the «east-voyagers», the trading ships, had posts for defence both fore and aft. The longships in process of time evolved exclusively for war service. But it is none the less of great interest to follow their development in seaworthiness, their qualities as rowing and sailing craft. Material for estimating these points is almost overwhelmingly abundant, especially in the later sagas. But it is practically limited to cruises off the Norwegian coast from Viken to Trøndelag. On ocean cruising we have in fact only two statements in the sagas.

Toraren Nevjolvsson, at King Olav's command, sails out to sea (Greenland was his real destination) and takes four days and nights from Møre to Eyrar in Iceland. This is of course mentioned as a record voyage, and is included in the saga as such. But then indeed it *is* a record! The distance is about 600 sea-miles, perhaps a little more. That gives a sailing speed of 150 miles a day, or an *average speed* of 6 miles an hour – and note, for four days and nights! Even with a favourable wind, such a performance is conclusive proof of the superb qualities of well-built longships as sailers. By examining a fairly large bulk of material illustrating these ocean voyages, I showed in my book on the Vinland expeditions that the long-distance average from harbour to harbour was between 3,5 and 4 miles. As Shetelig has related in the last chapter, writing of the Gokstad ship and of Magnus Andersen's voyage to America with the *Viking* in 1893, with a very favourable wind they succeeded in reaching an average for *24 hours* of about 11 miles. It is fantastic. But true. Finer sailing-vessels than these simple longships on the high seas have never been built until our own day.

Naturally fair winds counted for much. Håkon Håkonssøn took 48 hours

A 13th century drawing from Fide church in Gotland shows a ship of ancient type, but with stern rudder.

to sail from Bergen to Shetland on his Scottish expedition. The distance is not more than about 180 sea-miles, which gives an average speed of about 3.7 miles, and therefore tallies pretty well with the norm.

Another question arising from the subject of ocean voyages in the longships must also be touched on. When they were sailing to the western isles and to Iceland and Greenland – did they always reach the right place? Navigation is outside the scope of this chapter. In my book on the Vinland voyages I have shown that they had a very good knowledge, built on their experience as coastal seamen, of navigation on the high seas. Cf. Leiv Eirikssøn's fairly precise landfalls on the voyage to America. The occasional instances we know of their going wrong are carefully recorded in the sagas. We have therefore every reason to believe they seldom went wrong, although from time to time it did happen.

Then, in the same connection: They were surely wrecked sometimes? Again the sagas are very punctual in recording when this took place. We need only mention the time when Earl Håkon, who had been in England to negotiate with King Canute, was returning home to Norway in the autumn of 1029. His ship sailed round the west of Scotland and through the Pentland Firth. There it ran into a storm and was lost with all hands.

Another incident recorded in the saga is the homeward voyage of King Håkon's daughter Cecilia from Bergen in the autumn of 1248, after her marriage with the Hebridean king Harald. They had a great ship with many eminent men on board. It never arrived. Most thought it had gone down in the Roost, south of Shetland. Wreckage was washed ashore in Shetland during the winter.

The position is quite different with *coastal voyages*. Here we can scarcely expect to learn anything of the longships' qualities as sailers; they were really just as much rowing craft, and everywhere in enclosed channels could use the oars equally with the sail. So there is nothing of real significance to tell about record voyages. One or two may be singled out, as when King Håkon's messenger Gunnar, in July 1217, took three days and nights from Tunsberg (or Horten) to Bergen with the news of Philip's death. Of course at that time of year he could row and sail day and night. It really means so little. Another time, when Earl Skule – in winter, to be sure – was sailing from Tunsberg to Bergen (1221) to keep Christmas with the King, he took 8 days. And yet the saga says he had a fair wind.

Another point which has a natural interest is that throughout these very animated centuries, when everything or at least most things happen at sea, they cease to bother about *seasonal* obstacles when movement is required. Of course the old and proper system was that in winter ships should be laid up, well protected and carefully prepared for service next summer. In the *King's Mirror* we have the magnate's maxims and advice on this head.

At the battle of Strindsjøen in June, 1199, where it was a feature of King Sverre's tactics to lure the Baglers' ships further and further up the fjord, the Baglers lost more and more way, because their ships were «sodden and heavy-rowing after lying in the water all winter.»

rawing from the seal of Nieuwoort, Belgium, 1237.

rawing from the seal of Elbing, ast Prussia, 1242.

As far as we can see, all the more decisive naval battles took place in summer – to repeat only the most important, Norefjord in June, Strindsjøen also in June, etc. But this is less material when it comes to the mobility of the ships and fleets at *all* seasons, in the years when the struggle for power, and showing oneself in all waters, was of military significance. This almost incredible defiance of obstacles is limited to the years of fighting in King Håkon Håkonssøn's reign.

The *longship* held out latest in Norway, long after new types of ships had made their appearance in the 13th century. As late as 1429 we hear of the muster fleet in action in Norway.

The Trading Ships

The nature of the sources has obliged us to devote all this space to war and military history in our account of the ships and shipbuilding. It gives a very onesided picture of both, and of society as a whole. In spite of this continual sea-fighting, rivalry in naval armament and so on, the people of the country were going quietly about their work, though with that restriction and insecurity of working life which followed from the everlasting levies and the useless wars. Things must have been gravest in the period after King Sverre's death, with its growing uncertainty, increasing faction, national division all over the country. Kings and pretenders, the magnates' bands, the demand for contributions from the big landowners, the burdens of shipbuilding, the calling out of land workers in the middle of harvest, everything helped to impoverish the nation in the course of ten or fifteen years.

In the sagas we often come upon a reference to merchant ships, freighters, cargo-boats, «easternes», etc; also to cargo vessels, *byrdinger,* which the armed forces calmy seized on and converted for naval use, by, for example, furnishing them with oar-holes. From this point emerges, that the freighters and trading ships were as a rule more sailed than rowed. Naturally to exploit their carrying power. Also it appears that they were higher-built than the longships, for the same reason.

Trading ships was the collective name for these many different types and editions of craft. Of their build and appearance we know unfortunately much less than with the longships. Several times in the sagas we hear of *sea ships,* plying to Iceland. The main difference was undoubtedly that they were higher-built. We never hear of longships sailing to the Faeroes, Iceland or Greenland; on the other hand, we often meet them in Orkney. But this may just as well be due to military political and administrative conditions. In the old colonies – Man, the Hebrides and Orkney – the King of Norway had preserved a claim to military aid. No such claim was ever asserted in the Faeroes, Iceland or Greenland.

Historical sources are far more meagre for the trading ships than for the longships. Several historians have tried to work out a kind of classification. Sverre Steen, who has written on these matters with great insight, distinguish-

The shape of the viking ships survived in the north of Norway until the end of the 19th century, in the fishing vessels used in these parts.

es between the smaller vessels, the *karve* and *skute*, and the lighters. The *karve* seldom exceeded 13—15 rooms, and could obviously serve both uses, war and commerce. Of the *skute* much the same is true. The same was commonly applied to light, fast-sailing craft for all purposes.

The merchant ships were known as *cheaping-ships*. Till about 1300 there was no great difference of basic type between them and the warships. But the different use led by degrees to an inevitable change in shape, so that the building method had also to be different. The main object in the warships was sailing speed, in the merchant ships a large capacity. And gradually another standard of measurement creeps in for them than we are used to with the warships, which are measured in rooms. The trading ships are measured in *lasts,* according to capacity. A last was about two tons. This way of measuring maintained itself over a long period, and acquired in supplement a varying sense according to the cargo.

For the varieties of trading ship, three terms especially came into the foreground: *knarr, busse* and *byrding*. All trading ships were broader in proportion to their length than warships. They had a rounder form, a bigger freeboard and a deeper draught than the longships. As they were designed almost exclusively for sailing, in most cases the mast was fixed. On the permanent deck fore and aft it was possible to stand or sit and row if necessary, for here (but not amidships) there were oar-holes in the ship's side. All the middle part of the ships was occupied by the cargo.

Whereas at any rate we know a certain amount about the warships, their building, form and equipment, we have not much detailed knowledge of this kind about the trading ships. We know that the older types, till around 1300, were essentially the same in their main features as the warships, with pointed stem and stern, side-rudder, square-sail etc. But otherwise we are not told a great deal.

The biggest of them was the *knarr*. There is no doubt that in the Viking Period and early Middle Ages it was also used as a warship. But it never came to mean the same as longship. The *knarr* was the genuine sea craft used on trading voyages to all the Norse Atlantic islands as far as Iceland and Greenland. The vessel in which the King, by the agreement of 1261, was to send goods to Greenland was called simply the *Grønlandsknarr*. The original settlers of Iceland, in the 9th and 10th centuries, sailed in the *knarr*. And it was in the *knarr* and not the longship that both Greenland and Vinland were discovered. There were slightly different types of *knarr,* adapted to the different waters, one for the Baltic trade, one for the Iceland trade, and so on. In comparison with the warships the *knarr* had a small crew, because rowing was inessential. An ordinary Iceland ship had 15—20 men.

As we have seen, in earlier times the *busse* was a war ship, but in the 13th and 14th centuries it comes to be a term exclusively for merchant ships. In English customs-registers after 1300 it is the usual word for a Norwegian trading ship. The name is widely diffused, all over the north, as far as England and Holland. Both *busse* and *knarr* were ocean-going ships of about the same size, but they must have been distinct in type. The words are never used alternately of the same vessel. The difference may have been in the shape of prow and stern. At the close of the 13th century, it looks as if the *busse* had displaced the *knarr* as an ocean-going ship. And in this, it is believed, lies something more than a change of name. It is a new type of ship displacing the older one.

In historical times *byrding* was the name for a merchant vessel designed chiefly for the coastal trade, and as a supply ship for the fleets. But it was also ocean-going and sailed to Iceland and the Faeroes, and right down to England. All we know of the *byrding* is that it was short and broad, and smaller than both the *knarr* and the *busse*. It had usually a crew of 12—20, never of more than 30 men.

The report (p. 178) that some *byrdinger* were converted into longships by lengthening the keel, etc., shows that at any rate there was no great structural difference between the two.

All the vessels which have now been mentioned were Norse or Nordic types. And all had one common property, warships and trading ships alike. They were all built for rowing, or for rowing and sail. Not one was built exclusively for sail. Which means, for one thing, that the trading ships needed a large crew in proportion to their cargo capacity. Therefore it goes without saying that the practical demands arising from the development of trade and business were bound to produce a change and lead to new types.

Commonly, indeed in almost all accounts, it has become something of a generally accepted and established view that this change derives from the

Hanseatics, who in their turn borrowed something from the Frisians. As early as the 9th century the Frisians had ships which were propelled by sail alone. The Hanseatics also adopted this type – how early we have no exact knowledge. But at any rate they were plying to Norway by the 12th century. These were the so-called *cogs*. They were big, broad vessels, high in the gunnel and built up high in the fore and after parts. They made their way in Norway with difficulty, in Sweden and Denmark with greater ease; but once the Hanseatic entry had taken place, change was comparatively rapid as regards the merchant ships. It occurred in the latter half of the 13th century, and around 1300 the cog was the usual merchant ship for ocean voyages throughout Scandinavia. And the old name *busse* was gradually transferred to the cog.

The cog was a middling or bad sailer, but was at any rate enormously more dependent on the wind than any ships of the old type. It never carried oars, and thus required a much smaller crew. It could take far more cargo than our old ships, even with a corresponding crew and of the same size. This came to be of decisive importance, especially in the import of heavy goods, corn, salt and ale, and in the export of hides and fish. Indeed we cannot venture to reject the general opinion at the close of the Middle Ages that our growing inferiority in shipping was due to the want of this type of roomy vessels with a small crew.

Later, after 1300, new types of ship come in, answering to the new and changed conditions. The warship *holk* in the 14th and 15th centuries was allied to the cog. The *caravel,* at the close of the Middle Ages, possibly from Holland, was also a warship. The advance lay in the opportunity for several masts and a new rig. The *galley* is later and falls outside the period we are treating. Clinker-building is to a great extent displaced by carvel-building, that is, the strakes laid edge to edge. The transition takes time, and in Norway it could never wholly displace clinker-building, which had grown so spontaneously from our ancient boat-culture.

In general it may be said that the innovations which took place in western Europe in the latter half of the 12th century left Norway somewhat out of date. Early, perhaps earlier than any other West European people – except the Frisians, indeed – the Danish and Norse race had achieved superb boat-types, especially for fast ocean sailing. It is highly possible that the superiority thus won had made them more conservative and disinclined to changes. Also, the innovations which really count may not have been very well adapted to Norwegian conditions. Take, for example, a feature like the introduction of a *stern-rudder* in place of the side-rudder. With the Norwegian type of ship this change must have appeared very difficult to accept. Moreover the stern-rudder necessitates a *deeper-drawing hull,* and this transition was at least as difficult to manage. Finally, both these changes lead inevitably to a modification of the sail and rigging.

Where and how this was effected need not be explained here. In any case we know too little of it. But we may conjecture that it was a victory for the trader over military interests, and that in Norway, therefore, the transition

The seal of Wismar, which belonged to the German Hansa.

The seal of Bergen from 1299 shows a ship with a dragon's head decorating the prow and stern.

came with the ebbing of the long period of naval warfare, about 1300. The trader's interest was to load his boat as heavily as possible. Naturally he then found that with a deeper draught the sailing speed was reduced. But to make up, it was possible to take a good deal more advantage of all winds. A boat lying deeper in the sea can be sailed much closer to the wind than a light and shallow one, which makes too much leeway in tacking. To get the best advantage from the wind, the sail has to be kept in the right position. When the old boats had sailed close-hauled as far into the wind as they could go, the leading edge of the squaresail would flap, and twist out of the wind. To correct this, as has been said, they attached bowlines to the sail and hauled it forward. On a short craft with a large sail it needed hauling as far forward as possible, and so they hit on the idea of lengthening the prow with a *bowsprit.*

Of course it may be said that this is theory, but on the other hand there is no denying that it may very well have happened so. To some extent the same will apply to a reflection on the old side-rudder. With a hull of deeper draught and for clause-hauled sailing, the side-rudder naturally becomes less efficient. With a starboard wind and the ship heeling to port, it may cease to work at all. For a time they actually tried to correct this by having two side-rudders. So it is almost a matter of course that the final solution was the stern-rudder. Certain 12th and 13th century pictures serve to confirm that this was more or less what happened. On a baptismal font of about 1180 in Winchester cathedral there is a ship of the old type, tapering at both ends, but with a stern-rudder. And on the seals of several English towns in the first half of the 13th century there are ships of the old type with a stern-rudder.

Thence it is not far to the next step. The coming of the stern-rudder means the disapperance of the old pointed stern. It is exchanged for a transom. And with this change we say goodbye for ever to the fine old ships of the Gokstad era, the fast and pliant sailers. It enforces a novel type of hull with quite different lines, a development which proceeds briskly in the 14th century in Holland, England, etc. And here Norway lags behind. It is the death of an epoch, not merely an external change. It is the ebbing of a style, a working life hundreds of years old, a close and confidential fellowship with the sea.

And when we speak of the «decline» of Norway in the Middle Ages, this symptom is among the most profound. Cause or effect — it really comes to the same thing. A working problem, a problem of goods transport has been solved, certainly. But it is no less certain something has been lost. And slowly the old Nordic seas are lost to Norwegian ships.

In the 14th and 15th centuries the development of this «improved» ship evolved the standard sea-going type in North and West Europe. And from the transport ships it spread to every kind of craft, even to warships. They are clumsy and graceless, they do not «stand to» the sea, they express the retrogression of a new era. Then, at the end of the 15th and in the 16th century come the more radical modifications of both hull and rig, and the results emerge in the 17th, and still more in the 18th century, in the form of the full-rigged ship. And then once more the men of the Norwegian coast appear

babtismal font in Winchester thedral shows the oldest known presentation of a ship with stern lder.

on all the seas. But this development takes place in the main outside Norway. It had been very different in the four centuries from 800 to 1200, when Norway took the lead in an important cultural evolution. In the 14th century the very basis, the Norwegian ship is at a standstill. But happily it is preserved, as we have pointed out already, in the Norwegian boat in all its local forms from south to north.

Yet another aspect of these problems may be mentioned, though here we cannot enter on the question of how much is cause and how much is effect. This is a trend in purely general history: the gradual shifting of the centre of gravity from the west coast to the east of Norway, symbolised by the removal of the king, the machinery of higher administration, from Bergen to Oslo. This must link up with the «removal from the sea», the reduction in overseas trade, the disappearance of seafaring and seamanship — things which were making themselves felt both in Iceland and Greenland by the 14th and 15th centuries.

No doubt it is also bound up with a stronger consolidation of Continental Europe. The commercial empire of the Hanseatic League, although in some ways its effect on Norway was positively good, cut off both East and West Norway from their old and natural overseas connections. It repressed shipbuilding and seafaring with an iron hand. This harmful influence cannot be ignored, yet need not blind us to the fact that it had a strong ally in Norwegian incapacity and impotence. The commercial empire developed into a kind of political power blockade, engaging kings and magnates in a tremendous and protracted political game. Against such a power movement Norway in the early days could do nothing much.

There are no finds of buried medieval ships, nor is there any rich pictorial evidence, which might confirm this outline of events. But with such means of checking it as we possess in other sources, it would appear that we have gained a fairly accurate impression of what was going on. In a single instance we have had very interesting confirmation of the fact. In 1946, in Siljan church above Skien, a number of old frescoes were uncovered which depict ships of various kinds. One or two main features are common to all. They still seem to have preserved the lines of the early ship, the same at either end: also the ancient square-sail with the mast amidships. But there is a novelty in the stern-rudder, which is still attached to the old, pointed stern – a striking feature, very unpractical, but deriving from the transition period. Judging by these details, it is probable that the Siljan ships are 14th century.

The transition announces a change of style, matching historial conditions. The old longships had grown up in Norway and the Nordic countries over hundreds of years. They also showed their expansive power in relation to all the North Sea territories. Incentives to the new come from without, and encounter a certain passivity in Norwegian shipbuilding after the latter half of the 13th century. The mercantile element takes the lead and gradually expels the longship types. And it was a long time before Norwegian shipbuilding found itself again.

The trading ships imposed a different pattern from the warships on working life as a whole. This may bee seen at once by merely glancing at the chapter in the *King's Mirror* which deals with the trader and trading voyages across the sea – at that time (the 1250s) chiefly to England.

«Maintain your ship so that it looks well,» says the father in the *King's Mirror*. Naturally enough, he is thinking chiefly of the trading ship in his advice to his son. But what he says of it would apply also to the longships. They had to be carefully looked after, not least in winter. «You are to tar your ship well in the autumn,» says he, «and let it stand so through the winter.» (He does not mention a good boathouse, but that is implied.) «If the ship comes so late under a roof that it may not be tarred in autumn, do it in early spring and let it dry well after. Seek to have your ship clear by summer, and fare out in the best of the summer season. Take heed that all is in good order on your ship. *Never be long upon the sea* in autumn by your own will.»

This advice, as will be seen, applies to a sea voyage abroad, and therefore is less relevant to the coastal cruising of the longships. They can always find a harbour which will supply their needs. It is different for a man about to cross the sea on a trading voyage. He has to take precautions against finding himself stuck in a difficult situation. «Mind this», says the father, «whenever you fare out to sea, have with you in the ship two or three hundred ells of frieze-cloth, such as is fit to mend the sail at need. And many needles and

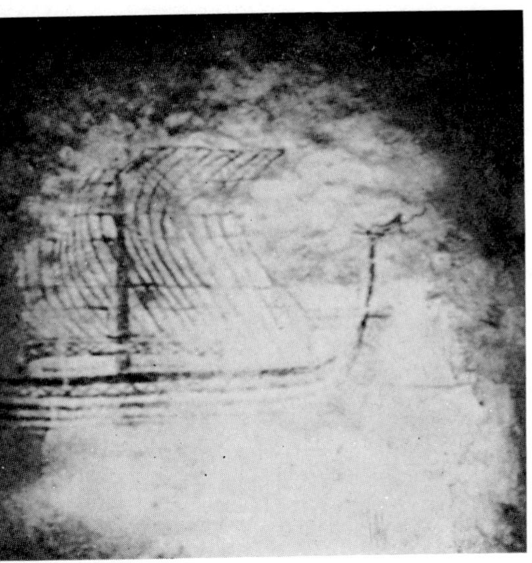

Murals in Siljan Church, Telemark.

abundance of yarn and reefbands. Though these be little things to talk of, yet it is often one shall need the like. Nails, also, you shall ever have good store of in the ship, and of that size that is convenient for the ship you have, both spikes and rivets, good deepwater grapnels, carpenter's axes, gouges and augers, and all such tools as shipbuilding requires.»

With the sagas the rich material we had for some part of the history of shipbuilding comes to an abrupt end. And a great vacuum succeeds. This is no mere chance. It is not only the sagas that stop. There comes a decline in shipbuilding, and by degrees also shipping, following the downward curve in the history of the country. Even at the beginning of the 14th century the old English ports are full of Norwegian ships, and from the customs registers we learn their names and cargoes, and occasionally their size as well. And a genuine medieval ship may actually be found here and there. From the 14th century official records increasingly fill up the gap, but in the nature of the case they are much more prosaic and utilitarian in content than the old sagas.

It is significant that not till seventy years after the building of *Kristsuden* do we meet a document about a Norwegian vessel for home use. This is an attestation drawn up in Tunsberg on December 15th, 1333, that Hr. Guttorm Kolbjørnssøn bought of one Orm Smørsvein a wherry of 8 lasts (or about 16 tons). Orm bought it of the priest at Borgestad, and sells it with the sail and all tools. An eight-last wherry was certainly not much of a trading ship. Yet the payment was no trifle. Ships had risen well in price.

One of the few magnates who still amounted to something as a shipbuilder and owner and in the shipping business was the well-known Håkon, Bishop of Bergen. In 1339 we see that he has many ships and runs a boat-building concern; for instance, in 1340 Hr. Pål Erikssøn is building him a *karve,* he is laying in material, mast-timber from Trøndelag, etc., and later he builds a *busse.* In 1341 he has occasion to approach Hr. Jon Haftorssøn with a commission for a boat to be «rowed by 8 men» — the scale was no bigger than that.

The *levy ships,* indeed, had still to be maintained, and of course it was desirable to have them reconditioned and new ones built. This last, I believe, was done less and less. We have a late reminder of the situation in a letter which King Olav the Young (that is, his mother the Danish Queen Margrete) issued in Tunsberg in 1382 to Våle and Slagen, levy districts of Vestfold, directing them to build a «ship for defence» — that is, a levy ship — with a keel of 20 ells, or about 11 metres (the Gokstad keel measures about 20), «till somewhat be resolved on further building.» They are to have leave to burn the old ship *Borrebranden* and use its rivets for the new ship. And the latter is to be finished with all tools appertaining, within *three years* of this day (April 20th). But if the Realm has need of it before, the shipowners are to *hire* or *buy* a vessel of like size.

When we think of the old longships and muster ships, poverty and decay shine out of such a document from start to finish. The old unserviceable ship may be burnt, the rivets may be used, and on this petty vessel they may spend three years. In the great days of old, ships twice the size and more were built in half a year, often in a couple of months.

This is the last we hear of the building of these ships, or about any «good-sized» craft. On the latter point we have a possible exception in the letter of a canon of Nidaros in 1381, bequeathing to the church of Hadsel, his native parish «my ship, the biggest that I have, with *yard and fittings* and all appurtenances.» It seems highly probable that it was meant as an addition to the levy ships.

Apart from that, most of the allusions are boats of four or six oars, which cannot be included here. Only now and then is there a reference to bigger ships.

When we get into the 16th century, information about ships and prices grows more abundant. But strictly speaking it falls outside the limits of our theme. We may just mention that in 1532 the bishop and chapter of Bergen owned a ship which was bought in *Holland,* and certainly built there, for five hundred Rhine-guilders. Here is another interesting reference, of 1524: Michel Blik has gone to Norway (from Denmark) in King Christian II' ship, with 90 men aboard. It sprang a leak in the North Sea, but was brought safely into *Oslo. But here were neither carpenters nor ship's parts for its repair.*

In 1524—29 we find a number of ship's prices quoted. They are all German, Scottish or Dutch, a few of them as high as five thousand guilders.

Only once in these years is building mentioned — when Vincens Lunge, in 1525, writes to his bailiff at Vardøhus about the building of a *north-going ship* of about 45 lasts. He does not say where the ship is to be built, but the most likely places are Bergen or Hardanger. In 1531 the King talks of building a sloop at Oslo.

As a final document we may include Frederik II's renewal of the privileges of Oslo in 1548. The burghers of the town had complained, for one thing, that the local *peasants* were engaged in sailing and commerce, and *had been having bigger ships built* than the law allowed. And the King naturally put an end to this. It was the same with the privileges of Konghelle in the same year.

Here we place a full stop, after following the evolution of the Norwegian boat from the Stone Age to the close of the Middle Ages.

It reached its grand climax with the viking ships and their successors the longships, and then with all the peasant-built sloops and other craft along the whole Norwegian coast down to our own time. It is the judgment of all experts, foreign as well as native, that better sea-going boats for coast and ocean were never built.

INDEX

Page numbers in *italics* refer to illustrations.